THE
AGE
OF
DECAY

THE AGE OF DECAY

How aging and shrinking populations
could usher in the decline of civilization

SHAMIL ISMAIL

Quickfox

What others say about the book

"This book explores in magnificent detail just how much this long-term trend can reshape the world's economy as well as the lives of ordinary people. Much credit must go to the author for the research he has done and the fascinating way he has used it to demonstrate the challenges we face as a species in the next hundred years."

—Clem Sunter, former CEO and Chairman of Anglo American Gold and Uranium, and internationally acclaimed authority on scenario planning

★ ★ ★

"Peeling back the layers of life in a rapidly depopulating world, the unique writing style reveals a complexity that catapults you into a future scenario that cannot be ignored."

—Dr Pali Lehohla, Head of Statistics South Africa (2000–2017) and Chair of the UN Statistics Commission(2008-2009)

★ ★ ★

"An intriguing analysis of how our lives could be impacted by the changing demographic trends. A must-read for anyone interested in how the future could unfold. Captivating, carefully considered and well-argued."

—Darrell Bricker, co-author of *Empty Planet: The Shock of Global Population Decline*

★ ★ ★

"Most countries' declining birth (fertility) rates are now well below the sustainability level, with several adverse economic implications. In this tautly written and well-researched book, Shamil Ismail focuses on whether there will remain enough essential workers to maintain our urban infrastructure, or whether the lonely old (with little family support) will be living in crumbling dwellings. Malthus must be turning in his grave!"

—Professor Charles Goodhart, London School of Economics; co-author of *The Great Demographic Reversal: Ageing Societies, Waning Inequality, and an Inflation Revival*

★ ★ ★

"The lockdowns in our economies were perhaps the only times in our lives that we truly appreciated our dependence on the workers we rarely notice. Shamil Ismail's welcome focus on this critical and inelastic portion of the workforce—essential workers—requires a refinement in the definition of the dependency ratio. If an increasing portion of a shrinking workforce is required to look after the elderly and another rising share to maintain Ismail's focus—essential work—the effective labour force available to generate economic growth as we know it just got smaller."

—Manoj Pradhan, Talking Heads Macroeconomics; co-author of *The Great Demographic Reversal: Ageing Societies, Waning Inequality, and an Inflation Revival*

★ ★ ★

Published by Quickfox Publishing
Cape Town, South Africa
info@quickfox.co.za
www.quickfox.co.za

*The Age of Decay: How Aging and Shrinking Populations
Could Usher in the Decline of Civilization (Revised Edition)*

ISBN Paperback 978-0-6397-9137-1
ISBN Hardcover 978-0-6397-9138-8
ISBN Kindle 978-0-6397-9139-5

First edition 2023
Revised edition 2025

Editor: Deborah Rudman
Proofreaders: Vanessa Wilson and Barbara Wood
Cover image: Jim Felder

To Echi, Ansaar, Imraan and Sakeena

CONTENTS

APPENDICES

INTRODUCTION

On 15 November 2022, the global population passed the eight billion mark. The milestone was reached without much fanfare and elicited only minor news coverage. The world was too preoccupied with more pressing current news such as the war in Ukraine and surging inflation. Yet, it had taken a mere eleven years to add a billion people to the seven billion on the planet in 2011, and less than fifty years for the population to double from the four billion alive in 1974. As the growth rate of the human population exploded, we became more aware of the impact of human activity on the environment. More people need more things—food, clothing, consumables and assets—which require an ever-expanding industrial base to produce. The effects that these escalating activities may have on climate change are becoming evident. Summer heat waves drag on longer with new record temperatures, storms are more intense, and floods have become more devastating. Some may be justifiably concerned that this rate of human population growth cannot be sustained.

However, in recent decades a long-term trend has gathered pace that not only renders such concerns unnecessary, but could also dramatically change our societies and our quality of life. Reproduction, one of the most basic of human functions, is on the wane. Around the world, birth rates have declined as populations transitioned from large families in rural settings, to smaller families in urban areas. The trend itself is not new—it started more than a century ago, in the late 1800s. Initially, though, this development proved to be positive. With fewer children, more of the family's resources could be allocated to each child and, over time, standards of living improved. But in many developed countries, the fertility rate (that is, the average number of children born to a female) has now fallen well below the replacement rate, which is the rate required to maintain a population. We have not yet seen the effects of this too-low fertility rate in declining global population, mostly because life expectancy has increased (which means there are more older people who can offset the decline in the number of young people). At a country level, immigration has propped up the ranks of shrinking domestic labor markets. However, a handful of countries are already experiencing a decline in their total population—in 2023, Italy's population fell by 33,000, Japan's by 861,000, and China's by 2.1 million.

A decline in the total population may not be a concern for most people. Many may think that a smaller population would reduce the strain on the environment. Imagine if we could gently transition towards a more ecologically sustainable population level—the outcome could be quite beneficial. But this is, unfortunately, not that simple. Such a transition will be incredibly challenging and will fundamentally disrupt our current way of life because we have built systems and infrastructure that cannot scale down commensurately with our population decline.

Like most people, I was alarmed by the disruptions caused in the early stages of the COVID-19 pandemic in 2020—supermarkets running low on stock as supply chains faltered, or chronic patients unable to get routine medical check-ups—the pandemic showed how vulnerable our modern societies are to systems breakdowns, especially when they are caused by a shortage of essential workers. This made me wonder—is there a minimum level of essential workers needed to keep a society functioning? How would the trend of declining populations square up against this minimum essential worker requirement? What would happen if we passed the tipping point when there are not enough essential workers to deliver the basic services we have become accustomed to?

This book explores what would happen when declining populations result in countries reaching a tipping point where they have too few essential workers to keep their societies functioning optimally. Labor shortages, which are already evident in some developed countries, will worsen as more countries scramble to fill the ranks of their essential workforce. To make matters worse, the future generations that will have to deal with these challenges may be ill-prepared, given the current path of social development in developed countries, as this book will show. There are several other implications that can only be appreciated once we evaluate the impact on the most primary level— the effect it will have on our daily lives and activities.

Issues at the top of our minds now, such as over-consumption, pollution and environmental sustainability, will fade in significance as we have to deal with new challenges such as a lack of consumption and declining living standards. While we slate over-consumption, the modern economy has evolved to be dependent on growth—growth in sales and profits means more products and services must be provided by a growing workforce and sold to an expanding customer base. When the feedstock of such growth—the number of people— starts to diminish, consumption will naturally decline, and shrinking consumer markets will decimate economies.

The phenomenal progress and technological advancement that we have achieved over the past few centuries may make us overconfident in our ability to deal with the challenges that lie ahead. We expect that solutions will be provided by technological advances such as artificial intelligence and robotics, but this may not be the panacea we hope for. Most importantly, though, past achievements that improved the quality of our lives—notably the complex infrastructure and systems that support our societies—will come undone if there are not enough essential workers to maintain it.

With hindsight, we will come to realize that we peaked as a civilization between 1990 and 2020. It was as if the COVID-19 pandemic sounded the bell to the end of an era—a time when life was generally good and things were working fine. But now we will start to traverse the slippery slope downward. When are we likely to see the first major signs of this new reality? Which countries will be first impacted, and by when? What can we expect the world to look like in the decades to come? And what will this mean for the future of our children and our grandchildren? This book attempts to answer these intriguing questions and will, hopefully, allow us to prepare for the incredible transformation that lies ahead.

* * *

CHAPTER 1

WAKING UP TO A HARSH REALITY

As usual, Eva woke up at 5am. There was no particular reason for her to wake up so early, but having retired only a year ago at the age of 75, the habit is difficult to break. She ambles sleepily to the kitchen to prepare a cup of tea. The cat is still fast asleep in the corner, oblivious to any of the existential concerns that agitate people on a day-to-day basis.

As Eva waits for the water to boil, she stares out of the window at the surrounding cityscape. The previously gleaming buildings have lost their luster in the moonlight. But even in the harsh light of day, they are not their former selves. Years of neglect and being left vacant have caused many to be almost derelict. The vacancies, in turn, decimated the property market—who would want to buy a residence In a building or a suburb where half of the homes are abandoned?

She turns her head to the ceiling. The water is still dripping but it seems to be quicker now. The apartment above hers is vacant. No one has lived there since Mr Alpert passed on five years ago. Last week, a pipe burst in that apartment, but none of the residents of the building wanted to contribute to repairing it. They say it is not their responsibility, and as they are not affected by it, they just ignore it. Eva tried to call a plumber, but their rates are exorbitant. The shortage of labor has caused wages to skyrocket. Eva lives on a fixed pension and barely manages as it is. Instead, she does the next best thing and empties the bucket under the drip when it fills.

The kettle whistles as the water reaches boiling point. Eva slowly pours a cup, savoring the fragrance wafting up from her teacup. Shuffling to her living room, she contemplates how the disrepair in her apartment building simply mirrors that of the rest of the city. The same neglect can be seen in the city's infrastructure. Roads are crumbling and water leaks run for days or weeks before being repaired. Maintenance crews are understaffed and lower tax revenues make basic maintenance a luxury these days. Signs of decay are everywhere...

Throughout our history, we have almost always had growth, progress and development. Sometimes growth slowed, sometimes it paused and, occasionally, it contracted. But in the fullness of time, we have, invariably, always progressed toward better living conditions. From the Stone Age to the Bronze Age and into the Iron Age, extending into the Renaissance, and then the Industrial Revolution—each era provided us with technological advances that have improved our quality of life. Driven by the desire to innovate and improve our conditions, humans have succeeded in molding our environment for our convenience. We have flattened forests for farmlands, built highways to speed up transport, and consumed fossil fuels voraciously to drive our civilization forward. Today, we find ourselves in the Information Age, where we harness the power of information technology in remarkable ways to advance civilization along a new developmental path.

But this could be the last stage of growth for us. Several trends are coalescing that compromise this growth, ushering in a new era that will be characterized by continuous contraction and decline. The change will not be brought about by any external threat—it is driven by our choices and changes in preferences. The change will not come about suddenly. It is already creeping up on us slowly, being hardly noticeable at first. It will steadily gain pace and its consequences will snowball as it progresses. The Age of Decay has already commenced.

The main cause of the impending transition is the rapid decline of fertility rates around the world. In the 1970s, when the global population passed the four billion mark, there was a generally held view that the global population was exploding and that Earth would not be able to sustain such an escalation in numbers. The book *The Population Bomb*[1], published in 1968, became a bestseller with sensational predictions that hundreds of millions of people could starve to death by the 1970s. A report published in 1972 by the Club of Rome titled *The Limits to Growth*[2] concluded that if growth trends in the world population, together with industrialization, pollution, food production problems, and resource depletion continued unchanged, then the limits to growth on the planet would be reached at some point within the next 100 years. The report predicted that this would result in a sudden and uncontrollable decline in both population and industrial capacity. These alarming scenarios echoed the 18th century Malthusian theory, which held that the rapid rise in population would result in mass starvation in some parts of the world, leading, ultimately, to economic decline. Fortunately, these apocalyptic scenarios did not come to pass. Instead, more and more countries will come to experience declining populations in the decades ahead, not by starvation or due to a lack of resources—rather, through the choices and circumstances of individuals choosing to have fewer or no children at all.

Almost as soon as *The Population Bomb* and *The Limits to Growth* were published, the rate of population growth started to slow. Annual global population growth peaked at 2.1% in 1970, but had eased to 1.8% by 1980. By the year 2000, it was at 1.3%, and two decades later it had decreased to 1.1%. The corresponding demographic data have shown a precipitous decline in fertility rates, especially in developed countries where women have been exposed to more educational and career opportunities, which competed with child-rearing as a defining purpose in life. The latest United Nations forecasts show that the world population is not on a continuous upward trajectory, and may not be heading towards unsustainable levels of population. Instead, the growth trend may taper off in the next few decades, and then start to reverse.

While the forecasts show the global population only peaking several decades from now, and then decline by the end of the century, the global data mask significant variations in population trends between countries and regions. Low fertility rates in some regions are offset by higher rates elsewhere. Viewed at the level of individual countries, though, the impact of declines in population will be evident in a few countries within the next decade. From there, the situation will quickly worsen, initiating a trend that will be difficult, if not impossible, to reverse. The handful of countries that will initially experience these challenges may find them relatively easy to deal with, but a cascading effect will be set in motion when several countries grapple with similar labor and consumer shortages.

Indeed, the generations to come will face some incredible challenges, unlike anything we have experienced in modern history. But their challenge won't be unique. After all, ancient civilizations have fallen, including the empires of the Romans, Mayans, Byzantines and Sumerians. These empires fell for a variety of reasons—be it battle losses, civil strife, and the splintering of the populace into smaller factions. The difference this time around is that our decline is by choice. We choose to thin out our numbers voluntarily, and the consequences will be far-reaching.

Can we avoid this future? The forecasts and predictions in this book may seem grim, but there are opportunities too. The most exciting potential development is that the 22nd century could become the "African Century". Unlike most of the rest of the world, many African countries will still boast fertility rates well above the replacement rate for the next few decades. The continent could therefore become the primary source of surplus labor supply, and would play a vital role in filling the growing labor gaps in the West. It would be in the interest of developed countries to invest in education and training on the African continent, as they could draw on this skills base when their own labor pool thins out.

★ ★ ★

CHAPTER 2

FROM BABY BOOM
TO BABY BUST

———

Eva had dozed off after enjoying her cup of tea. Waking up early and watching the sun rise had always been a routine that she preferred enjoying alone, basking in her own random thoughts. But every now and then, a feeling of loneliness crept in, and she would become aware of her isolation.

Eva was raised a single child in a doting family. This was common at the time and most of her friends also came from single-child homes. Growing up, she did not have to compete with any siblings and her parents spoiled her. She became accustomed to this family structure, and when she married Sam at the age of 30, having one child was the only sensible option for them too. Eva thought about phoning her son, Matthew, but decided against it. He is probably very busy with his work—he seems consumed by it and hardly has a social life. Matthew will turn 40 in September and is still single. He seems in no hurry to get married or start a family of his own. He could be the end of their family line, she thinks morbidly, and momentarily regrets not having had more children.

The small, urban family is a fairly recent development. Before the mid-twentieth century, large families were the norm. The number of children in families often extended into high single-digits, and sometimes even into double-digits. A large brood was a source of wealth and pride. Children were valuable assets who could contribute to the household's productivity and were also a useful retirement policy, as they could care for their parents when they grew old. Children provided extra pairs of hands that helped with chores and shared in the workload of the rural home—after all, more hands make light work. As recently as 2011, children in Uzbekistan were still taken out of school for up to two months, so that they could help pick cotton during the harvest season.[3] And as a retirement plan, the value system into which children in rural areas were born placed a great emphasis on family duties and responsibilities. Children were obligated, out of respect for their elders, to provide and care for their parents in their old age.

In the past, infant mortality rates were high and having more children increased the probability that some would survive—to work the farm and look after their parents in later years. Limited birth control and family planning services also resulted in more unplanned pregnancies and births in the past. In short, the fertility rate was high.

All this began to change during the Industrial Revolution in the 18th century. Factories and industries sprang up in cities and needed labor. Rural workers were drawn to cities in search of exciting new employment opportunities. The migration from the countryside to cities—urbanization—has been a trend in all countries that have undergone industrial development. Industrialization and urbanization have generally resulted in improved standards of living for the population. But urbanization has also led to a dramatic change in the traditional family structure.

As people move from rural to urban areas in search of better jobs and higher income, parents realize that raising children in cities is very different to raising them in a rural community. Rearing children in the countryside is a hands-off affair: Children can be left to their own devices to play and explore with their friends in familiar surroundings, with the community on hand to ensure they are safe. The African proverb, "It takes a village to raise a child", neatly encapsulates child-rearing in rural environments. In cities, however, children require much more resources from parents. They need to be fed, clothed and schooled. They need after-school care and parents are more involved, because they cannot simply expect children to go play outside in a much more menacing environment. A large family needs a larger home and these are significantly more expensive in cities. Consequently, instead of drawing on children as an economic resource and a source of labor in the countryside, children in the cities become an expense as they need to be educated and cared for. And as standards of living increased in cities, parents in developed countries became less reliant on children to care for them in their old age. They could save and have retirement plans that are independent of children. City-dwelling parents soon realized that smaller family sizes made more sense—it was less expensive, and it allowed parents to give more attention and resources to each individual child, which improved the prospects of their offspring. And raising one child gives the maximum benefit of channelling all possible care and attention to a single recipient.

Besides the additional cost and effort involved in raising children in cities, women are also afforded greater opportunities in urban areas. Women can attain higher levels of education than they might be able to in a rural community. And once they are educated and qualified, the career opportunities that open up for women can be appealing enough to delay starting a family. Accordingly, women in developed countries with high levels of urbanization tend to have children later in life. This results in a shorter period of reproductive time available—a woman in her early thirties may only have about ten years left to bear children, whereas someone in their early twenties could have twenty years to build a family. Often, women who choose to start a family later in life may not have the time to have a second or third child before their biological clock runs out. Some of those women who delay this step may find that when they do feel they are ready to take the plunge, life's circumstances may not be aligned for them — for instance, they may not be in a healthy relationship or their partner may not share their desire to start a family at that time. All the while, their fertility window is closing. The documentary film *Birthgap — Childless World* presented interesting research findings in this regard; it concluded that the majority of childless women at the end of their fertility window in low birth-rate nations did not intend to end up in that situation. Writer and researcher Stephen J Shaw terms this "unplanned childlessness".[4]

The introduction of reliable contraception from the 1960s was yet another important disrupting force in the fertility rates of developed nations. Contraceptive use among women in urban areas is generally higher than in rural areas,[5] which further contributes to smaller family sizes in cities.

As a result of these factors, global fertility rates more than halved from 5.3 in 1963 to 2.3 in 2020.[6] The situation in high-income countries is much more acute, with the fertility rate dropping to 1.5 by 2020, which is well below the replacement rate of 2.1 (basically, two children are needed to replace the mother and father, while the additional 0.1 accounts for children who may not reach adulthood).

Consequently, average family sizes have steadily decreased in developed countries. The average number of people per household in the United States dropped from 5.6 in 1850, to 2.6 in 2018.[7] Furthermore, the proportion of mothers at the end of their childbearing years in the United States who have borne only one child doubled from 11% in 1976 to 22% in 2014.[8] And across the pond, the trend was even more pronounced. In the European Union, about 49% of families had only one child by 2021, with Portugal recording the highest ratio at 59%.[9] There is also a growing trend of childlessness among women at the end of their reproductive period. Research shows that the rates of childlessness at age 40–44 have increased in most OECD countries, with around 20% of women in this age group childless in Spain, the United Kingdom and the United States.[10]

Figure 1: Fertility rates globally

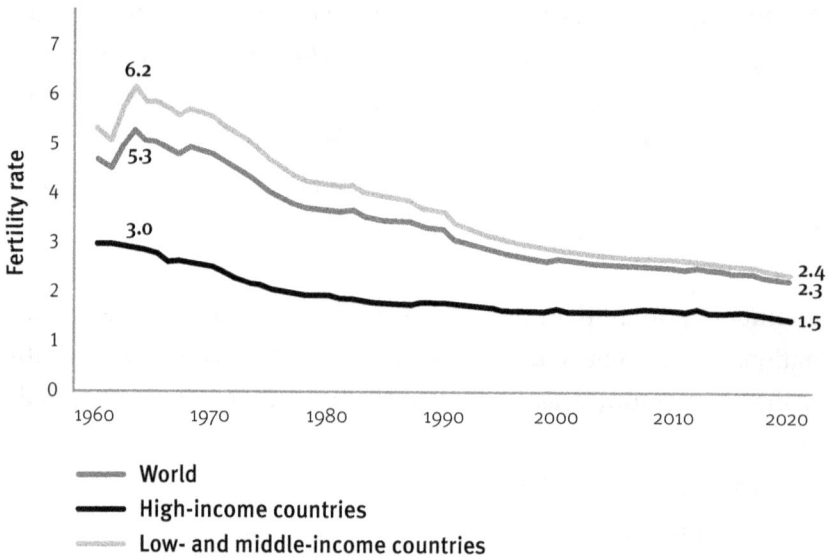

World
High-income countries
Low- and middle-income countries

Source: United Nations

Mobilizing women in the urban workforce has undoubtedly been an important step for gender equality. But having fewer children slows population growth and opting for only one child (or no children at all) can shrink population sizes significantly within only two generations. The impact that single-child family structures across multiple generations can have on population growth is demonstrated in Figure 2.

If two sets of parents had one child each, and their children marry and, in turn, have one child only, then after only around 90 years, the size of this family cluster would drop from four people in the first generation to three people two generations later (after the passing of the grandparents). While this may not, at first glance, seem too concerning, it is a reduction of 25%. Consider the impact of this pattern on a larger scale—if most families in a population were to follow this trend (which seems to increasingly be the case), the overall population could drop by as much as 25% in less than a century. This is a major population reduction, but it could be even worse. For example, China, which applied a strict one-child policy between 1980 and 2016, is forecast to experience an even more dramatic decline in population of 56% over the next 80 years. This may be a consequence of the preference for male offspring during the one-child policy period (which means there are fewer potential mothers), as well as a rising proportion of Chinese women preferring to be childless.[11]

Figure 2: Impact of single-child families

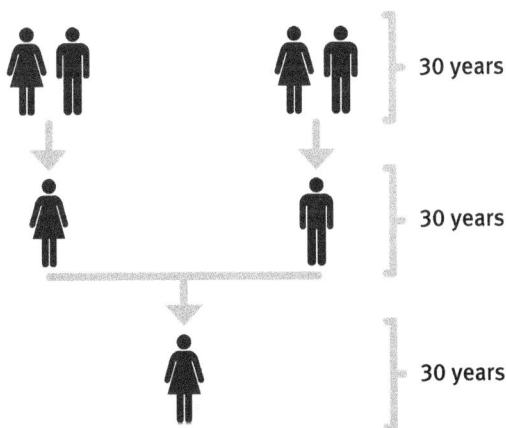

In the illustration above, the fertility rate is equal to 1, which means that, on average, a woman has one child during her lifetime. To keep population numbers constant, a fertility rate of 2.1 is required; in other words, on average a woman should have 2.1 children in her lifetime.

Falling well short of this rate results in a significant population decline in a matter of decades.

The world population grew exponentially in the last century despite the continuous decline in fertility rates over this period—this was mainly due to increased life expectancy. The global population had been mostly stable for millennia as, in the past, population numbers were kept in check by wars, famines and short life expectancy. However, with advances in technology and healthcare, life expectancy has increased and episodes of famine and disease have been all but eradicated in developed countries. The global population remained below one billion for most of history and only surpassed that milestone in the 19th century. The graph below shows that, after the end of the Second World War in 1945, the population grew at a rapid rate, with one billion people added roughly every 12 to 15 years.

Figure 3: Global population over the past millennium (millions)

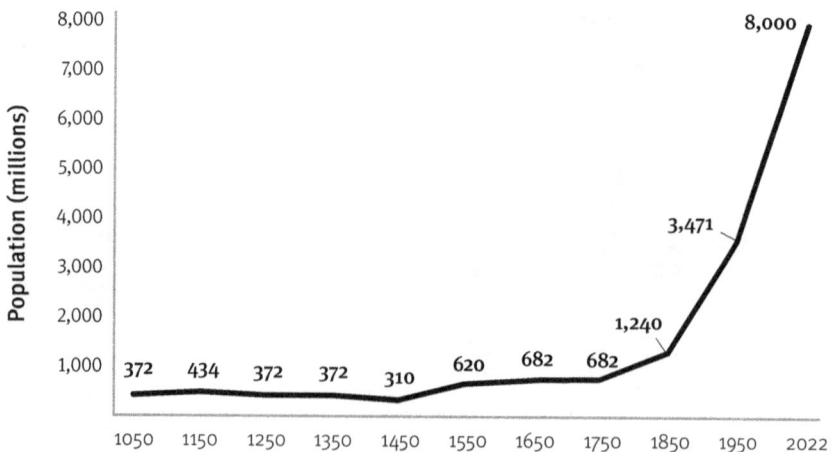

Source: United Nations

The alarming increase in the population size by the late 20th century raised some fears that population growth would outpace food production, and would cause mass starvation and suffering—echoing the Malthusian theory. The concerns resulted in some radical actions being adopted, none more so than China's one-child policy. This policy, which was implemented in 1980, restricted families to a single child, with penalties imposed to enforce the rule. In hindsight, though, this harsh policy may have been unnecessary, as it coincided with two key developments taking hold in China at the time, both of which would naturally drive fertility rates down: urbanization, and increased education opportunities for females. Let's briefly consider both.

When China adopted the one-child policy, the country's urbanization level was low at only 19%, which meant that 81% of the population lived in rural areas. But as the Chinese economy opened up in the mid-1990s, its urbanization increased dramatically and reached 64% by 2020. This was actually the largest migration of people in the history of the world[12], representing a transfer of about 726 million people from rural areas to urban locations in the space of only 40 years.

Figure 4: Urbanization rate in China: 1980–2021

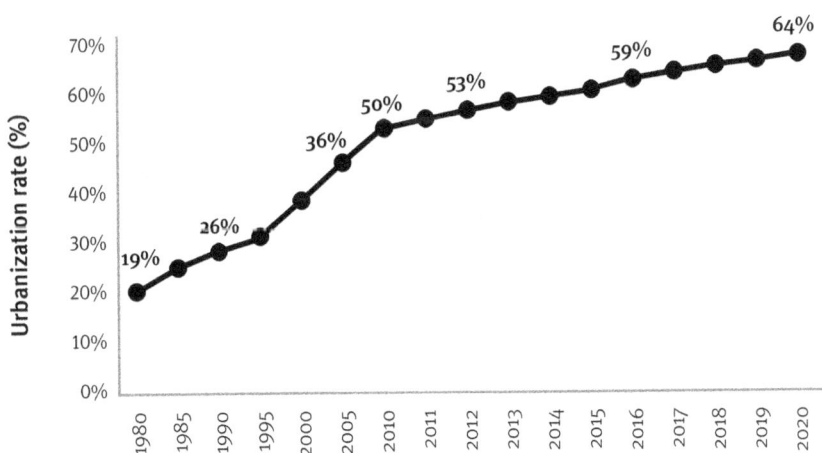

Source: China CDC Weekly

As urbanization increased in China, more female children gained access to better education in the cities. Female secondary school enrolment in China increased substantially from 23% in 1983 to 88% by 2010,[13] and women now outnumber men in tertiary enrolment in that country.[14] As noted earlier, higher urbanization and better education opportunities for women would have naturally lowered the fertility rate. Thus, China would have experienced an easing in the fertility rate even without a state-enforced birth-control policy.

Globally, other factors have also contributed to lower fertility rates. For example, religious households tend to have larger families and over the past few decades there has been a decline in religious conformity—which, in turn, would result in more small families. The movement away from religion is generally associated with higher-income countries,[15] which would partly explain the lower fertility rates in most developed countries.

So, over the past 60 years we have moved from being concerned that exploding population growth could lead to an overcrowded planet and rampant famine to the realization that, in the near future, the global population will start to decline. The United Nations forecasts that the population of 8 billion people in 2022 will peak at 10.3 billion by 2084. Other forecasts, such as those of the International Institute for Applied Systems Analysis,[16] are more sobering. They project the global population will peak at 9.7 billion in 2070 and drop to 9.3 billion by 2100. Regardless of which demographic forecast model is more accurate, the underlying message is clear—the next generation will live through a time when the world undergoes some dramatic changes as more and more countries' populations begin to shrink.

We noted earlier that a fertility rate of 2.1 (the replacement rate) is needed to maintain a population. In 2022, though, 110 countries had fertility rates below the 2.1 replacement rate.[17] This means that more than half of the world's 195 countries do not have sustainable fertility rates, and are at risk of declining in population within the next few decades. The problem is not a short-term trend either, as 81 of these

28

countries recorded a rate below 2.1 in 2012, and 68 countries were already below the replacement rate in 2000. If anything, the list of countries with below-replacement fertility rates will only increase in the years ahead.

Figure 5: Global population projections (billions)

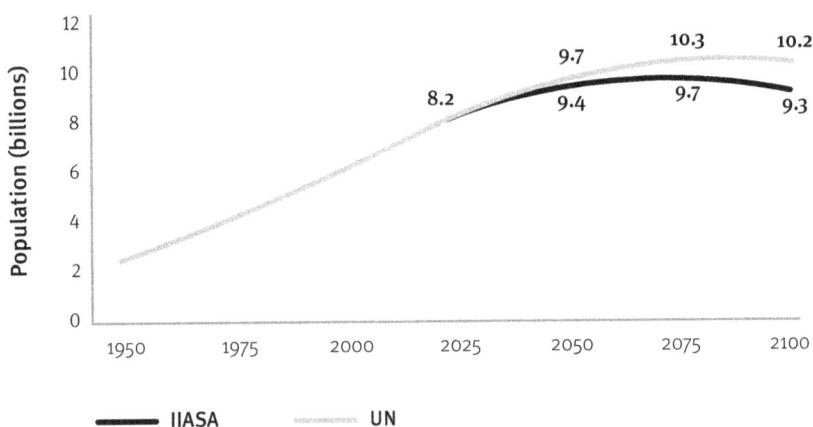

Source: United Nations, IIASA Wittgenstein Centre

Table 1 lists the 20 countries with the lowest fertility rates in 2022.

South Korea heads this list with an astonishingly low fertility rate of 0.78, which means that on average women there bear fewer than one child. In the top 20 list, thirteen countries are in Europe, six are in Asia, and one is in North America. All the G7 countries (which are seven of the world's most advanced economies) have fertility rates below the replacement rate of 2.1, with Italy being the lowest at 1.24, followed by Japan at 1.26. Clearly, the decline in fertility is most prominent in the developed world. A full list of fertility rates for each country is provided in Appendix 1.

There are very important social and economic consequences of not meeting the replacement rate. As fertility rates drop and life expectancy rises with improved healthcare, there is an increase in

Table 1: Top 20 countries with the lowest fertility rates (2.1 is the replacement rate)

	1990	2000	2012	2022
South Korea	1.57	1.48	1.30	0.78
Singapore	1.83	1.60	1.29	1.04
Spain	1.36	1.22	1.32	1.16
China	2.51	1.63	1.80	1.18
Italy	1.33	1.26	1.43	1.24
Japan	1.54	1.36	1.41	1.26
Poland	2.06	1.37	1.33	1.26
Ukraine	1.85	1.12	1.53	1.27
Finland	1.78	1.73	1.80	1.32
Thailand	2.09	1.61	1.59	1.32
Canada	1.83	1.51	1.63	1.33
Bosnia And Herzegovina	1.79	1.28	1.29	1.35
Switzerland	1.58	1.50	1.52	1.39
Austria	1.46	1.36	1.44	1.41
Norway	1.93	1.85	1.85	1.41
Russia	1.89	1.20	1.69	1.42
Greece	1.39	1.25	1.34	1.43
Portugal	1.56	1.55	1.28	1.43
United Arab Emirates	4.54	2.73	1.67	1.44
Germany	1.45	1.38	1.41	1.46

Source: World Bank

the ratio of aged people (those older than 65 years) to working-age people (those aged 15 to 64 years, whom I will refer to as "workers" for brevity). The conventional measure used by demographers is the age-dependency ratio, which calculates the number of dependents under the age of 15 and over the age of 65, compared with the working-age population of 15 to 64 years old. This ratio is usually expressed as a percentage, and the global average was 54% in 2023. However, it is intuitively easier to understand the inverse of this ratio, that is, the number of workers per dependent, which we can refer to as the worker-to-dependent ratio. The age-dependency ratio of 54% in 2023[18] is equivalent to a worker-to-dependent ratio of 1.9, meaning there are on average 1.9 workers per dependent.

For the purposes of demographic planning and forecasting, the conventional age-dependency ratio's treatment of children as a burden to the economy may be misleading, because children are only temporary dependents, and more importantly, they do not draw pensions. Within a few years children will become productive contributors to the economy, while the aged will remain permanent dependents and continue to draw on the social welfare system. In faster-aging countries, the number of people entering the aged bracket (older than 65 years) is often higher than the birth rate, which means that including children in the calculation may obscure the severity of the situation. This can be seen in the example of Italy in the chart below, where the worker-to-dependent ratio excluding children is dropping at a much faster rate than the traditional measure including children. For the remainder of this book, I will exclude children and focus on the worker-to-aged ratio.

Figure 6: Dependency ratio (number of workers per dependent)—Italy

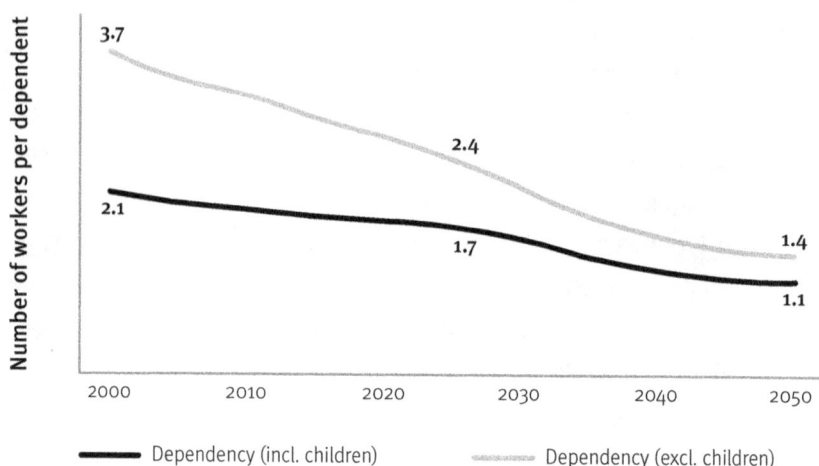

Source: United Nations

Let us now consider the worker-to-aged ratio across different regions. The table below shows that the ratio of worker-to-aged people has dropped dramatically over the past 60 years on all continents, except Africa. Note that although Africa's worker-to-aged ratio has also declined somewhat since 1960, the drop is not as significant. Africa's worker-to-aged ratio remains much higher than the rest of the world, and will continue to exceed the other regions by the end of the century.

Table 2: Ratio of worker-to-aged people

	1960	1990	2020	2050	2100
Europe	7.4	5.3	3.4	2.0	1.7
North America	6.9	5.4	4.0	2.6	2.0
Latin America	16.6	12.8	7.6	3.5	1.7
Asia	15.2	12.7	7.4	3.5	2.0
Africa	16.9	16.6	16.2	11.0	4.4

Source: United Nations

In Europe, there were 7.4 workers for every aged person in 1960. By 2020, this more than halved to 3.4 workers per aged person. By the end of this century, this ratio will further reduce to 1.7 workers per aged person in Europe. Similar declines are forecast for the Americas, as well as Asia. On the other hand, while Africa's ratio is also expected to drop, it will still be comparatively high at 4.4 workers per aged person by 2100 (which is higher than the figure for Europe and North America in 2020).

The decline in the number of workers supporting a growing cohort of aged people will present massive challenges to governments, corporations and households. I will explore the impact of this in detail in subsequent chapters. But first, there is another problem that may be even more consequential, and could result in us experiencing the effects well before the global population starts to decline. That problem is the decline in the number of essential workers needed to sustain a functioning society.

★ ★ ★

CHAPTER 3

ESSENTIAL WORKERS WILL DETERMINE THE TIPPING POINT

———

The water seems to drip faster now. How much damage will the burst pipe upstairs cause before others in the building are also affected, wonders Eva. Perhaps then the residents will come together and pay for the repairs in the vacant apartment above hers. But that faintest glimmer of hope quickly disappears when she thinks about the other issues in their apartment block. Regular maintenance has long since ceased, and now many things are falling into disrepair. The elevators are unpredictable and to avoid getting stuck overnight waiting for a repairman to come, most residents use the stairwell. At her age, though, walking up and down the stairs to her seventh floor apartment is difficult. So she limits her trips outside to just once or twice a week. It is a pity being cooped up in her apartment, because the park is just across the road. She misses her early evening walks in the park and chatting with the locals from the neighborhood.

In 2020, the world stopped dead in the face of a highly infectious virus, which spread rapidly across the globe. Countries closed their borders and implemented radical policies to try to curb the spread of this deadly virus. Mandatory lockdowns forced people to stay at home. Only the most essential workers were allowed to ply their trades. It was during this time that the world learned to appreciate the important role that essential workers play in society. The essential workers who were often hailed as heroes in the media at that time were mainly those on the frontline of the pandemic—doctors, nurses and hospital staff. These workers put themselves in harm's way by tending to others afflicted by the virus. But the caste of essential workers extends well beyond the healthcare sector. For example, staff in supermarkets, garbage removers, and truck drivers moving produce from farms to retailers all form part of the intricate backbone of the society we take for granted. And when these essential workers fell sick and had to quarantine, we were impacted by delays and shortages of the goods and services we needed. The COVID-19 pandemic gave the world a preview of what life could be like should we face a shortage of essential workers.

We also became aware of the downsides of globalization with its complex, integrated global supply chains. The COVID-19 pandemic exposed the vulnerability of global supply chains as factories in distant lands stopped production and borders closed, disrupting the flow of goods. One of the earliest manifestations of the broken system was a shortage of products in stores as consumers rushed to buy products they considered essential (which curiously often included toilet paper!). The panic buying only exacerbated the shortages. But the pandemic did provide us with a taste of what life might be like when the systems that keep society functioning start to falter. Cracks in the system appeared all over. For instance, the United Kingdom faced a critical shortage of truck drivers, which delayed products getting to stores and then to customers. There was a global shortage of semiconductor chips due to factory closures in Taiwan and South Korea, affecting the supply and prices of computers, cars and even washing machines. Italy had to deal with a shortage of farm workers, as seasonal migrant workers could not travel across borders. Not only were the logistics of the transport of products affected, but the supply of human labor was also disrupted. All of this had a direct impact on consumers.

Fortunately, the COVID-19 pandemic was only temporary, and as it receded, supply chains returned to normal, pre-pandemic operations. Those system malfunctions and challenges will soon fade from our memories. But what would happen if labor shortages and supply chain disruptions are not a temporary inconvenience to bear, but rather a permanent feature of life that we must learn to live with?

The structure of the underpinnings of our society has evolved over time and become highly intricate as our standards of living improved. Piped water and sewage systems were only rolled out to households from around 1900,[19] and this created the need for plumbers to expand and maintain this essential service. After the provision of electricity to homes (also from around 1900), electricians were needed to take care of this critical service for households. The list of services we depend on has grown considerably and includes a diverse range of jobs. Every essential product or service we use is supported by an army of essential workers toiling in the background to support and maintain the system.

What we have learnt from the COVID-19 pandemic is that if the number of essential workers drops below a certain minimum threshold, service provision will begin to fail. Some essential services will not be delivered timeously, and if this persists, the very structure of society could start to unravel. Essential workers span a wide range of occupations—the jobs are often unglamorous and serve functions we hardly take much notice of. And yet, these functions and services hold up our organized societies. These workers include plumbers, electricians, bus drivers, truck drivers, retail workers and farmworkers, to name but a few.

We emphasize the importance of essential workers, but what is the difference between essential and non-essential workers? Put simply, non-essential workers provide services in the absence of which society would still be able to function. For example, a shortage of architects, accountants or lawyers may very well disrupt our modern lives, but we would still be able to function and meet our basic needs without those services. Indeed, non-essential workers are important for economic development and the advancement of civilization. Non-essential workers are often highly skilled, knowledge workers whose services add considerable value to the foundations laid down by essential workers. Their services allow us to prosper and, while their absence would certainly hinder growth and development, it would not cause society to regress and go backwards.

By contrast, the absence of essential workers such as plumbers or truck drivers would cause our quality of life to deteriorate rapidly and affect us on a more fundamental level. To appreciate their value, imagine a major water mains pipe bursts and your water supply is cut for several days. Without easy access to water for drinking, food preparation, bathing or even flushing toilets, life will become un-pleasant very quickly. Or imagine if power lines that were damaged in a storm are not repaired for weeks—without electricity, lighting and internet access, life would be miserable indeed. Or if your garbage is not collected for several weeks—as happened in Paris in March 2023, when a three-week strike by garbage collectors left the city with 10,000 tonnes of rubbish piling up to two meters high in the streets. One can certainly appreciate the indispensable role these essential workers play in making our lives more comfortable and pleasant. In terms of societal functioning and importance, not all workers are equal.

As we noted earlier, when a population ages, the proportion of workers compared to the number of aged people decreases. In Europe, this proportion dropped from 7.4 workers for every aged person in 1960 to 3.4 workers per aged person in 2020. However, the number of essential workers needed to provide critical services to that population would remain relatively constant. This is because, regardless of the age or working status of the citizen, they will still need essential services such as piped water, electricity and sewage systems. This means that essential workers become a larger part of the shrinking workforce.

The situation is worsened when infrastructure built to serve large communities becomes under-utilized when the population declines. During its growth phase, a city's population may, for example, grow to four million people over time. There would be enough housing and related infrastructure constructed to cater for the population of four million. But if that population then drops by a quarter over the next 90 years, around 10% to 20% of the housing units will become vacant (depending on the average size of the households). The problem is that the infrastructure that was built to serve a population at its peak, is still there and will need to be either maintained or demolished. In cases such as vacant freestanding homes and buildings, demolition can solve the problem, although it will come at a substantial cost with no real economic benefit or cash return on the spending.

But in many other instances, demolition is not an option and the infrastructure must be maintained. Vacant units in a large apartment building cannot be demolished, and neither can large-scale, integrated civil services such as water reticulation and sewage systems. This infrastructure will require maintenance as it ages, but in a future with fewer workers available to provide these essential maintenance services, there is a risk that the infrastructure will decay. Burst water mains or electrical power outages that happen in abandoned parts of a city could have a widespread impact, disrupting the entire infra-structure network.

Can we then quantify the minimum number of essential workers needed for different population sizes? This is possible if we develop some benchmark, which we could base on the current levels in a developed country. Let's take the United Kingdom as an example, and assume it had an optimal number of essential workers to keep its society functioning in 2021 (a reasonable assumption given there were no significant service failures in the country at that time). In 2021 there were about 170,000 plumbers employed in the United Kingdom. These plumbers were servicing a population of 68 million people, meaning that there were about 2.5 plumbers per 1,000 people.

But what would happen if there were only 150,000 plumbers in the country? The impact of the lower number of plumbers would be felt, as the shortage would naturally lead to higher wages and slower service, as they would be unable to respond to all service requests timeously. Invariably, the quickest fix would be to fill the void with immigrant labor (which the United Kingdom did in the 1990s). Our hypothetical reduced number of plumbers of 150,000 is equivalent to 2.2 plumbers per 1,000 people in the UK, and this level may well be considered sub-optimal for that society. Similar calculations can be made for other occupations as well. For instance, the 2021 figure of 241,000 electricians in the United Kingdom amounts to 3.5 electricians per 1,000 people, while the 58,000 dental practitioners means that there is just less than one dentist per 1,000 British people.

Using this approach, an estimate of the number of essential workers needed to support a society comes to about 185 essential workers per 1,000 people in a population (see Appendix 2 for more details on how this number is calculated). The accuracy of the number itself is not that important, as it does not affect the trends to unfold in the future—only the timing of those events may change by about a decade or so. The key point is that the essential workforce is relatively constant as a proportion of the *total population*, but as the population ages, essential workers will become a higher proportion of the *total workforce*. This situation could have significant implications for future progress and development. Some might argue that artificial intelligence and robotics can reduce our dependence on manual labor and essential workers, but later in this book I will highlight the limitations of technological solutions in addressing this looming problem.

Therefore, as essential workers progressively form a much greater share of the workforce, they could crowd out other non-essential, but higher-skilled and advanced jobs. The chart below shows the proportion of essential workers to all workers at various levels of worker-to-aged ratios—from 4.0, the North American level in 2020;

to 0.5, a level not yet seen anywhere in the world. When the ratio of worker-to-aged persons is higher than 2.0, essential workers account for a relatively low and stable share of the total workforce—below a third of the total workforce.

Figure 7: Essential workers as a percentage of all workers

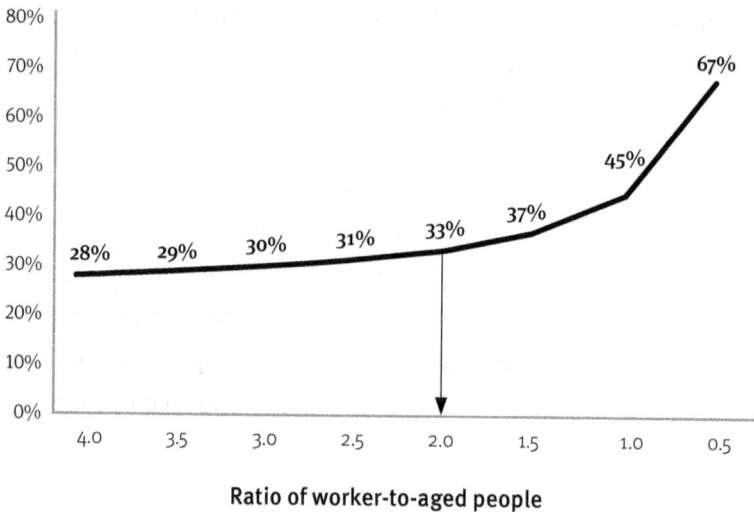

Ratio of worker-to-aged people

Source: Author's calculations

But once the ratio of worker-to-aged people drops below 2.0, the increase in the *proportion of essential workers to all workers* rises at a much faster rate. At the parity ratio of 1.0 (meaning that the number of workers equals the number of aged people in the population), the essential workers needed to sustain a society could account for 45% of the total workforce. And when aged people eventually outnumber the workers in a population, most of the workers would have to work in essential services to support the systems underpinning that society. This could limit future progress and development, as the pool of potential talented innovators shrinks. As a result, the critical tipping point when we will really experience the effects of a too-low birth rate is not when the fertility rate drops below the replacement rate of 2.1—rather, we will start seeing the consequences when the ratio of worker-to-aged people drops below 2.0.

Which countries, then, are close to this tipping point of a ratio of 2.0 workers-to-aged people, and is there any evidence of a growing labor shortage in those countries? Japan hit this mark in 2020 with a ratio of 2.0 workers-to-aged persons. Several other countries including Italy, South Korea, Spain, Portugal and Germany will approach and pass the ratio of 2.0 by 2040. The rapid pace of the decline in some countries—such as South Korea, which will drop from 4.1 to 2.6 workers per aged person within a decade—will exacerbate the situation, as those countries may not have enough time to properly plan and prepare for this momentous transition.

Figure 8: Countries with the lowest ratio of worker-to-aged people

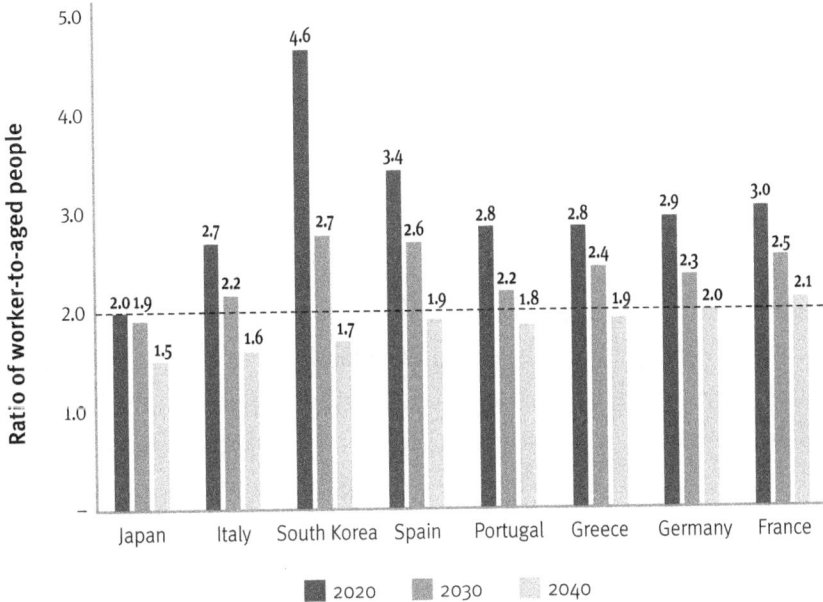

The tipping point of 2.0 workers per aged person is indicated by the dotted line.

Source: United Nations forecasts

Let's now consider the individual circumstances of these countries in turn. There is ample evidence that Japan is already grappling with severe labor shortages. Japan is a notably insular nation, with one of the lowest levels of immigration in the world. But despite their aversion to immigration, in 2019 the Japanese government passed legislation expanding the number of semi-skilled foreign workers who are permitted to live and work in the country. The move was seen as a measure of last resort in addressing a severe shortage of workers in 14 industries, including restaurants, nursing, construction and agriculture. Note that these were often not high-skilled jobs. With its shrinking workforce and aging population, Japan has become increasingly reliant on foreign workers, whose numbers have increased from 700,000 in 2011, to over two million in 2023[20].

The shortage of labor in Japan has resulted in higher wages and, in some cases, companies had to close stores because they were unable to hire enough staff. It was reported that the number of bankruptcies in Japan caused primarily by staff shortages doubled between 2016 and 2017.[21] (Note that this was even before the COVID-19 pandemic.) Other examples of companies grappling with acute labor shortages in Japan include the electronics retailer Nojima, who raised its retirement age limit from 65 to 80, and zipper maker YKK Group, who eliminated the retirement age of 65 for full-time employees.[22]

Japan certainly is a striking example of age-affected employment trends. However, another country worth examining is Italy. Italy is a particularly interesting case because in 2020 it reported a high unemployment rate of 9.2%, yet it still suffered severe staff shortages in the agriculture and hospitality sectors following the pandemic. This is partly due to a very low labor participation rate in the country. In 2020 there were 2.6 million people available for employment in Italy who were not seeking work.[23] Italy has one of the most difficult school-to-work transition paths in the world, which is often blamed on the failure of its education system to prepare students to be adequately work-ready.[24] The Italian tertiary education system has been described as excessively rigid and disconnected to the labor market. This results in a significant mismatch between supply and demand for jobs—the lack of demand for some specialized qualifications they have trained for leaves young people having to consider "trading down" and taking jobs with lower qualification requirements and lower wages. The low labor participation rate suggests many Italians are not willing to accept this transition, forcing employers to look for migrant workers to fill the void instead.

The lack of suitable jobs at home has prompted many young Italians to seek better job opportunities abroad. Between 2006 and 2021, the number of Italians living outside their home country has increased by 82%, with 5.6 million now living abroad. That figure is equivalent to almost 10% of the 59 million Italians residing in Italy.[25] Meanwhile, a near-corresponding number of immigrants—5.2 million—live in Italy, having stepped in to fill the labor void. The growing trend of young Italians emigrating coupled with a low fertility rate of only 1.2 exacerbates Italy's already chronic labor shortage.

Labor shortages in Italy are especially acute in primary sectors such as agriculture. In Puglia, a southern region of Italy, the farmers' association stated that over a quarter of food products in Italy come "from the hands of foreign workers".[26] The labor shortage in Italy was so severe during the COVID-19 pandemic that the government sought to legalize the status of 200,000 migrants who were living in the country illegally. This was a significant policy development, given the vocal opposition of right-wing parties in Italy's political arena at the time. It shows how social needs may eclipse political will when the effects of a shortage of essential workers are felt.

The situation in Italy also shows that the official unemployment rate of a country may not actually be a good indicator of labor shortages. In developed countries, young people who attain higher education levels may not be keen to work in sectors that do not fit their field of training, despite the availability of alternative jobs. This increasing educational attainment and higher-level skills of the labor force in developed markets creates a void in lower-skilled jobs, which we will explore in Chapter 7.

Portugal recorded an unemployment rate of 5.7% in 2022, but, as with Italy, significant labor shortages were also reported. However, economists generally consider an unemployment rate of around 4% to 5% to be close to full employment, which means that Portugal's unemployment rate is actually quite low. Employers' confederations in Portugal have asked the government to streamline immigration rules as there were not enough workers available in sectors such as hospitality, agriculture and construction. In September 2022, the Portuguese government announced that it would speed up the granting of visas to citizens of other countries in the Community of Portuguese Language Countries (CPLP), which includes Angola, Mozambique and Brazil.[27] Under the new rules, visas for citizens of any CPLP member state must be granted immediately by the Portuguese consular services.

Portugal is a popular tourist destination and that sector alone employed around 400,000 people in 2018. But by 2022, the tourism sector was suffering from a shortage of around 50,000 workers. While there is much hope pinned on the CPLP agreements, Portuguese tourism is also seeking to attract labor from ten other countries, including Morocco, India and Indonesia, who have shown willingness to replicate these mobility agreements.[28] The shortage of labor has resulted in higher wages in affected sectors such as tourism, which has in turn, impacted the competitiveness of Portugal's tourism offering—holidays have become more expensive in Portugal relative to other global destinations.

Lastly, Germany recorded a very low unemployment rate of only 3.5% in 2021. Like Portugal, Germany is faced with the challenge of addressing a growing worker shortage across its entire job market.

Shortages were particularly acute in the healthcare sector, as well as social services, education, architecture, engineering, and construction.[29] The labor shortage affects the everyday life of Germans in tangible ways—there may be vacant tables at a restaurant, but there may not be enough kitchen staff or waiters to serve customers; trains and airplanes run late or get cancelled due to a shortage of workers at rail stations and airports. The German Chambers of Commerce and Industry have stated that about 56% of companies reported being under-staffed in 2022.[30] The problem is no longer restricted to specialist fields; it has become a general staffing problem across all sectors of the economy. Germany loses about 350,000 working-age people every year as its post-war baby-boom generation retires, but there are simply not enough younger people available to fill those positions. The German labor market is projected to have seven million fewer workers by 2035. The German government has moved to ease immigration rules, hoping to attract skilled workers from abroad. The measures include making it easier for foreign workers to bring their families into the country.[31] In 2022, due to the impact of unprecedented labor shortages on spiraling inflation, Germany allowed around 130,000 resident foreigners to regularize their immigration status.

The examples highlighted in this chapter show that as developed countries with low birth rates approach the tipping point ratio of 2 workers for every aged person, they are confronted with acute labor shortages. These countries have no other option than to try to plug the labor gaps through immigration. As a result, governments have to improve immigration policies in order to attract foreign labor. But the competition for essential labor is hotting up. For instance, Germany used to rely on workers from other European Union countries to fill its domestic labor shortages, but those sources are now drying up. With low birth rates across the continent, other countries in the European Union are struggling to fill their own job gaps. There is no surplus supply, and therefore the cost of labor has also increased significantly.

But most importantly, these examples show that the problem is already on the doorstep of developed nations. Labor shortages, a direct result of changing population dynamics, are already impacting economies and driving policy.

* * *

CHAPTER 4

IT COULD HAPPEN SOON

Eva stares out the window onto the deserted street and just beyond, to a park, complete with a swing, see-saw, and jungle-gym, that is being reclaimed by nature. There is not a single child to be seen, excitedly running ahead of anxious parents towards the playground and squealing with delight. This morning, the activity is limited to two feral cats rummaging through the garbage bins, and some birds feasting on early-morning worms. The scene is tranquil but somewhat ghostly. It was not always like this, Eva thinks to herself.

She smiles, however, as she reminisces about her carefree youth over sixty years ago, when the community was much livelier. She can still distinctly recall the joy that she felt growing up, when she pleaded with her parents to buy ice cream from the friendly vendor selling in the park, and the relish of its cool sweetness in the summer heat. Years later, as a teenager, she had strolled through the park at sunset, feeling butterflies in her stomach, smitten with the young man walking alongside her. It is as if those moments remain etched in her memory, remnants of a markedly different world, when excitement permeated the air and everything seemed possible.

Things have slowed down so much now. The world seems quieter and less ambitious. She waits for the predictable arrival of the garbage-removal truck. It used to come once a week, but this has been pared back to collections every two weeks. The number of workers has been scaled back too: a single person driving the truck and having to load and disgorge the garbage bins. The worker is a young man, whose enthusiastic spirit seems out of place here. She can tell he is new, one of the many immigrant laborers the city continuously has to recruit to fill the growing void left by its own diminishing workforce.

The labor shortages experienced after the COVID-19 pandemic were sporadic aberrations in a few countries around the world. For the most part, governments could handle these challenges with relative

Table 3: Worker-to-aged ratio—countries that will drop below the ratio of 2x

Countries	2020	2030	2040	2050
China	5.5	3.8	2.4	1.9
South Korea	4.6	2.7	1.7	1.3
Germany	2.9	2.3	2.0	1.9
Albania	4.6	3.1	2.5	2.2
Chile	5.5	4.0	3.0	2.3
Taiwan	4.5	2.7	1.9	1.4
Ukraine	4.0	3.2	2.7	2.1
Singapore	6.6	4.2	3.1	2.4
Lithuania	3.3	2.8	2.3	2.1
Poland	3.7	2.9	2.5	1.8
Cuba	4.4	3.1	2.1	1.9
Turkey	7.6	5.4	4.0	2.8
Japan	2.0	1.9	1.5	1.4
Italy	2.7	2.2	1.6	1.4
Uruguay	4.2	3.8	3.2	2.7
Spain	3.4	2.6	1.9	1.5
Croatia	2.9	2.4	2.1	1.8
Greece	2.8	2.4	1.9	1.5
Colombia	8.3	5.5	4.1	3.2
Thailand	5.5	3.5	2.4	2.0

Source: Author's calculations based on United Nations population forecasts

ease, as there was still a strong demand from migrants to relocate to where the job opportunities were. However, this will change in future: The trends that appeared during the pandemic were a foreshadowing of what is to come. The competition for migrant labor is about to intensify.

The table below shows that over the next three decades, several countries are projected to drop below the ratio of 2 workers for every aged person, which could be the tipping point for critical labor shortages (the full list of the 69 countries that will reach this mark by 2100 is shown in Appendix 3). Japan is projected to dip below this threshold by the end of this decade, with five other countries

2060	2070	2080	2090	2100
1.5	1.3	1.0	0.9	1.0
1.1	1.0	0.9	0.9	1.0
1.8	1.9	1.9	1.8	1.8
1.5	1.2	1.1	1.1	1.1
1.7	1.4	1.2	1.1	1.1
1.2	1.1	1.1	1.1	1.2
1.6	1.5	1.2	1.1	1.2
1.6	1.1	1.1	1.2	1.2
1.7	1.5	1.4	1.3	1.3
1.4	1.5	1.4	1.3	1.3
1.7	1.5	1.4	1.3	1.3
2.2	1.8	1.5	1.4	1.4
1.4	1.4	1.4	1.3	1.4
1.4	1.5	1.4	1.4	1.4
2.2	1.8	1.5	1.4	1.4
1.4	1.5	1.4	1.4	1.4
1.8	1.7	1.5	1.5	1.5
1.6	1.7	1.5	1.5	1.5
2.3	1.8	1.6	1.5	1.5
1.8	1.6	1.5	1.5	1.5

(including South Korea, Spain and Italy) joining this club by 2040. The ratio in Germany will drop to 2 workers per aged person by 2040 as well. Thereafter, several other countries will join those ranks. The countries mentioned here will be the first to contend with what the rest of the world can expect in the decades to follow: increased competition for labor, with countries going to ever-greater lengths to secure their share of essential workers.

In the previous chapter, we noted that the minimum threshold of essential workers-to-population ratio is about 185 essential workers per 1000 population, or 18.5% of the population. Below that point, essential labor shortages will become much more evident and could impact the supply and pricing of essential products and services. To this we can add the constraint that essential workers should account for *at most* around 32% of the total workforce, after which the higher proportion of essential workers may distort and disrupt the overall labor market. When the proportion of essential workers rises above this level, it could crowd out other non-essential, yet innovative and growth-producing, occupations. This could have severe long-term developmental implications for a country.

With these two variables in place—that is, the minimum proportion of essential workers needed to support a population, and the maximum proportion of essential workers to the total labor force before it distorts the labor market—we can calculate the quantity of labor shortages that could arise in various countries over the next few decades as their populations age and decline in number. The charts below show the number of countries that could experience labor shortages over the next few decades, as well as the total shortfall in the number of workers. The forecasts indicate that by 2030, the situation could still be fairly benign. However, by 2040, four countries—Japan, Italy, Portugal and Germany—could have a combined shortage of about six million workers. By 2050, 13 countries could have a labor shortfall totaling around 19 million workers.

Figure 9: Number of countries with a projected shortage of workers

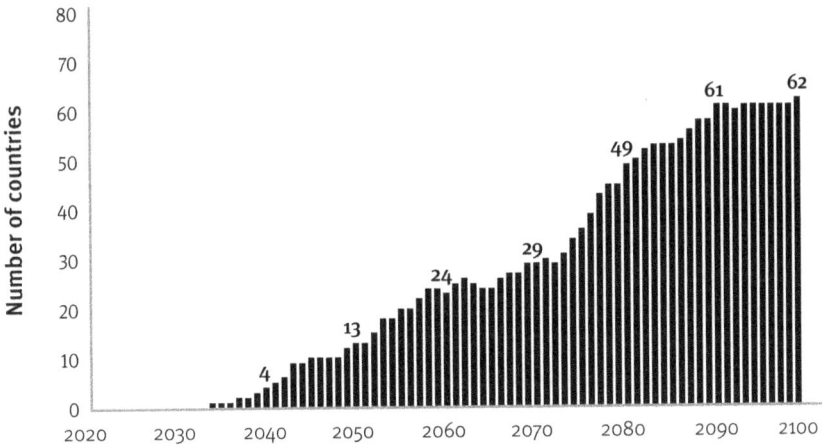

Source: Author's calculations based on UN Population forecasts

Figure 10: Projected shortage of workers (millions)

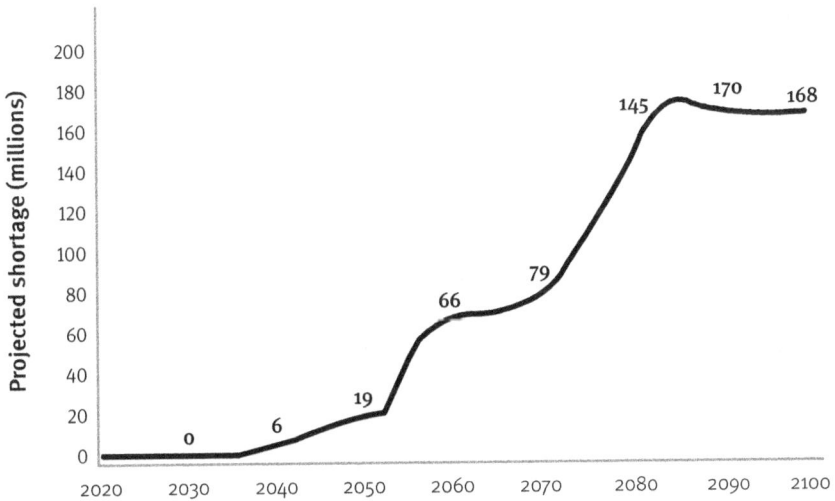

Source: Author's calculations based on United Nations population forecasts

The projections also show that there could be two periods of rapid increases in labor shortages based on the current demographic forecasts and our calculation method. Between 2050 and 2060, the number of countries with labor shortages could grow from 13 to 24. The corresponding shortage of workers would increase *threefold* from 19 million to 66 million workers. Then, between 2070 and 2080, the number of countries grappling with labor shortages could increase from 29 to 49 countries, while the total labor shortfall *spikes* from

Table 4: Projected labor surpluses and shortages (shaded) (in millions)

Countries	2020	2030	2040	2050
China	165.2	163.7	83.2	16.7
India	132.2	171.5	179.5	163.1
Bangladesh	11.8	15.6	19.5	19.7
Brazil	24.7	22.8	19.1	10.9
Japan	1.3	0.8	(4.0)	(6.9)
Turkey	9.0	9.7	8.7	4.7
Iran	9.8	11.9	11.6	4.8
Mexico	11.1	13.8	13.4	11.5
United States of America	26.2	19.8	15.6	12.1
South Korea	7.4	4.4	0.3	(2.4)
Colombia	6.1	6.1	5.5	4.2
Italy	3.6	2.0	(1.4)	(2.9)
Vietnam	10.0	10.9	9.6	5.7
Thailand	9.4	7.0	3.3	0.7
Germany	5.5	1.7	(0.0)	(1.0)
France	2.6	1.8	0.2	(0.6)
Spain	4.0	3.0	0.1	(2.4)
United Kingdom	3.8	3.9	2.9	1.9
Argentina	3.0	4.8	4.8	3.3
Poland	3.3	2.5	1.9	(0.4)
Chile	2.2	2.2	1.7	0.8
Peru	2.6	3.4	3.3	2.8

Numbers in brackets indicate projected labor shortages.

79 million to 145 million workers. Labor shortages of this magnitude have not been experienced in history. An avalanche is potentially building, and the cascading effect of growing labor shortages could fundamentally impact how many countries view immigration.

So, which countries are most vulnerable to the looming crisis? The table below lists the countries that could face the most significant labor shortages over the next few decades.

2060	2070	2080	2090	2100
(43.1)	(53.0)	(98.0)	(99.9)	(72.7)
118.8	60.7	19.5	(2.9)	(22.3)
14.7	7.8	1.9	(3.4)	(7.5)
4.2	(0.8)	(3.6)	(5.5)	(6.1)
(6.0)	(5.0)	(5.9)	(5.8)	(5.1)
1.7	(1.1)	(3.5)	(4.5)	(4.3)
(1.0)	(0.9)	(2.7)	(4.3)	(4.1)
8.1	4.0	(0.1)	(2.4)	(3.8)
9.5	6.4	(0.1)	(1.3)	(2.6)
(3.6)	(4.0)	(4.3)	(3.4)	(2.5)
1.6	(0.9)	(1.9)	(2.3)	(2.5)
(2.5)	(2.0)	(2.6)	(2.5)	(2.2)
2.6	2.6	(0.3)	(1.7)	(2.2)
(0.5)	(1.5)	(2.5)	(2.4)	(2.1)
(1.7)	(0.8)	(0.8)	(1.7)	(1.9)
0.0	0.0	(1.5)	(1.9)	(1.9)
(2.3)	(1.6)	(2.1)	(2.1)	(1.9)
1.1	0.8	(1.0)	(1.8)	(1.9)
2.0	0.6	(1.3)	(1.7)	(1.6)
(1.6)	(1.2)	(1.5)	(1.7)	(1.4)
(0.3)	(1.0)	(1.5)	(1.5)	(1.3)
1.7	0.6	(0.3)	(0.8)	(1.2)

Source: Author's calculations based on United Nations population forecasts

Developed countries could experience labor shortages much sooner than less developed countries, but in time, the developmental status becomes less relevant as most countries will be exposed to this crisis.

Japan is projected to have a shortage of 4 million workers by 2040, increasing to a peak of 6.9 million by 2050. China could have significant labor shortages from 2060 onwards (43 million), despite having a forecast population of 1.1 billion at that time—this is due to their aged persons accounting for 37% of the Chinese population by 2060, a threefold increase from the 12% in 2020. By the end of the century, China could have a shortage of 73 million workers. It is sobering to consider that this is nearly equivalent to the 71 million people projected to populate the entire country of Germany at that time.

The competition for labor will heat up and lead to interesting new dynamics that could fundamentally change political attitudes toward immigrants. Countries will have to work much harder to claim a slice of the foreign labor pie. Local opposition to immigration will have to change in countries suffering a continuous decline in their workforce, for several reasons that will be explored in more detail in the chapters ahead.

These forecasts are based on the estimate that the proportion of essential workers needed to sustain a society is 18.5% of the population. This ratio is based on 2021 data from the United Kingdom. If the definition of essential workers is expanded and the essential worker requirement increases to, say, 20% of the total population, the labor shortages could be significantly higher. For example, China's labor shortage would increase to 102 million workers by 2100 if the essential worker-to-population ratio requirement is at 20%. Conversely, a lower ratio of essential workers required to sustain society will decrease the need for labor. Automation and artificial intelligence could help in reducing labor dependency to some extent, but, as we will see in the next chapter, it will not be the silver bullet solution for this problem.

Further academic research into quantifying the minimum levels of essential labor needed to support economies and populations can refine estimates and provide more accurate forecasts for the timing and impact of the shrinking workforce.

It should be noted that the estimates that I use have been calculated on the more conservative United Nations population forecasts. If the forecasts of the International Institute for Applied Systems Analysis or *The Lancet*[32] are used instead, both of which predict a faster decline in population numbers, the critical tipping point could be reached even sooner. But regardless of which forecast is used, it is clear that trouble is brewing—and it is likely to arrive before we are ready to deal with it.

★ ★ ★

CHAPTER 5

CAN AUTOMATION, ROBOTICS, AND AI SOLVE THE PROBLEM?

Eva relies on her robo-cleaner to help tidy her apartment. She named the robot Annie, and she can tirelessly vacuum the apartment and mop the bathroom floor. She gives automated responses, but you can then direct her to where you would like her to clean.

Hearing Annie's movements from a different room as she cleans is oddly reassuring for Eva. She can imagine, for a few moments, that these are the sounds of another person living with her in the apartment. She fondly remembers the sounds of her husband beavering away on one of his projects—but this has long since fallen silent.

Shuffling into the living room, Eva peers at Annie, who is making a gentle humming noise as she meticulously vacuums the carpet from one end of the room to the next. There is a newer and quieter model with additional features, but Eva can't afford it. Besides, she has somehow grown attached to Annie and can't just replace her.

As Eva walks back into the kitchen, she wishes that Annie or her robotic ilk could do maintenance repairs such as fixing the leak in the apartment above hers. But technology seems to have come up against its limits in that regard.

We like to imagine that the future will have advanced solutions for every problem we might face. So it is the conventional view that technological advancements will, through automation and artificial intelligence (AI), address labor shortages in the future. We envisage a future filled with driverless trucks and robots that serve our every need. Our exaggerated expectations are based on the pace of past achievements. For example, we progressed from the first self-propelled flight by the Wright brothers in 1903 to a commercial jetliner in less than fifty years. The first mobile phone developed by Motorola in 1973 was a two-pound block measuring over nine inches long and only capable of making patchy calls; less than 40 years later we have sleek 7-ounce smartphones capable of 4K video and providing countless apps at your fingertips. From this we extrapolate further feats, thinking much more will be possible and any future problems could be solved by the relentless march of technological progress. The launch of ChatGPT in 2022, an artificial intelligence chatbot, raised expectations even higher. Undoubtedly, innovations could ease labor pressure in some areas, but technology may have limitations in addressing the shortage of essential workers.

To understand why technology may not help us avert the looming essential labor crisis, we need to reflect on the recent history of our progress. The Industrial Revolution changed the way labor was utilized, transitioning from hand production methods to machines, which were fueled by rapid advances in power generation—first steam, and later electricity. But instead of countless artisans losing their jobs and their trade, employment and economic growth surged as increased industrial output stimulated a prosperous cycle of lower cost, higher demand and more economic activity. This, in turn, contributed to a rapid rise in population growth. Machines did not end up replacing people in the economy, nor did they leave large swathes of the population without work. Instead, the technology of the Industrial Revolution stimulated human economic activity and boosted growth.

The key point is that technological advances often only change the *nature* of jobs and not the quantity. For instance, advances in the textile industry during the Industrial Revolution meant that labor was displaced from hand-picking cotton and hand-crafting garments to operating machinery that performed these tasks. With workers freed up from just producing basic clothing items by hand, mechanization allowed a whole new ecosystem to evolve, creating a host of novel roles in the textile industry. The scope of jobs within the textile sector expanded to include a vibrant design industry, conjuring up new fashion and brand design ideas that were enabled by the new technological advances. And downstream, the increased output needed an efficient channel to the market, fueling the growth of large retail chains, distribution centres and mall developments, all of which created more employment.

Similarly, in the pre-motor vehicle era of the late 19th century, horse-drawn carts were the primary mode of transport. The advent of motorized transport certainly made many jobs obsolete. For example, the blacksmiths and farriers who replaced worn horseshoes, as well as the carriage manufacturers and repairers, found themselves with a shrinking market for their services. But at the same time, the motor vehicle created an explosion in demand for its own support services. Mechanics were needed to repair cars, along with fuel stations, tire suppliers and parts shops. Labor was reallocated and people adjusted to this technological advance. In a similar manner, future technological developments will make some jobs obsolete, but it will also create an extensive ecosystem of new jobs. Driverless delivery vehicles may lower the demand for truck drivers, but there will be new jobs to support this new mode of logistics. Staff are required to monitor a growing fleet of robotic drivers; programmers are needed to deal with glitches and to continually improve algorithms; and all the while, the traditional repair and maintenance services will still be required for these driverless vehicles.

Furthermore, the transition to a more automated economy may not be seamless and could result in other complications. Take, for example, the introduction of self-checkout counters in supermarkets. The concept of self-checkout by customers was first introduced in 1986 and, contrary to expectations that it would revolutionize the retail industry, this technology continues to frustrate customers four decades later. Self-checkout lines in supermarkets often become congested: Some customers require assistance with scanning, making payments, or redeeming coupons. A 2021 survey in the United States found that 67% of customers said they experienced problems at the self-checkout counter.[33] Self-checkout automation has not proved to be smooth sailing for the retailers either, who have often found that the expensive self-checkout stations are not totally autonomous and required regular maintenance and supervision.[34] Although self-checkout counters eliminated some of the tasks of traditional cashiers, staffing requirements ended up being redirected to supervisors and higher-wage information technology jobs. Retailers have also found that self-checkout leads to more losses due to errors or theft than is the case with human cashiers. It turns out that customers are not very good at scanning products reliably, as they have not been trained in the way that store staff would probably have been. Customers can make innocent mistakes, but some "mistakes" take the form of intentionally pilfering items at self-checkout machines.

In some areas, automation works exceptionally well—for example, performing repetitive tasks in a controlled environment. Think of an assembly line in a factory or the harvesting of a field of crops. In fact, the first wave of automation targeted low-skilled, menial work. Many jobs on farms, for instance, were made redundant by the development of combine harvesters in the early 20th century. Similarly, many assembly line jobs were rendered obsolete after the deployment of the first industrial robot, named Unimate, at a General Motors assembly line in New Jersey in 1961. In the decades since Unimate, many

THE AGE OF DECAY

opportunities to automate manual labor have been exploited. Today, most manufacturing and agricultural jobs in developed countries that can be automated have been automated. The lower-skilled manual labor that remains most probably does not lend itself to automation. For example, tomatoes that will be processed into pastes and sauces can be efficiently harvested by machine, but whole tomatoes for the fresh produce market must still be picked by hand.

As a result, the latest wave of automation has mostly targeted higher-skilled jobs, and draws on AI and machine learning to replace human effort. The preparation of legal agreements, accounting financial statements and even medical diagnoses are within the capabilities of current software applications, and the skill of such applications will be enriched by artificial intelligence. We might envisage the significant encroachment of AI-enabled solutions into many high-skilled occupations in future, putting those professions under the same pressure that the 19th century blacksmiths and farriers experienced with the advent of motorized transport. But today this leads to an interesting conundrum. As countries and economies develop, the levels of education increase, and a larger proportion of their populations attain tertiary qualifications. This means that more people are being trained for higher-skilled jobs that may be under threat from AI.

Another area where automation works effectively is with rule-based applications. That is why applications can be developed to provide accurate medical diagnoses or legal services through question-and-answer processes. But many other jobs—often blue-collar type work—may remain beyond the ability of robots. For example, as far as we can foresee, a robot is unlikely to fix a leaking pipe under the kitchen sink or clear a blocked drain on its own. And the skills of a person with considerable experience in their trade may be difficult to code. In New York City, for example, water maintenance crews rely on their experience and listening skills to pick up and locate the tell-tale signs of a leaky pipe, which has a distinctive "whooshing" sound.

Or, another example: How do you automate nursing care for the aged, which requires compassion and interpersonal engagement?

There are numerous other cases where the automation of some essential service is very difficult, if not outright impossible. These often basic services will likely continue to need the human touch, and a human workforce will be required. And even when automation is possible, humans will still be needed to monitor, manage and maintain automated solutions. Automated medical diagnostics may be very useful in sifting through all possible diagnoses and isolating those that are most likely. However, the risk of an inaccurate diagnosis means that these readings must be checked by a medical professional—that is, a human.

In the messiness of real life, there are countless different scenarios that could impact the performance of a programmed device. Artificial intelligence applications aim to deal with these new situations by constantly learning and adapting. However, in real-life settings, where the vagaries of weather and light conditions can affect the interpretation of the sensors that are the eyes and ears of the AI device, the permutations of conditions are infinite. Despite the best efforts of machine learning, there will always be something new that could throw a spanner in the works. Human oversight will always be needed to ensure things don't go awry.

Consequently, the risks associated with widescale automation and AI applications, even in some lower-skilled jobs, must be carefully considered. When a truck driver crashes his vehicle, it is treated as an isolated incident—that incident has no impact on the other trucks in the supply chain system. However, should a driverless vehicle be involved in an accident, it would immediately raise questions about systemic risk. Could the same issue recur with the other driverless vehicles operating on the same software, and be a risk to the public? Thorough investigations would be required and in a worst-case scenario, a product recall may be implemented. And as such technologies are likely to be widely adopted, the ramifications could span several countries. Such a widespread recall could cripple large parts of the supply chain.

We may think that modern innovations and changing consumer behavior would lessen the need for human resources. For example, online retailing is a fast-growing sector that has resonated with consumers, allowing them to shop from the comfort of their homes or workplaces. And as the user interface is laden with sophisticated technology, we may think it has a much lower worker requirement. In reality, it is a very inefficient form of trading, as each retailer takes the responsibility of delivering directly to individual customers. The traditional, store-based retail model is much more efficient, as it represents a hub-and-spoke system, whereas online retailing is a wasteful point-to-point system (see Figures 11 and 12). With traditional retailing, a customer visiting a mall could shop at multiple stores during one trip. By comparison, if that customer instead purchased the same items online, each checkout would initiate a separate delivery event. The situation is exacerbated as online shopping tends to have smaller basket sizes (that is, customers buy fewer items per checkout, compared to the prepared shopping list of items in traditional retail). This results in more frequent purchases, which require even more delivery trips.

The shift to online retail has already resulted in a dramatic increase in traffic levels. In the United States, the per capita rate of deliveries remained remarkably stable between 1963 and 2009, at about one freight trip a day for every ten people in the country. But this increased significantly to an average of 2.5 freight trips a day for every ten people between 2009 and 2017,[35] coinciding with the surge in online retail in that country. The number of freight trips per capita is forecast to rise even further in the years ahead as online retailing becomes more prevalent. So, as e-commerce continues to grow, the demand for drivers will increase in tandem. And even if driverless truck technology does become a practical and safe option, the issue of traffic gridlock is still there.

Figure 11: Traditional, store-based retail

Figure 12: Online retail, direct-to-customer

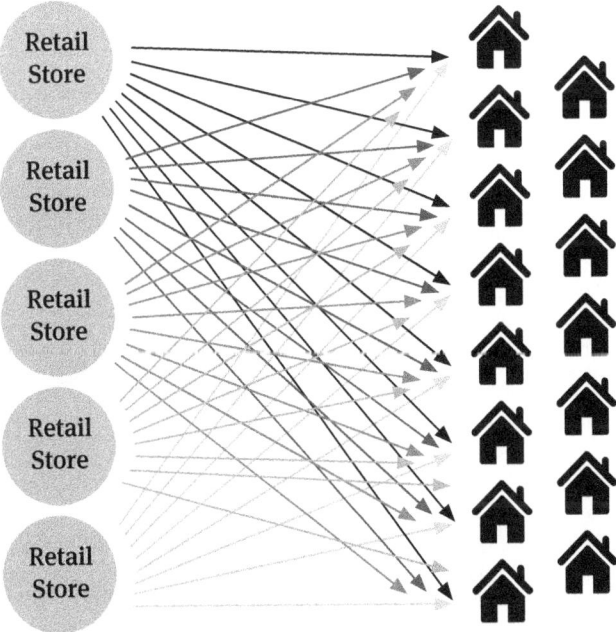

Most importantly, though, from an economic viewpoint, automation cannot replace consumers. A driverless vehicle or other robots do not go shopping, they don't go to restaurants, they don't go on holiday, and they certainly don't pay taxes. So, while robots may take over the tasks performed by some workers, they cannot replicate the spending that workers do with their wages. And that spending power forms a critical part of economic growth. Making up for the deficit of labor supply with automation, AI and technological advances does not solve the fundamental problem of there being fewer wage earners, and hence fewer consumers. An economy is hollow without consumers.

★ ★ ★

CHAPTER 6

RAISING THE RETIREMENT AGE HAS LIMITATIONS

━━━━

Eva retired at the age of 75 from her job as a legal advisor at an insurance company. This was the norm, as the retirement age was raised many years ago. Governments tried to compensate for the shortage of labor by delaying the age of retirement—first it was raised from 65 years to 70 years, and then to 75 years. Most of Eva's friends also worked to this age, although a few did not make it, having, literally, worked themselves to death.

By the time Eva retired, she was exhausted. Her mental acuity had already been softening for several years. After her husband Sam died, two years before her retirement, she had started to dread the lonely days when she would no longer be distracted by her work. She had begun to live for work. Now, a year into her retirement, she feels that her old age has caught up with her. Although the state provides the essential healthcare she needs, she sometimes wonders if more time spent with her loved ones would have been more beneficial to her overall well-being.

One of the proposed solutions to address labor shortages is to "rethink retirement"—that is, to *delay* retirement. Because people are living longer and have access to ever-improving healthcare, it stands to reason that they should be able to spend a longer time in the workforce and retire later. For example, the retirement age could be raised from 65 years to 70 or even 75 years. This would increase the longevity of the existing labor pool and dampen the negative impact of fewer young workers entering the workforce. The tax base will be maintained for a longer period and, theoretically, the number of workers available to perform essential tasks will not drop as abruptly.

But there are important practical limitations to raising the retirement age. This solution could certainly be feasible in some occupations, typically those that require less physical exertion and do not expose other parties to physical risk. Suitable occupations could include office, managerial and administrative roles, which might even be able to accommodate retirement ages approaching 80 years old. This is becoming more plausible, given improved healthcare and longer life expectancy. Over the past 60 years, life expectancy at birth has increased from 52.6 years in 1960 to 72.8 years in 2020. Less developed, low-income countries have lower life expectancies, but even there, life expectancy at birth has improved from 39.7 years in 1960 to 64.1 years in 2020. High-income countries boast life expectancies averaging 80.2 years in 2020, with 44 countries having life expectancies higher than 80 years. (At 84.6 years, Japan has the highest life expectancy in the world.)

Unfortunately, extended retirement-age policies will not have much impact on the problem of a shortage of essential workers in future. This is because jobs demand different levels of physical and mental aptitude, and these attributes wane with age. Some jobs require a level of physical effort that is not reasonable to expect from the elderly. Raising the retirement age, therefore, will not address shortages in physically demanding fields, which in many cases are the jobs of essential workers. For example, construction, maintenance and repair tasks need stronger workers who are capable of doing some heavy lifting.

Figure 13: Life expectancy at birth

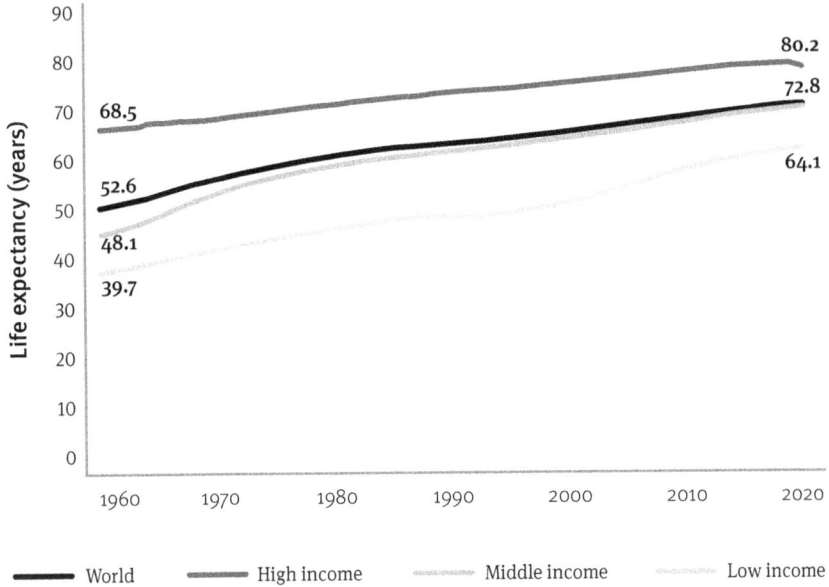

Source: World Bank

Besides the physical limitations that come with aging, the extension of the retirement age will also need to consider gender disparities in jobs as well as the difference in life expectancy between males and females. Data from the United Kingdom shows that while there is gender equality across the whole workforce, with males accounting for about 51% of all jobs in 2021, specific jobs may feature significant gender disparity. For instance, 99% of vehicle mechanics in the UK are male, while 98% of nursery school nurses and assistants are female. Figure 14 shows some of the roles that are dominated by gender.

Figure 14: Jobs by gender (United Kingdom, 2021)

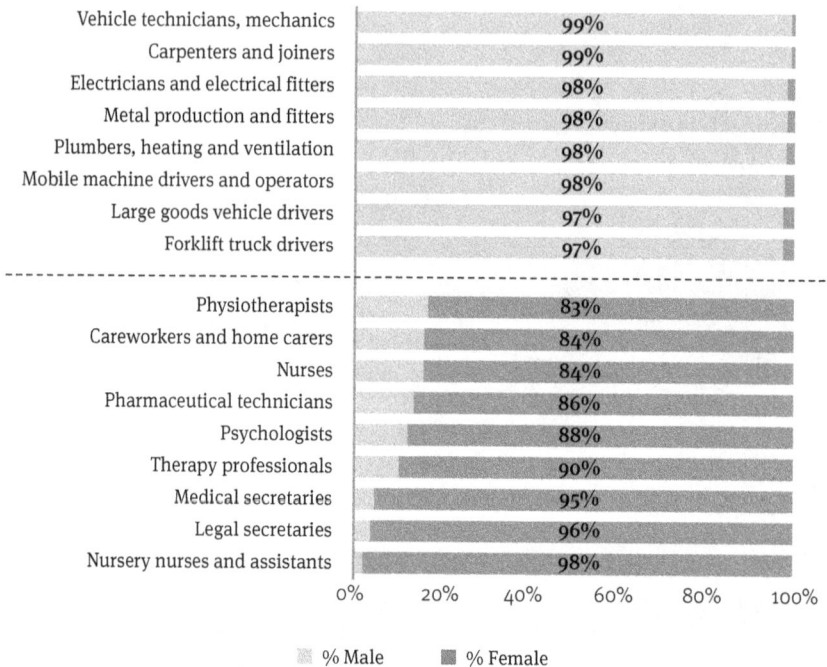

Job	%
Vehicle technicians, mechanics	99%
Carpenters and joiners	99%
Electricians and electrical fitters	98%
Metal production and fitters	98%
Plumbers, heating and ventilation	98%
Mobile machine drivers and operators	98%
Large goods vehicle drivers	97%
Forklift truck drivers	97%
Physiotherapists	83%
Careworkers and home carers	84%
Nurses	84%
Pharmaceutical technicians	86%
Psychologists	88%
Therapy professionals	90%
Medical secretaries	95%
Legal secretaries	96%
Nursery nurses and assistants	98%

% Male   % Female

Source: Working Futures, Careersmart

Many of the jobs we consider critical to the functioning of society appear to have a gender-bias—for example, the vast majority of plumbers and electricians are male, while most nurses are female. The gender disparity in some jobs is important because women, on average, live about seven years longer than men.[36] This means that, as the world population ages, there will be relatively fewer older men to step into these male-centric roles. Females account for 54% of the population in the 70-year age group, and the disparity increases with age—in the 80-year age group, women account for 58% of the cohort.

So, even if the extension of the retirement age could be applied in some fields, the roles typically taken up by males could still be affected by labor shortages as there are proportionately fewer older men in the labor pool.

Figure 15: Gender mix by age group (global, 2021)

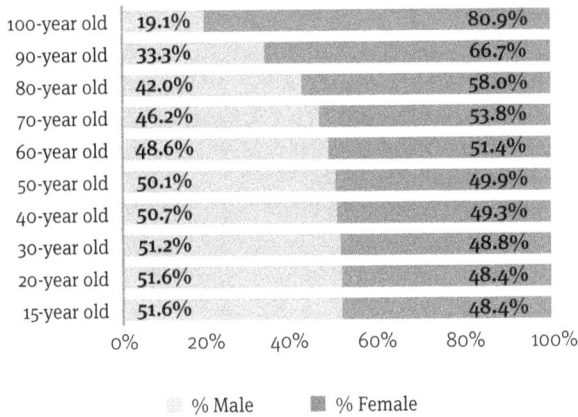

Age group	% Male	% Female
100-year old	19.1%	80.9%
90-year old	33.3%	66.7%
80-year old	42.0%	58.0%
70-year old	46.2%	53.8%
60-year old	48.6%	51.4%
50-year old	50.1%	49.9%
40-year old	50.7%	49.3%
30-year old	51.2%	48.8%
20-year old	51.6%	48.4%
15-year old	51.6%	48.4%

0%   20%   40%   60%   80%   100%

% Male   % Female

Source: United Nations World Population Prospects

Another factor to consider is the risk associated with specific jobs, which could limit the extension of retirement ages within these fields. People aged 65 and older are more likely to suffer a sudden catastrophic life event such as a heart attack or a stroke.[37] There could be considerable risk to the general public in having a 73-year-old person operating heavy machinery, driving a truck or a bus, or piloting a commercial aircraft. We may find sector-specific regulations put in place to address such risks. For example, the US Federal Aviation Administration rules require that air traffic controllers must retire at the age of 56 due to the higher probability of memory or hearing loss, inattentiveness, or reduced eyesight in older individuals.[38] Another interesting nuance is this: Jobs that carry a greater responsibility because of the risk of potential harm to others (for example, a driver losing control of an 18-wheeler truck) are often taken up by male workers—for instance, truck drivers and aircraft pilots are more than 90% male. With the shorter life expectancy of males, these higher-risk essential jobs may still suffer significant labor shortages.

It seems unlikely that improved healthcare will mitigate such age-related risks to an acceptable level, and so age will still be a limiting factor to a variety of essential services. Efforts to stave off critical labor shortages through an extension of the retirement age will be blunted by these constraints.

Lifting the retirement age is also not a popular move and often incurs vociferous public opposition. When France tried to lift its official retirement age from 62 to 64 years in 2019, it resulted in its longest workers' strike in decades. The French government resumed the effort in 2023, after the pandemic, and when it faced similar opposition, it pushed through the reforms regardless. But lifting the retirement age will only buy some time. Figures 16 and 17 show the impact of lifting the retirement age by five years on the ratio of worker-to-aged people. In the case of France, if the retirement age was increased from 65 to 70 years, the initial boost to the ratio of worker-to-aged people is significant (increasing from 2.6 to 4.0). However, the difference is whittled down over time, and by the end of the century, France could still have a worker-to-aged ratio below the tipping point of 2.0, even with an elevated retirement age of 70 years. Another example is the case of South Korea, where the benefit of lifting the retirement age diminishes much faster due to its older population pyramid profile.

Ultimately, though, the most important reason why extending the retirement age may not work as a strategy to address labor shortages in the future, is the changing attitude towards work of the younger generations. Previous generations were willing to commit to long job tenures and "lifers" were the norm. Receiving a gold watch on retirement after 30 or 40 years of service was a symbolic gesture, where the company acknowledged that "you gave us your time, now we are giving you ours". Long periods of service were considered to be a badge of honor. But the Millennials (those born between 1981 and 1996) and Generation Zers (or Gen Zers, those born between 1997 and 2012) have very different attitudes towards jobs. They want a better work-life balance, with more flexibility and more time off. Loyalty to an employer is less important to them, and consequently, they change jobs more frequently. Data from the United States indicate that the average tenure of workers aged between 25 and 34 years decreased from 3.2 years in 2012, to 2.8 years in 2022.[39]

The COVID-19 pandemic caused many to reflect on what is important to them. Many are no longer willing to put up with jobs that are not aligned with their goals in life. This has resulted in trends such as the "Great Resignation" and "Quiet Quitting". These shifts towards

Figure 16: Impact of lifting retirement age by 5 years—France

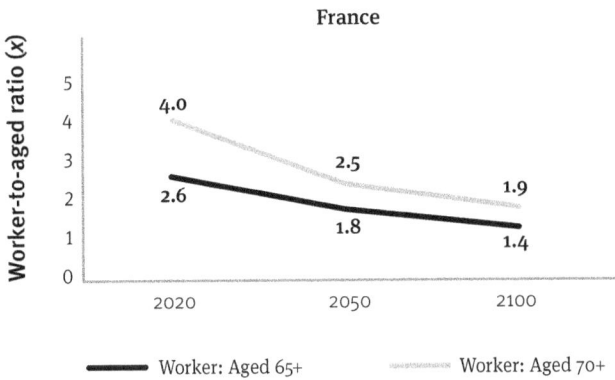

Figure 17: Impact of lifting retirement age by 5 years—South Korea

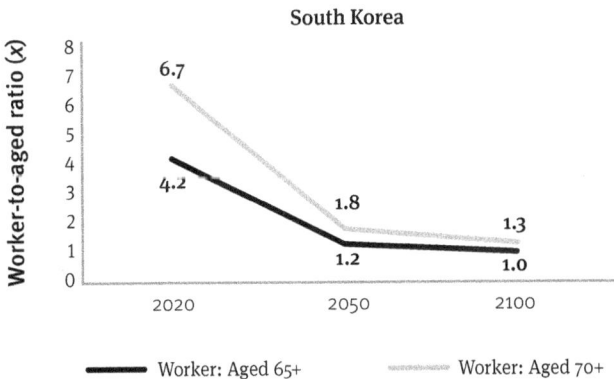

Source: Author's calculations based on United Nations data

greater self-interest and more concern for self-care means that Gen Z workers and those who come after them may desire shorter work lives, possibly aiming to retire earlier than previous generations.

Think about it from their point of view—the average life expectancy in high-income countries is around 80 years, which means that with a retirement age of 65, they can look forward to around 15 "golden years". If the retirement age is increased to 70, their "golden years" period is cut by a third and they may only have 10 years left to enjoy their retirement. And as males have shorter life expectancy than females (77 years, compared to 83 years for females in high-income countries), men could end up enjoying only seven years of retirement, on average, with these policy solutions. Expecting Gen Z workers and subsequent generations to toil longer in their jobs with only a handful of sunset years may well prove to be unrealistic.

We will return to the topic of the attitudes of younger workers in a later chapter. For now, what is important to realise is that raising the retirement age will not solve the problem of a shortage of essential workers. Tweaking the retirement age will only provide a temporary reprieve in some non-essential jobs—the looming shortage of essential workers remains largely unaffected.

★ ★ ★

CHAPTER 7

BAD EDUCATION—THE JOBS DISCONNECT IN DEVELOPED MARKETS

As an only child, Eva had all available opportunities for success presented to her. Her parents worked hard. They were not rich, but as a solid middle-class family with their joint incomes concentrated on a single child, they could afford to give Eva an excellent education. After graduating with a law degree, she found a job as a compliance officer at an insurance firm. Throughout her career, she switched jobs often, moving to new roles every few years. She ended her career as a legal advisor, returning to the same insurance company she started her career at.

She had been fortunate in her professional life, always finding work that was in line with the expertise her studies had afforded her. Jobs for some highly skilled people had become more and more scarce. All her friends graduated with advanced degrees, but some of them had ultimately not been well-rewarded for their choices. Her parents taught her that a good education would guarantee a comfortable life. This may have been true when those with advanced education were in the minority, but now, when most people had tertiary qualifications, the value equation had changed dramatically.

As countries develop and their citizens' general standard of living increases, the quality of education also improves. The trend over the past few decades has been that each successive generation typically matches or beats their parents' educational level. The young stand on the shoulders of the generation before, and seek to reach greater heights with their accomplishments. While this is a noble ambition and has contributed to the advancement of economies in the past, this relentless upward progression in educational attainment can lead to a severe mismatch between supply and demand in the workforce, especially for essential labor jobs.

The chart below shows how education to a tertiary level has grown over the years. By way of example, in 1970 only about 3% of South Korea's and Singapore's adult population were educated to degree level. By 2020, their proportion of adults with degrees had increased to 33% and they are projected to pass the 50% mark by 2050. In younger age groups, the proportion of university graduates is already very high. For instance, in the European Union, 40% of people aged between 30 and 34 had a tertiary level of education by 2017.[40]

Figure 18: Percentage of adults educated to degree level (1970 to 2050)

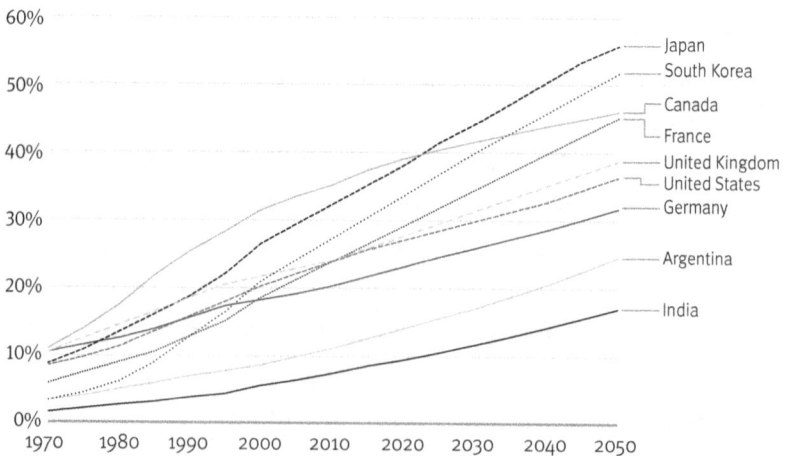

Source: *International Institute for Applied Systems Analysis (IIASA)*

In 2020, only 18 countries had 25% or higher of their adult population educated to degree level, with Canada leading the pack at 39.2% and Japan at 38.1%. By 2050, it is predicted that 56 countries will achieve this milestone of educational advancement, with Japan leading with 55.8% of its adult population projected to have completed university degrees.

While this is commendable, there is an awkward problem brewing. If a high proportion of the population have achieved tertiary education and are skilled in specific, advanced fields, who then will perform the less glamorous yet essential "blue-collar" work? If most people in developed countries qualify as doctors, lawyers, software engineers, and in other professional fields, who will pack the supermarket shelves or collect the garbage? Who will repair roads and bridges, and who will fix the plumbing? As countries develop and incomes rise, their respective workforces naturally shift away from these traditionally lower-paying jobs. At some stage in future, there will be too few locals available to do some of these basic, yet essential, tasks in countries with high levels of educational attainment. There is already evidence of this unintended consequence of extensive tertiary education in some developed countries.

Canada provides one such example. At 39.2%, Canada had the highest proportion of adults with degrees in 2020. In 2021, it was reported that in some Canadian provinces, the highest job vacancies included those for cooks, home support workers, material handlers, cleaners and carpenters.[41] These are not high-skilled jobs and may fall well below the aspirations of many of the country's highly educated population. Young Canadians have a higher level of education than the national average, with 63% of Canadians aged 25 to 34 years in possession of a college or university education. Higher education is often funded by student debt, which compels young graduates to look for high-paying jobs, so they can service their student debt. The result is that more and more Canadians are not interested in essential jobs, and these vacancies have to be filled by immigrant labor.

Some 38.1% of Japan's adult population is educated to degree level. But Japan is also one of the world's most homogeneous societies, and the country has long maintained a closed-door policy on immigration. Historically, the percentage of immigrants in the total population was very low at about 1% (compared to 11% in Europe and 12% in North America).[42] When the country did experience labor shortages, it filled the gaps with foreign technical interns. For example, the Japanese Technical Intern program was created in 1993 to give young people from across Asia an opportunity to gain professional experience in Japan, while completing an internship for a period of two to five years. Japan, in turn, benefited from a temporary labor pool without having to revamp its immigration policy. But the number of technical interns in Japan has been steadily increasing in recent years, from 150,000 in 2012 to 412,500 in 2023, mostly from Vietnam, China or the Philippines.[43] The rising number of technical interns is a reflection of the growing gaps in the Japanese workforce. Now that it is facing acute labor shortages, the Japanese government is planning to allow more foreign workers in blue-collar positions to stay indefinitely, along with their families.[44]

In the United Kingdom, the "Polish plumber" and the "Romanian builder" were stereotypes for cheap labor coming from Central and Eastern Europe in the 1990s. But stereotypes aside, these workers filled a critical void in the labor market left by young British people aspiring to better jobs more suited to their higher education levels. By 2016, though, fears that cheap Eastern European labor was threatening the jobs of locals contributed to a referendum on the continued British membership of the European Union, which resulted in a 52% majority voting to leave the Union. This response to anti-immigrant rhetoric has led to labor shortages in the UK in some critical areas, such as truck drivers.

The perpetual quest to better ourselves and improve the education levels of our children is contributing to a growing mismatch in the labor market in developed countries. Regardless of how advanced and well-developed a country may be, there will always be some sort of basic labor functions that will need to be performed. Even in developed countries, employment in the agriculture, construction and mining sectors (which typically employ lower-skilled workers) account for around 10% to 15% of the total workforce.[45] And with the local population attaining higher levels of education, a vacuum develops in the lower-skilled jobs segment. That gap must be filled, and it is most likely to be filled by immigrants.

Italy, for example, had a high unemployment rate of 9.8% in 2021, but at the same time there was a severe shortage of labor in the agriculture and hospitality sectors. The country had 2.3 million people available to work, but who were basically unwilling to take on the jobs that were available. Italy has an advanced economy, but still has a substantial labor-intensive agriculture sector employing 3.6% of the workforce. And as a major global tourist destination, its hospitality sector employs some 14.7% of the total workforce. These two sectors alone account for almost a fifth of Italy's workforce, paying relatively low wages to lower-skilled workers. Young Italians, 28% of whom have attained a tertiary qualification, may not find these sorts of jobs appealing. This creates a demand for immigrant labor.

Let's consider these trends from a broader perspective. Each of the examples above suggests an interesting correlation that unfolds as countries develop and their population's education levels rise. The rise in the standard of living is accompanied by a rise in immigration, because the rise in educational attainment by the local population creates a void in the lower-skilled, lower-paid jobs space. Data from the United States, represented in the chart below, shows the near-perfect correlation between the increase in educational attainment and an increase in immigrants as a proportion of the population.

Figure 19: Immigrant population compared to adult education levels (United States)

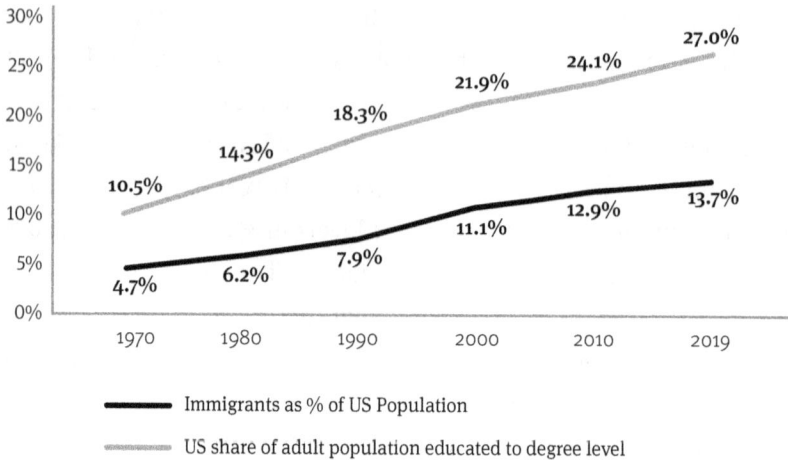

Immigrants as % of US Population

US share of adult population educated to degree level

Source: Author's analysis, Migrationpolicy.org, World Bank

As the number of people attaining tertiary education in developed countries is projected to continue increasing, demand for immigrant labor will increase proportionately. In the short term, these gaps can be filled by foreign workers, often from poorer countries with lower education levels. However, as more countries join the list of recruiters, the supply from traditional sources may not be sufficient. Western European countries who preferred hiring from Eastern European countries may find that the supply of labor there has dried up. Similarly, Japan's traditional recruiting ground in Southeast Asia may be close to depleted. In the decades ahead, the source of immigration will need to shift to Africa, which would still be capable of providing surplus labor. As will be seen later, the shortages in essential workers in developed nations will place African countries in a strong position in the future labor market.

In this chapter, we have seen that rising education levels in developed countries have led to a workforce that often isn't willing to settle for blue-collar jobs—many of which can be classified as essential to support societal functions. But there is another reason why younger people are becoming less suited to the demands of the job market. The change in family dynamics, where parents have fewer children and focus more resources on them, has created a generation that may not be temperamentally suited to what the market will soon demand. We will explore this dynamic in the next chapter. The capacity of the future working-age cohort to deliver essential labor is under relentless pressure from all sides.

* * *

CHAPTER 8

HANDLE WITH CARE

——

Eva trembles. She needs to take her medication for anxiety. She has been on medication since her student days, and it has become a part of her daily regimen. When she worked, she regularly took time off for sick leave, mental wellness breaks, and annual holidays. Her employers were always very accommodating, as greater awareness of mental health became the norm.

Eva takes a big gulp of water to wash down her medication. Leaning back in her chair and closing her eyes, she contemplates how dependent she has become on medication. Even in her school days, she can recall taking some form of medication to calm her nerves. And along with the medication came the therapy and counseling. Over the years, she has had several different therapists. To Eva, they became friends and confidants, despite still charging on the clock. But hers was not a unique situation. Having a therapist was as normal as having a dentist, and everyone she knew went for regular therapy sessions.

There was a time when excellence was celebrated and competition encouraged. Individual achievement was highly prized, and innovation was born out of hard work, talent, and determination.

But somewhere around the early 2000s, with the nurturing of a new generation (specifically Gen Z, those born after 1997), the thinking shifted towards increasing inclusivism. Instead of only celebrating those who excelled, we thought it would be better to acknowledge and reward everyone who participated in an activity. It seemed like a good idea at the time—leave no child behind, and ensure that every child in a class or in a sports team feels appreciated and has their self-confidence boosted. Anything and everything was recognized and acknowledged. There were prizes for the most improved, the most diligent, the best attendance. As long as no child's feelings were hurt.

The decline in the fertility rate and smaller family sizes may have contributed to this change in mindset. With only one or two children, instead of a squad of four or more children that earlier generations would typically rear, parents were more protective of their smaller families. They were able to concentrate their resources on one or two children and wanted to make sure that those children were afforded the best opportunities, to give them the greatest chance of success. Parents became over-protective and intervened whenever a perceived threat or obstacle arose, whether it was challenging a teacher about poor grades for a project, or taking the coach to task if the child was not selected for the team. Children were thus shielded from many early experiences of setbacks and failure. Whenever things did not go their way, a child could bank on a doting parent sweeping in to make things right.

These behavioral changes spread beyond the schoolyard. They led to sensitivity-awareness practices being applied in other areas, with the aim that nobody would feel offended or be aggrieved. Universities became hyper-sensitive to topics raised in debates and discussions. "Cancel culture" took hold, snubbing out anything that may even vaguely be perceived as potentially insensitive to some groups. Safe spaces were conceived where individuals could shelter from any harshness that they thought was out there threatening them. This movement coincided with the rise of social media, which spread its influence among young people.

While the intention of promoting better mental well-being and softening the harder edges of life for young people was noble, there have been unintended consequences that could have a profound impact in future. These outcomes may well surface at a time when the seismic changes in demographics would present this generation and future ones with uniquely challenging situations.

In the book *The Coddling of the American Mind: How Good Intentions and Bad Ideas Are Setting Up a Generation for Failure* (2018), the authors Greg Lukianoff and Jonathan Haidt argue that over-protection is having a negative effect on university students. They contend that embracing "safetyism" (a culture in which safety, including "emotional safety", has become sacrosanct) interferes with young people's social, emotional, and intellectual development, and makes it more difficult for them to become well-adjusted adults who can navigate the challenges of life. Living organisms generally grow stronger and better adapted to the world's demands through exposure to stress and challenges. One example is the immune system, which grows stronger by developing the antibodies required to combat antigens. The body uses exposure to foreign microbes to develop immunity against them. There are therefore benefits to being exposed to some of the microbes that lurk about in the messy, real world. Avoiding danger by over-sanitizing can make us less resilient and, contrary to our intentions, can make us *more* vulnerable to increasingly drug-resistant bacteria.[46] The old adages "what doesn't kill you makes you stronger" and "no pain, no gain" hold considerable truths. The equivalent when confronted with a perceived psychological threat is to avoid that threat, instead of dealing with it. In so doing, the person does not develop the ability to navigate these situations with resilience.

This is reminiscent of the parable of the butterfly, which goes something like this. A man found a cocoon in his garden. He noticed a small opening in the cocoon, and watched the young butterfly for a while as it struggled to force its body through that tiny gap. After a while, the butterfly stopped making progress. It appeared as if it had gotten as far as it could, and could go no further without help. Thinking he could help the butterfly, the man took a small twig and carefully widened the gap in the cocoon so that the butterfly could emerge easily. When it emerged, however, he noticed that the body was swollen, and the wings were shriveled. The man thought that the condition of the butterfly was probably due to having been cooped up in that tiny cocoon. So, he watched the young butterfly for a while, expecting that the wings would open up and expand to support the body. But this did not happen. The struggles of the butterfly in the cocoon were actually needed to strengthen and develop its new body, so that it would be able to use its wings to fly away. The butterfly spent the rest of its short life crawling around with a swollen body and shriveled wings, unable to fly. Through this misplaced act of kindness, the man had prevented the young butterfly from fully developing and becoming strong enough to face the outside world.

Our own acts of misplaced kindness may well be setting up a generation that will be ill-equipped for the demographic transition that will unfold over the coming decades. The novel efforts taken to "help" young people at school and universities could have similar consequences. By removing obstacles, creating safe spaces, and eliminating any supposed psychological threats, we are preventing this generation from developing the necessary skills to prepare them for a world that will be getting harsher with every decade.

China's one-child policy provides a fascinating real-life example, on an immense scale, of how individuals raised in an over-protective environment may turn out. Research published in 2013 by Cameron, Erkal, Gangadharan and Meng[47] argues that the one-child policy has given rise to a land of "little emperors" whose parents dote on them excessively. The study concluded that single-child households have produced individuals who are significantly less trusting, more risk averse, less competitive, more pessimistic, less conscientious (that is, less diligent and with a lower motivation to achieve) and more neurotic (more sensitive and less confident).

The Chinese research study findings are consistent with widespread concerns that were apparent within that country before the abolition of the one-child policy in 2016. Concerns about the social skills of the single-child generation, and the observation that these children tend to be more self-centered and less cooperative, were prevalent in the country. In some cases, Chinese employers even included phrases like "no single children" in job advertisements (in effect limiting recruitment to the older generation born before 1980). In addition to the risk of population decline, the behavioral consequences of the one-child policy may have been a key reason for its abolition in 2016. As early as March 2007, delegates in the Chinese People's Political Consultative Conference called on the government to abolish the policy, citing concerns about "social problems and personality disorders in young people".[48]

Importantly, the Chinese study's authors noted that their findings were based on cohorts born around the time of the introduction of the one-child policy in 1980. The effect of the policy on the behavior of people born long after its introduction may differ, as later cohorts will have grown up with very limited extended family and in a society dominated by children growing up without siblings. The researchers believe that the impact on later cohorts may be magnified. If this turns out to be the case, it has significant ramifications for the rest of the developed world. Developed countries, without any coercion from their governments, have also trended towards single-child families— they too could experience similar social consequences, perhaps only with some time lag.

In a world where fertility rates are dropping, and one-child families are becoming the norm, the observations from the study on the effects of the Chinese one-child policy serve as a harbinger of what could come.

These findings are ominous, as they suggest that future generations of workers could be more risk-averse, less competitive, less diligent, more sensitive and nervous, and less confident. This means that these young people are less likely to choose risky occupations including entrepreneurship, which is a key driver for economic development. The traits of being less competitive and less diligent could impact the quality of their work, while increased sensitivity and nervousness may result in more down-time and lower productivity. Overall, these traits do not bode well for businesses in the future.

It is perhaps no coincidence that the "quiet quitting" movement which started trending in the West in 2022 was preceded by the Chinese social movement "*tang ping*" (which translates to "lying flat") the previous year. *Tang ping* was a social protest against the societal pressure to overwork in modern Chinese culture, which included the "996 work culture" (where people work from 9am to 9pm, six days a week). Quiet quitting is a movement where mostly younger employees choose to do the bare minimum at work, and not go above and beyond the requirements of their job descriptions. This can be problematic for employers because most jobs, particularly jobs requiring highly skilled workers, need some level of extra effort when collaborating with co-workers to meet customer demands. A growing pool of disengaged employees can cause a decline in the company's customer service levels and undermine its performance.

In China, the *tang ping* trend was soon followed in 2022 by the more extreme *bai lan* (which literally means "let it rot"). Some disillusioned young Chinese are deciding to "let it rot" and giving up on striving for high achievement (or any achievement at all) in modern Chinese society.[49] It remains to be seen if this trend will spread to the West and if a more extreme version of "quiet quitting" will arise. Nevertheless, the renewed popularization and widespread acceptance of a slacker culture among younger workers could not have come at a worse time.

In a future where there are proportionately fewer workers relative to aged people, there will be much more pressure on those workers to perform. The fewer workers will be expected to work harder and shoulder a greater burden. However, what is suggested by the research findings on China's one-child policy and trends such as quiet quitting, is that many in this generation may not have the inclination to rise to the challenge.

Members of Gen Z have decidedly different attitudes to work than their immediate predecessors, the Millennials. Indeed, Gen Z views regarding work would also be completely alien to those of Gen X (who were born between 1965 and 1980). Whereas Millennials entering the workplace valued career progression and personal development over compensation, the top priority for Gen Z workers is higher pay.[50] They also want a better work-life balance, with more time off, and have clear boundaries between work and personal life. A 2022 survey conducted in the United States showed that 82% of Gen Z respondents wanted mental health days as a perk. Companies have to respond to these demands because Gen Z is not bluffing—unlike the Millennials, who may have only wished for similar benefits, Gen Z workers readily quit their jobs if they are unhappy with the workplace environment. Another study from the United States, conducted in 2021, found that 77% of the Gen Z members surveyed were actively on the hunt for a new job. By comparison, a similar survey from a decade earlier found that 38% of Millennials were looking to change jobs at the same stage of their careers.[51] Attitudes toward job loyalty have clearly changed: so far as Gen Z is concerned, being a lifer at work is a thing of the past.

The apparent Gen Z attitude towards work is being abetted by two key factors. The first is social media, which allows for greater transparency and awareness, and the second is that this generation is entering the workplace in a post-pandemic world. A 2022 LinkedIn survey found that Gen Z workers are far more willing to share their salary details with others, compared to older working generations.[52] Given all their social media proclivities, pay levels and the achievements of others serve as a benchmark against which they measure themselves. Previous generations were blissfully unaware of what other workers in their organization or field were earning, and tended to stick to the job at hand. As Gen Z workers observe the financial successes of others, a fear-of-missing-out (popularly termed "FOMO") reaction may set in. This contributes to an almost perpetual dissatisfaction with their career paths and results in shorter workplace tenures, as workers regularly seek greener pastures. The fundamental qualities of our future business leaders are being shaped under these conditions; and when they are required to step up, their performance could echo their experience.

Besides the disruptive impact of workers changing jobs with more frequency, there is also a tangible financial impact on businesses. Investment in training and skills development by companies could yield lower returns if those employees being trained change jobs more frequently. For example, training as a heavy goods vehicle (HGV) driver in the United Kingdom costs about £3,000 per driver in 2021. Between 2011 and 2021, about 250,000 people under the age of 40 were trained as HGV drivers in the United Kingdom. Subsequently, though, around 150,000 of these drivers left the industry. This means that almost half a billion pounds has been invested in training drivers, who then did not go on to practise their trade.[53] Such fruitless expenditure could well be repeated across a wide spectrum of industries where training is required. In time, companies could become disincentivized from investing in costly skills development programs if employees are unlikely to remain in their jobs for long. This could have significant knock-on effects for the quality of their products and services and ultimately, their competitiveness and financial performance. The erosion of skills in the workforce ultimately disadvantages both the worker and the employer, and in the long run, the very foundations of large organizations may come under threat.

The decline of institutional memory and the end of corporate culture?

Establishing and maintaining a strong corporate culture is one of the fundamental building blocks of modern business management. "Corporate culture" refers to the shared values and behaviors that characterize a company and is crystallized in its mission and vision statements, as well as in the leadership style. A strong corporate culture helps to create a positive and productive work environment, while a toxic corporate culture can lead to low morale and high staff turnover, which can impede the company's performance. Developing a successful corporate culture takes time, and in the case of large organizations, it could take many years, if not decades, to build.

A critical element in building and maintaining corporate culture is institutional memory—the stored knowledge within the organization that is developed over time and shared with new staff. Institutional memory is not saved in a database or printed in manuals. It is preserved in the collective experience and skills of staff who have been with the organization for long periods. The longer the tenure of individual staff members, the stronger the institutional memory is likely to be. The converse is that shorter staff tenures would lower institutional memory significantly, and thus undermine the corporate culture. Think about it this way—if after every five years, 90% of the company's staff is new (that is, they have been with the company for less than five years), what possible long-term institutional memory would the staff have? How could any corporate culture be maintained with such constant changes in the composition of the team? And what happens if that time frame shortens to an average of three years? Such high staff turnover rates would cause institutional memory to fade— effectively, a form of "institutional amnesia". The collective learnings of past experiences would be lost, and strategic mistakes of the past may be repeated.

Would large, transformative projects ever again be possible with a labor force that is so fickle? For example, the Apollo space program in the United States, which succeeded in landing humans on the moon, ran for more than a decade and at its peak employed 400,000 people.[54] Such projects require long-term commitments, dedication and sacrifices—attributes which may not be in abundance among workers in the future. The era of the large multinational corporation could come to an end, as businesses shrink in number of staff—not only because the pool of labor will be smaller, but also because of the difficulty in managing and maintaining large teams when there is high staff turnover.

Analysis of resume data by CareerBuilder in 2021 provides an indication of how long a typical member of each generation stays in their job in the United States.[55] Whereas the older generations might spend up to eight years in a job, the average Gen Z and Millennial worker spends less than three years in a role before moving on to other opportunities. The rate of staff turnover for workers in the younger generations is therefore more than twice that of the past.

Figure 20: Average length of time spent in a job per generation (US, 2021)

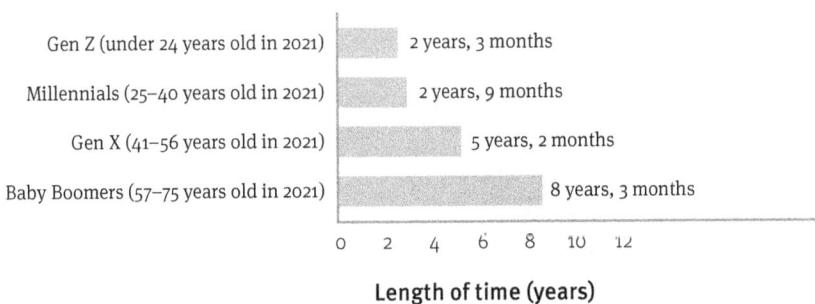

Gen Z (under 24 years old in 2021)	2 years, 3 months
Millennials (25–40 years old in 2021)	2 years, 9 months
Gen X (41–56 years old in 2021)	5 years, 2 months
Baby Boomers (57–75 years old in 2021)	8 years, 3 months

Length of time (years)

Source: CareerBuilder

The oldest Gen Z workers finished school just before the onset of the COVID-19 pandemic, and the remote-working situations that resulted from lockdowns fitted in well with their views on the work-life balance. Even as the pandemic restrictions fade into memory, many of them still prefer remote or hybrid working arrangements. While many modern roles can accommodate remote working, there are significant drawbacks for a young person learning the ropes of a new career remotely. Not all skills transfers can take place in Zoom meetings, and the transfer of institutional memory is certainly less effective in scheduled online interactions. Similarly, the assimilation of corporate culture by remote-working staff would be less than ideal.

In the past, trusted and valued employees with deep corporate experience acquired over many years would eventually progress to become leaders within the company. In the future, however, the corporate professional may well be a new breed of consultant-type manager, with a succession of short-term experiences; someone who views jobs as discrete and temporary "projects" instead of milestones along a career path. They may view leadership roles as just another gig in their career, and another entry to be added to their constantly circulating CVs. A *Harvard Business Review* study found that the 2019 list of the world's best-performing CEOs held their jobs for an average of 15 years.[56] Future corporate leadership is unlikely to exhibit such stability. Future business leaders who do not have a history of long tenure, or the inclination towards job longevity, may cause companies to vacillate from one strategy to another, as it switches from one CEO to the next every three to five years. Ultimately, companies could pay a high price for this evolution in management.

Companies face not only a projected shortage of workers in future, but a radically different type of workforce: one that is less ambitious, less loyal, and may not be committed for the long haul. This is in dramatic contrast to previous generations, and will have an impact on worker productivity, the effectiveness of management, and ultimately corporate performance. Companies too may suffer their own Age of Decay.

★ ★ ★

CHAPTER 9

A LIFE DISRUPTED

Eva is looking forward to an upcoming visit from her only son, Matthew. He last visited two years ago. He was supposed to visit last Christmas, but his trip was canceled on short notice by the airline, a routine occurrence in these days of chronic staff shortages. He only has two weeks of leave per year, due to his hectic work commitments. Eva had wanted to take him to her favorite Italian restaurant, but they closed down a few months ago. The eatery was very popular and seemed successful, but the owner continually struggled to find enough kitchen staff and waiters. Eventually, he couldn't cope with the stress of dealing with the shortage of labor, and just closed the restaurant down.

On a summer weekend late in June 2022, more than 1,500 flights were canceled in the United States. This caused major disruptions in travel ahead of the busy July 4th holiday weekend.[57] The flights disappeared quickly from previously arranged schedules, throwing air travel into chaos. And this was not an occurrence unique to the United States. North of the border, Air Canada canceled up to 10% of its flights between July and August 2022, amounting to around 150 abandoned flights per day. Flight cancelations in Europe were more than double the cancelations of American carriers between April and June of that same year.[58] Adding to the flight cancelation mayhem, airports were often congested with queues of passengers extending beyond the terminal doors. Camping out in departure halls was a common sight, due to delays with security and check-in procedures. Luggage collection became chaotic as bags piled up, separated from owners who left after frustratingly long waits, and instead hoped to retrieve their possessions the following day. The chaos was so bad that Heathrow Airport in London, one of the world's busiest international transport hubs, had to ask airlines to stop selling excess tickets, and set a capacity limit of 100,000 departing passengers per day. Prior to the COVID-19 pandemic, Heathrow Airport had comfortably processed 125,000 departing passengers per day.

What was the cause of the severe travel disruption that characterized the summer of 2022? At the root of the long queues, the canceled flights, and the overnight stays in terminals surrounded by abandoned baggage, was a lack of adequate staffing. In the midst of the crisis, the German airline Lufthansa lamented that their efforts to rectify the situation were thwarted because "many employees and resources are still unavailable". During the pandemic, many experienced people left the sector, either voluntarily or due to retrenchment. In the post-pandemic recovery, airlines, airports, and other key parts of the aviation ecosystem had been unable to hire enough qualified staff to replace them. Hiring new employees in the air transportation sector is not a simple process as it is slowed down by the tight security pass requirements that permit work on an airplane or even within the airport security zone. The German government said it would assist in bringing in airport security workers from places like Turkey to fill the void, while the Irish Transportation Ministry put the army on standby to help alleviate staffing issues at Dublin Airport. Clearly, the crisis was viewed with such seriousness that government resources were required to keep the sector running.

While the significant issues facing air travel in June 2022 were an unintended consequence of the layoff of workers during the COVID-19 pandemic, it gave us a preview of how our lives could be impacted if we experience chronic labor shortages in the future. Every aspect of our lives relies on some sort of human labor, and this dependency on labor will be threatened with regular disruption in a future that is starved of pairs of hands to do the work. What should make the transport chaos of the summer of 2022 particularly alarming is that it occurred in a sector that has embraced automation to a far greater extent than many other industries. Automation technologies pioneered by the airline industry include online and self-check-in systems and sophisticated bar-coded baggage handling systems that can count and weigh bags, balance loads, and direct luggage to departing aircraft automatically. Yet, with all this sophisticated labor-reducing technology, the system was ultimately still brought to its knees by a lack of workers.

A key insight from the travel chaos of 2022 is that as we increase automation, the number of jobs being performed by humans may well reduce, but the remaining workers are increasingly positioned at critical points in the system. So, when there is a shortage of labor in a largely automated system, it occurs at a critical point and bottlenecks quickly develop—soon, the whole system starts to unravel. A basic job, such as removing offloaded baggage from a cargo container and placing it on the luggage carousel, can bring an airport to a screeching halt. This problem occurred at Manchester Airport in July 2022, because there were too few workers to do the physical offloading. Returning holidaymakers were left frustrated and, in desperation, some even climbed through the carousel curtain in a bid to retrieve stranded bags, prompting armed airport police to intervene in what was effectively a security breach.

Such chaotic disruption will not be confined to the airline industry. Similar disruptions, with the same underlying causes, could be replicated across the entire spectrum of the economy. For example, your local supermarket might occasionally close on short notice, or operate with reduced hours, should there be insufficient staff available to run the store on any particular day. This has happened in the Netherlands, when there were about 40,000 job vacancies in the retail sector during 2022.[59] Many medium-sized retailers there were forced to shorten their trading hours to cope with the reduced staff complement, for example, closing two hours earlier at 18:00, instead of the normal 20:00. Some businesses even resorted to closing smaller branches entirely, in order to deploy staff to larger, busier stores.

Even if the store maintained scheduled opening hours, many shelves could be empty because suppliers are unable to produce enough products due to their own staff shortages. A similar situation would arise if there were a shortage of truck drivers, crippling the logistical operations that move products from factories to stores. This happened in the United States in January 2022, when the Omicron variant of the COVID-19 virus swept through that country. As more and more workers called in sick, severe labor shortages choked the supply chain. The logistics breakdown between factories, distribution centers, and stores resulted in empty shelves in supermarkets. And when consumers become accustomed to inconsistent availability in stores, they respond by overstocking when goods are in store—these panic buys put even more pressure on an already fragile supply chain.

Online retailing will not side-step these logistical challenges, even if it reduces dependency on costly bricks-and-mortar stores. As was noted in Chapter 5, online retailing is less efficient than traditional retailing and puts a huge strain on last-mile delivery execution. Online retailing is therefore just as exposed to critical labor shortages in the supply chain as traditional retailers are. Instead of finding empty shelves in stores, customers will find that many items are simply not available on the app, or there are not enough drivers to do deliveries.

Regular power outages could be another feature of our future daily lives. The staff needed to operate and maintain electricity generation plants and transmission networks could be overstretched, leading to flagging performance. An example of this is South Africa's power utility, Eskom, which has seen a consistent decline in plant generation performance since 2014. This decline was partly due to a dwindling skills base at the South African electricity provider. The reduction in energy generation resulted in nationwide loadshedding in South Africa, with debilitating power cuts of up to 12 hours a day by 2022.

Shortages of skilled labor could also hamper emergency mainte-nance in utility companies. For instance, restoring power supply following storm damage is likely to take much longer if fewer workers are available. After the superstorm Sandy hit in 2012, utilities in New York took 13 days to restore power to 95% of customers.[60] Hurricane Katrina in 2004 had been even worse, with local utilities only able to restore power to three-quarters of their customers after 23 days. In a future where human resources are severely over-stretched, power lines that go down during storms could take weeks or even months to repair. Think what life would be like without electricity—after a day or two, your mobile phone's battery will run out, leaving you disconnected from your community of friends and family; you have no internet connection, lights or television. A couple of days of this may be tolerable, but a few weeks may be unbearable for a generation that grew up always connected to the internet.

Burst pipes, water leaks and blocked drains are similar public-affecting problems whose repair we take for granted. However, with reduced availability of labor (such as plumbers and civil engineering workers), these breakdowns may not be fixed promptly. After an abnormally cold winter snap in Texas in February 2021, there were widespread incidents of frozen and burst water pipes.[61] Frozen pipes can burst when the water trapped inside freezes and begins to expand. The cold snap resulted in a sharp spike in the demand for plumbers to do emergency repairs, but there were too few plumbers in Texas to attend to all the service calls timeously. A plumbing contractor business in the city of Austin reported that at one stage, it had over 2,500 customers awaiting service. The governor had to sign orders allowing out-of-state plumbers to obtain provisional licenses to work in Texas, and to allow plumbers without current licenses to go back to work immediately. Imagine life without running water in your home—you can't wash or shower, or even flush the toilet.

Healthcare services will be in high demand as a larger proportion of the population becomes aged. The doctor-to-patient ratio and healthcare worker-to-patient ratio could drop significantly, driving up costs but also potentially diminishing the quality of care. The importance of healthcare workers, and the impact on society when they are overwhelmed by demand for their services, was made abundantly clear during the early stages of the COVID-19 pandemic in 2020. Doctors, nurses and other healthcare workers were required to put in long shifts to cope with the influx of sick people. Many struggled with the physical and emotional burden that society placed on them. In a study published by the *Journal of the American Medical Association*, the number of doctors who reported feeling burned out rose from 32% in 2019 to 40% in 2022, while nurses reporting long-term exhaustion increased from 41% in 2019 to 49% in 2022.[62] The situation will only get worse as the World Health Organization predicts a global shortage of around 15 million healthcare workers by 2030. The prospects of a healthcare system permanently under the strain it experienced during the height of the COVID-19 pandemic, should be very unsettling.

Chronic labor shortages could have another result: the reduction of public transport schedules. With fewer drivers, the number of bus trips and scheduled trains will have to be cut, causing longer waiting periods between trips. A shortage of transportation workers can have a knock-on impact on other sectors as well. When buses or trains run less frequently, commuters' schedules will be disrupted, affecting the broader economy. For example, workers might have difficulty getting to their jobs on time. In late 2021, several large cities in the United States experienced labor shortages in their public transportation systems.[63] New York's Metropolitan Transportation Authority, the largest public transit system in the United States, was so desperate for workers that it sent letters to 700 retired subway operators, offering them $35,000 to come back to work for three months (considering the average annual salary for a train operator in New York was $49,700 at the time, this was a substantial incentive).

Faced with a shortage of staff, restaurants could opt to shorten their business hours or even close for full days, because hospitality and catering staff would likely be in short supply. This happened in many restaurants in the United States during the summer of 2022, because staff did not return to the industry in sufficient numbers after the pandemic. If restaurants did maintain regular opening times, diners could be faced with longer waits for their food. During that summer, customers in the United States found themselves waiting for seating for 30 minutes or longer, even when there were tables available. This was a direct result of short-staffed kitchens.[64] In addition, the quality of service could drop as waiters and cleaning staff become hard to find.

The tourism and hospitality sectors are set to experience extreme difficulties in a future with a shortage of workers. An example is that of Benidorm, a seaside resort on the eastern coast of Spain. The town is popular as a Mediterranean holiday destination and is known for its nightlife and sandy beaches. In July 2022, some Benidorm bars and restaurants were forced to close at the height of their peak summer period, because they could not find enough staff.[65] Businesses had to close at least one day a week as there was no extra staff to cover "days off", while some outlets had to close temporarily until they could get more workers. The Spanish hospitality industry struggled to fill 200,000 vacancies that summer.[66] A large hotel chain even ran a trial recruiting people with no experience in the industry and provided them with only six hours of training before expecting them to continue to learn on the job.

Local amenities could also be affected. For example, a national shortage of lifeguards forced public swimming pools across the United States to limit operating hours or shut down entirely in 2022. Major cities were scrambling for staff, and the American Lifeguard Association said one third of pools in the country were affected. New

York City canceled its public swimming programs, while Houston and Chicago did not open some of their public pools as planned.[67] The shortage resulted in a bidding war for trained lifeguards, but higher wages alone could not solve the problem. The United States had about one million trained lifeguards in 2019, many of whom were students from overseas. The COVID-19 pandemic reduced the number of foreign student visas issued, which resulted in fewer people willing to train for the job. Trained lifeguards must get recertified every two years and after the pandemic, many lifeguards had let their qualifications expire. The result was that without the lifeguards, the public swimming pools could not open, depriving many communities of these facilities during the hottest months of the year.

The list of consequences is endless. Almost every aspect of our lives will be affected by a shortage of labor, and trying to cope with the situation will become the new norm. Most of the examples given here were those that came to the fore as a consequence of the COVID-19 pandemic, and the subsequent stuttering recovery towards economic normalization. Many of these issues soon passed. But a fundamental shift towards a life that could permanently be like this is already taking place. Situations such as those described in this chapter will become more frequent, and get progressively worse as the pool of labor continues to shrink relative to the total population it must support. When multiple systems, utilities and services fail concurrently, the effect can be felt at the level of entire communities. The example of a small Australian town, where severe labor shortages across several sectors all occurred at the same time in 2022, shows how the day-to-day life of an entire community can be disrupted.

A picture of life to come: Griffith, Australia

Griffith is located in the Riverina region of New South Wales, Australia. The town, 353 miles southwest of Sydney, has a population of around 27,000 people. The region's warm, dry climate is ideal for growing a variety of crops, including grapes, almonds, and citrus. But despite its idyllic surroundings, this town's residents had first-hand experience of living with widespread labor shortages in 2022.[68] Almost every business and service in the town was chronically understaffed. The shortage of general practitioners meant that there was a waiting list of about nine weeks to visit a doctor for a general consultation. The doctors left some slots open each day for emergencies, and if one of these slots became available, there was a waiting list of up to 30 patients willing to take it at short notice. The excessively long patient waiting list, together with overworked doctors, put people's lives at risk (fatal diseases might not be detected in the early stages; exhausted healthcare workers could make mistakes).

Outside the town, there are vast citrus orchards. One plantation holds around half a million trees, which would normally be picked by about 200 seasonal workers. But in 2021 and 2022, there were only 20 pickers available. As a result, the fruit was simply left unharvested, and fell to the ground to rot. The trees also needed to be pruned and irrigation channels had to be maintained, but there were not enough workers available to do these tasks. Thus, not only did current crops go to waste, but future yields were at risk because the orchards were not properly maintained.

Local businesses suffered too. In 2022, the pharmacy in town was short of four staff, the florist needed two more workers, a café needed a cook and two waiters, the two hotels were trying to recruit a total of 45 more staff, and the two McDonald's fast-food outlets together had about 50 vacancies. This lack of workers was choking economic growth. In some cases, operations were curtailed, resulting in a loss of revenue.

The crisis extended to the public sector too. There was an acute shortage of teachers at the regional high school and in the first four months of 2022, about 220 individual classes were merged. Teaching cannot take place in merged classes and children are then left to learn independently. Basic education is therefore compromised; and there were concerns that this situation could have a negative impact on the children's preparation for tertiary education.

Besides the physical exhaustion of working flat out all the time, the toll on the workers' mental health mounted. Some simply gave up and left their professions, putting even more pressure on the few who remained. The labor shortage in the town was a vicious downward spiral with no end in sight.

While the labor situation in Griffith in 2022 may seem like a peculiar anomaly, it could become the norm across most of the developed world in the decades ahead. This vivid example gives us a glimpse into the challenges that will be faced by communities in future, as they try to cope with the knock-on effect of a drastic reduction in the ratio of worker-to-aged people. Crops going to waste, a shortage of healthcare providers, businesses closing because of a shortage of staff, and general economic malaise—all seem like scenes from some fictional dystopian future. But with a rapidly aging population and a shrinking workforce across the developed world, Griffith may well soon be a town near you.

★ ★ ★

CHAPTER 10

CRUMBLING CITIES

On one of her occasional walks, Eva passes by several derelict buildings. Houses and apartments that were previously alive with the sounds of laughter and the cries of children are now silent and empty. As the years passed, nature reclaimed its property rights. Overgrown gardens have encroached and eventually breached the doors and walls—man-made barriers are futile against the unstoppable force of nature. Winter rain and snow wear down the edifices, and the wind brings seedlings that lay claim to growing patches of dirt. Over time, walls crack and timber rots. In a final act of submission, some of the structures collapse.

On her way to the supermarket, Eva stops briefly in front of an old train station that closed down a few years ago. Eva used to enjoying taking the train to the surrounding towns for a change of scenery. The trains had already been showing signs of aging and a lack of maintenance. Train trip cancelations had become more frequent, and some routes were even canceled outright—the result of a potent combination of a lack of commuter demand and a shortage of workers to operate the rail network safely.

As population numbers decline, a vicious cycle of decay will set in. This decay will eventually affect every facet of society, but will be most apparent in property and infrastructure. One can imagine what happens to an average suburb with 500 homes if the population drops by 20% over a 25-year period; around 100 homes in the suburb would be vacant. As a result, property values will collapse—first, there are fewer buyers available due to the lower population; and, second, with the excess supply of homes, there will be relentless downward pressure on house prices. And because homes have traditionally been the primary asset and means of building wealth for most households, the fall in property values could set in motion a general decline in the overall wealth of households.

The pattern will repeat itself across the entire property spectrum. The declining population will result in an excess supply of shopping malls, office space, and industrial facilities. Property as an asset class will be decimated, and investors could suffer significant losses. The situation will be exacerbated by the changing needs of the older demographic—pensioners may prefer to live in smaller retirement units or care homes, instead of their previous larger family homes; they will make fewer visits to malls and make fewer discretionary purchases. This is the reversal of consumer asset accumulation, which fuels strong economic growth when the population is still growing. When young adults set up a new home, they acquire lots of things—furniture, refrigerators, stoves, kettles, mattresses, linen, and many more items that must be bought for the first home. This spending dynamic is a powerful driver of consumer demand as populations grow and countries follow the path to prosperity. The rise of household income improves living standards and education levels, resulting in more aspirational consumers wanting to "trade up" to better things—a more expensive car, a better coffee machine, or a larger television with the latest technology. In time, they would have acquired most of the consumer assets that they would need for a comfortable life. But when they retire, the older folk want to scale down. They soon realise that over the course of a lifetime, they have accumulated too many things and now they may want to lighten the load in their later years. For example, they choose to move into smaller homes, reduce the number of vehicles in the household, and generally "declutter" their lives. They have no real need to acquire more things and when older people do buy items like clothing or appliances, the purchase is most likely a replacement of something that is worn out or broken. As aged persons form a larger part of the total population, foot traffic falls in shopping malls and eventually shops with low sales close down. When vacancy levels in shopping malls continue to rise, an irreversible decline sets in that culminates in the eventual closure of the mall—they become "ghost malls". In the United States, where the first modern mall was built in 1956 in Edina, Minnesota, mall construction reached a peak of 140 new malls per year by the mid-1990s. But the tide had turned by 2007, when for the first time in half a century, no new malls were built in America at all.[69] Since then, malls began to close at an increasing rate as shopping patterns changed and online shopping gained traction. These colossal buildings with their vast, cavernous spaces are often difficult to repurpose for other uses. In the end, they are either demolished or left to decay. Until recently, Randall Park Mall in Ohio was the largest abandoned mall in the United States, with a total floor space of 2.2 million square feet. When the online retailer Amazon acquired the property in 2017, it demolished most of the structures to build a new warehouse.[70]

While the thought of a growing number of derelict buildings and malls is worrisome, even more disturbing is the concealed decay that takes place below ground. The deterioration of the infrastructure systems hidden beneath the soil will be considerably more costly and more disruptive. Modern cities are serviced by intricate infra-structure systems, most of which lie underground. This includes extensive networks of water mains, sewage systems, electrical circuits, telecommunications and gas lines. These systems allow us to live a comfortable and civilized existence. But these networks do not have infinite lifespans—they age and degrade over time, and regular maintenance is required to keep them working reliably. This maintenance and repair is bound to become more challenging when fewer staff are available to do the work. To illustrate what can go wrong, let's consider the complexities of the underground infrastructure in a major city like New York.

New York City has nearly 7,000 miles of water mains, an astounding 97,000 miles of underground electric lines, 4,400 miles of gas mains, and thousands of miles of telephone and cable-television lines.[71] In addition, there is a maze of subway tunnels and other assorted equipment, all crammed beneath the streets and pavements of this bustling city.

But much of New York's underground infrastructure has become old and fragile. In 2020, the average age of water mains in the city was 66 years. In January 2020, the brittle condition of New York's infrastructure resulted in several major water mains failures. Two water mains pipes on the Upper West Side broke within days of each other, sending water gushing onto the streets. These incidents also underscored how tightly packed the underground systems are, because the breaks paralyzed several subway lines for hours. New York's underground infrastructure is getting older every year and is in various states of disrepair. It must be constantly tended to, upgraded and have critical components replaced, otherwise there will be more water mains failures, gas explosions and other breakdowns that disrupt life above ground. A gas explosion in Harlem in 2014, for example, which killed eight people and injured more than 70, was found to be the result of faulty maintenance of nearby gas pipes.[72]

The national average number of water mains failures per year in the United States is 25 breaks for every 100 miles of water mains[73]— this means a city like New York with 7,000 miles of water mains could average 1,750 failures per year, or almost five a day. This rate of failure may be similar in other developed countries. In New York, almost half of the city's water mains breaks happen in the winter months of December, January and February, when temperature changes lead to colder pipes at night than during the day. These temperature fluctuations cause valves and joints to expand and contract, which contribute to leaks and breaks. And with more extreme weather conditions brought about by climate change, we can expect more rapid deterioration of the old infrastructure. A 2013 report for the American Society of Civil Engineers calculated that at the current rate, it would take 150 years to replace every water mains in New York City, which is twice the life expectancy of most mains.[74] The enormity of the problem is clear to see. And this situation is not unique to New York—it is likely to be similar in other major metropolitan centres in developed countries, such as Tokyo, Paris and London.

One may think that when the population declines, our usage and demands on infrastructure will drop commensurately. But here lies the problem—even though population numbers may decline in the coming decades, the infrastructure will not reduce proportionately. Once the infrastructure is built, it is there to stay—and it needs to be looked after to ensure the longevity of the entire infrastructure system. A city like New York had infrastructure that could service 9 million people in 2020. If the population should drop by two million people at some point, the 7,000 miles of water mains and the 4,400 miles of gas mains will still be in place. If these systems are not maintained, they will wither and deteriorate, and cause service disruptions to customers. This is a useful example to understand why there needs to be a minimum level of essential workers to support a society, as we discussed in Chapter 3. In 2021, New York City had around 50,000 employees to support the infrastructure provided for 9 million people. Even if the city's population had to drop to 7 million people or less, it would probably still need the 50,000 workers to maintain the established infrastructure. Infrastructure is difficult to scale back and entire networks must be maintained regardless of how many people they service.

An interesting study in Germany in 2007 considered the effects of the underutilization of water and sewer networks arising from declining populations.[75] The context of the German study was peculiar—after the reunification of the former German Democratic Republic (communist East Germany) and West Germany in 1990, major investments were made in the former Communist country's infrastructure on the expectation that the region's population would grow rapidly. But this population growth did not materialize, resulting in local authorities and utility companies grappling with the challenges of maintaining, restructuring and deconstructing overcapacities in infrastructure, such as water supply systems, only 15 years later (which meant they were dealing with relatively new infrastructure, and not old, decaying systems as in many major cities in developed countries). The study noted that while social or education infrastructure can be closed down and public transportation can be phased out, shutting down water supply infrastructure is not possible because the remaining population must still be supplied by an interconnected network. In the case of water supply, lower consumption results in reduced flow quantities, which can impair the functioning of the supply network. For instance, the large diameter of water pipelines can cause the flow of water to slow when it is under utilized, leading to stagnation zones where sediment can build up and affect the quality of drinking water. With sewage, lower levels of usage results in decreased flows and a build-up of solids in oversized pipes. The deterioration of infrastructure can lead to the corrosion of sewage pipes. The study concluded that water supply and sewage systems are not flexible enough to respond adequately to declining population numbers. Moreover, the study noted that as these large-scale infrastructure systems have high fixed costs (in the case of water systems, up to 80% of the costs are fixed), a declining population means that the cost per user will rise, as the fixed costs are borne by fewer consumers.

So, as the population ages, the infrastructure ages as well. Combined with lower utilization, these systems will need more frequent maintenance and repairs, but the labor available to do this work will decline in future. Unless a solution is found, disruptions caused by infrastructure breakdowns are likely to happen more frequently, last longer, and be more damaging. One can imagine the damage to property and the disruption that a burst water mains on New York's Fifth Avenue would cause if it is left unrepaired for a few days.

The economic impact of a declining population in cities is vividly illustrated by the example of Detroit in Michigan. In the mid-20th century, Detroit was at the center of the United States' motor industry and an economic powerhouse. However, in the second half of the 20th century, the city experienced a dramatic collapse, as production shifted away to other centers and jobs dwindled. As employment evaporated, a rapid exodus of people followed. The population of Detroit dropped from 1.85 million in 1950 (when it was the fourth largest city in the United States) to 639,000 in 2020 (dropping to the 27th largest city in the country).[76] A direct result of a reduced population was lower tax revenues, and the city struggled financially. By 2013, Detroit was forced to file for bankruptcy—the $18 billion bankruptcy filing was the largest municipal bankruptcy in US history.[77]

The lower population in Detroit has resulted in massively reduced demand for housing (figure 22 below). Consequently, an excess supply of houses has depressed the property market, and thousands of vacant houses in the city have become derelict over time. Empty, neglected properties are a blight on neighborhoods and reduce property values for everyone in the area. Ideally, derelict buildings should be demolished to restore the demand/supply equilibrium. But this is costly and there is no direct cash inflow to offset demolition costs. Fortunately, in Detroit's case, federal funding could be used to demolish 15,084 abandoned houses between 2014 and 2020, knocking down an average 3,000 homes per year. This has improved the situation in some suburbs, but as of 2020 there were still around 22,000 vacant homes remaining in the city.[78] The situation is not limited to residential properties—shopping malls, office buildings and industrial parks in the city are shuttered and closed.

Figure 21: Detroit population—1950 to 2020

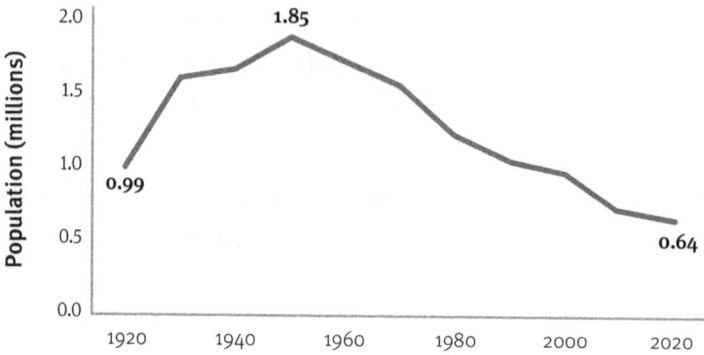

Figure 22: Detroit has a glut of housing stock

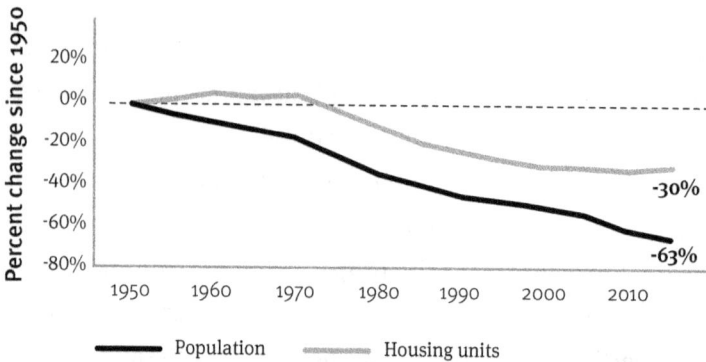

Source: US Bureau of Census; Zillow

While the impact of derelict buildings can be dealt with by demolition, the economic impact of a smaller population is more difficult to address. The decline in population erodes a city's property tax base and results in lower revenue, which in turn forces cuts in expenditure. The demolitions in Detroit cost an average of $17,500 per building. Because these properties were abandoned by their owners, the taxpayers must pick up the tab for the rehabilitation of neighborhoods. But as the tax base continues to shrink in future, it may become more difficult to find funding for such "aesthetic" demolitions. The consequence is that the remaining residents may have to learn to live with these derelict structures in their neighborhoods.

Japan offers a curious contrast to the property experience of Detroit. With Japan's population decreasing by 3.8 million between 2010 and 2023 and aging rapidly, one would expect a property market in turmoil. But this is, surprisingly, not the case. The reason for this phenomenon is rather unusual. Houses in Japan rapidly depreciate in a similar manner to durable consumer goods, because buyers prefer newly built homes. After 15 years, a freestanding home typically loses all of its building value and only the value of the land it is built on remains. When a property is sold, the purchase price is usually based on land value alone. The new owner demolishes the old house and builds a new one.[79]

There are very specific reasons for the unconventional view on housing property in Japan. Frequent earthquakes have conditioned the Japanese to not take buildings for granted, while poor quality homes from the post-War era instilled the belief that old homes are of lower value. Consequently, new homes are preferred by buyers and the resale values of homes are a lot lower than in other developed countries. So, despite its shrinking population, Japanese house-building activity remains steady with around 87% of home sales involving newly built homes (compared with the norm of 11% to 34% in Western countries).

Could the unique Japanese approach to homes be a solution for other countries with aging and declining populations, offering a way to deal with a glut of excess properties in a future with fewer people? It seems unlikely. Besides, tearing down and building new houses will require lots of labor, which will be a scarce resource in the decades to come. In Japan, the number of construction workers declined by a quarter from a peak of 6.8 million workers in 1997 to 5 million workers in 2018. One forecast is that Japan could have a shortage of 1.3 million skilled construction workers as soon as 2025.[80] Soon, Japan will have to deal with the same challenge of managing a surplus of excess property stock—the government's survey reported about 8.5 million vacant homes across the country, which is around 14% of the country's overall housing stock. The number of vacant homes (known as "akiya" in Japanese) is forecast to exceed 30% of all houses in Japan by 2033.[81]

Japan's low birth rate and declining number of children also means that it is ending up with a surplus of school buildings. About 450 schools close every year across Japan due to a drop in enrolment in the country.[82] The number of learners at Japanese elementary and junior high schools was the lowest since data was first collected in 1948. School enrolment is now about 54% lower than its peak in the early 1960s. With such a significant drop in enrolment, a large number of school buildings simply stood empty. The Japanese education ministry has been grappling with this issue for many years. About 8,580 public school buildings were closed between 2002 and 2020.[83] Besides the closed schools, many other schools are operating well below their capacity. For example, a school in southeast Osaka has a capacity of 480 students but operated with only 190 enrolments in 2022.[84] Operating and maintaining facilities that run well below their capacities is inefficient and expensive. It is only a matter of time before schools running below optimal capacity will have to be shuttered and the remaining buildings dealt with as obsolete infrastructure.

There are some attempts to stave off this inevitability. In Italy, for instance, 20 small towns began selling abandoned homes for only one euro. The towns were in rural areas and have been experiencing declining populations for decades.[85] As younger people migrated to the cities in search of better job opportunities and furthering their education, many rural towns were left with declining and aging populations. In some cases, older residents bequeathed properties to municipalities, while other owners simply abandoned dilapidated homes. The goal of the plan to sell the abandoned homes at a bargain price was to draw in new life into the ailing towns. The sales came with conditions, including that the properties must be renovated within three years. While these schemes attracted widespread interest and all the properties were promptly sold, it won't be a template for countering global depopulation trends. Most of the buyers acquired the houses as holiday homes and have no intention of living there permanently. Also, when many other small towns in other countries copy this strategy, there will soon be several options around the world to acquire homes at nominal prices. One example of the heightening competition for home occupants is the town of Presicce in southern Italy, where officials were planning a scheme to *pay people* up to €30,000 to buy an empty dwelling and take up residency in the town.[86] So, as competition ramps up, we will be back to square one—an excess supply of dwellings courting an ever-shrinking pool of buyers.

We are entering an era where we will be confronted with the hangover of past excesses. We have a built environment in developed countries that has catered for a much larger population than we will have in the future. One survey revealed that there were about 65 million empty housing units in China in 2017,[87] which is sufficient to house the entire population of France in single-person homes. Considering that China's population dropped for the first time in 60 years in 2022, and is forecast to continue to decline in the years ahead, this country may soon follow the path of Italy in dealing with a surplus of vacant homes.

The oversupply of the edifices of this infrastructure cannot be ignored and dealing with this problem will be costly. And the cost will have to be borne by a smaller population and a smaller workforce. Not only will there be fewer workers available for critical maintenance, but less labor means a smaller tax base to pay for the maintenance of the infrastructure system. The 1980s hit song by Starship exclaimed *"We built this city on rock and roll"*—when we get to unbuild the cities, the melancholic tones of the blues may be a more appropriate musical accompaniment.

★ ★ ★

CHAPTER 11

CREAKING SUPPLY CHAINS

Eva loathes going to the supermarket. There are constantly shortages of goods, and many shelves are empty, with ubiquitous "out-of-stock" signs. She tries to go to the shop early, often waiting outside the store an hour before its opening time. But she is not alone, as many others have now resorted to trying to be first in line. In winter, queuing is a dreadful prospect—standing in icy conditions, waiting for the shop to open. At least it won't snow today, she thinks, grateful for small mercies. She has tried using the online shopping apps to buy groceries, but online availability is even worse. She feels that she has a better chance of getting her hands on the products she needs by queuing herself.

After checking the weather, Eva musters up the courage to go to the supermarket. Best to get an early start, she thinks, as she plods toward her bedroom to prepare herself for the tiresome errand.

Since the advent of the Industrial Revolution in the 18th century, there has been a constant drive by businesses to improve efficiency and lower the cost of production. The division of labor revolutionized factory production and allowed for step-change improvements in output and productivity. Instead of one worker completing a product from start to finish, the manufacturing process was carved up into multiple steps. Each step was assigned to an individual worker, and this specialization resulted in higher output and more profit. This system was initially adopted in individual factories, but soon it became apparent that the division of labor for tasks need not be confined to specific locations or even within countries. Comparative advantages between countries mean that it is more efficient to produce items, or parts of products, in the country that can deliver them at the lowest cost—this ushered in the era of globalization. Manufacturing was soon distributed across the globe, with tasks allocated to regions where comparative advantages existed. Shifting production from countries with high-cost structures (often high labor costs) to countries that could deliver products much more cheaply, was generally a win-win for all parties. It stimulated economic growth in the countries where manufacturing was low-cost, while the importing countries benefited from low prices which, in turn, allowed for more consumption and the raising of living standards.

The outcome is a global production line and supply chain that is very cost-efficient, but also results in businesses and economies that are highly interdependent and potentially vulnerable. That vulnerability was on full display in 2020 when the COVID-19 pandemic disrupted global supply chains to an unprecedented degree—when borders closed, the flow of goods was disrupted, which led to shortages of many goods and services.

The events of 2020 were due to a highly infectious virus, but other factors, including chronic labor shortages, could also threaten global supply chains. It is useful to reflect on the instances of supply chain disruptions during the pandemic, to gain insights into what may happen in a future where labor shortages cause such disruptions to become endemic.

During the pandemic, one of the most severe bottlenecks was the shortage of semiconductors (that is, computer chips). The global chip shortage was a striking display of an imbalanced market—a spike in demand following the pandemic that could not be matched by a supply base which was, in parts, still impacted by lockdown restrictions. This sector also has a high concentration of supply, with the world's largest chip maker, TSMC in Taiwan, accounting for 28% of global semiconductor manufacturing capacity.[88] In response, some governments have resolved to increase local chip manufacturing capacity and reduce the dependency on key suppliers in foreign countries. In 2021, the United States Senate passed the CHIPS Act, which provides funding to semiconductor manufacturers in the country. The European Union is planning a similar "CHIPS Act" of its own, to increase the production of semiconductors within Europe. The shift to increasingly insular supply chains aims to reduce dependence on foreign supply, and thus reduce systemic risk to local economies.

As bad as the component parts shortages can be, they will pale in comparison to supply chain disruptions caused by a shortage of labor. Throughout the supply chain, from production and logistics to the end-consumer market, labor is both the key ingredient and the oil that lubricates the system. Even when production can be automated, the system will still be reliant on humans for process supervision, intervention, repair and maintenance, and the logistics of bringing the product to the market. As we noted in Chapter 5, driverless trucks and non-human delivery systems will still need to be supported by an army of workers who can supervise, maintain, repair and tend to any problems arising in fleets of automated vehicles.

The issues confronting the trucking sector in the United Kingdom after Brexit in 2016 provides another example of how supply chains could be hamstrung. The United Kingdom's Road Haulage Association (RHA) had estimated that there was a shortage of around 60,000 qualified HGV (heavy goods vehicle) drivers in the country, even before the COVID-19 pandemic in 2020. This was at a time when the industry already employed 600,000 drivers.[89] During the pandemic, the labor shortage increased to more than 100,000 drivers. Besides specific problems related to the pandemic and the Brexit vote, the

United Kingdom was facing structural changes that are remarkably similar to the future that awaits other developed countries. RHA research shows that the average age of an HGV driver in the UK in 2020 was 55 years, with fewer than 1% of the drivers being under the age of 25. There was a total of 95,000 drivers over the age of 55 years in 2021, and with the retirement age at 65, the industry will soon need to find a way to plug that labor gap. British truck drivers are aging and will be retiring in large numbers soon. But there are simply not enough young drivers signing up to replace them.

Haulage is by no means a glamorous job. The RHA has noted that industry standards for facilities, pay, and general public attitudes toward truck drivers all amount to a perception that haulage is not an appealing industry to join or stay in. The industry trained a total of 250,000 HGV drivers under the age of 40 in the decade before 2021, but since then 150,000 have left the industry.[90] The reasons younger people do not find the job appealing include relatively low pay, a poor work-life balance (the result of being away from home for long-haulage trips), and poor conditions and facilities (such as sleeping in a cab at truck stops). The only feasible solution for the industry in the short term is to use foreign drivers to fill the void, a solution complicated by the country's decision to leave the European Union. The RHA requested that the British government introduce a temporary working visa for HGV drivers, and for the occupation to be added to the Home Office's Shortage Occupation List. While we have looked at the experience of the UK here, the same situation is likely playing out in other developed markets as well. The poor job conditions and quality of life for an HGV driver are in direct conflict with the aspirations of Gen Z, and thus the industry is unlikely to appeal to young people in developed countries as an avenue for employment.

Other jobs in the supply chain network may be just as unappealing to Gen Z workers in developed markets. Being a forklift driver, a receiving clerk at a supermarket, or a stock clerk at a distribution center is unlikely to meet the aspirations of a generation that achieved significantly higher tertiary education levels than generations before. The United Kingdom had a shortage of 7,000 forklift drivers in 2019 alone. The chronic labor shortages in supply chains are already leading to some peculiar responses. For example, in 2022 the Australian Prime Minister floated the idea of lowering the minimum age of forklift drivers from 18 to 16, in an attempt to deal with that country's shortage of drivers. The Australian proposal was swiftly scrapped, as forklift driving is considered a high-risk occupation, which may not be appropriate for a 16-year-old. But such proposed solutions that push the boundaries of what is acceptable to societal norms are becoming more common. For instance, legislators in the US states of Iowa and Minnesota introduced bills in 2023 to loosen child labor law regulations around age and workplace safety protections. Minnesota's bill aims to permit 16-year-olds to work in construction jobs, while the Iowa measure would allow 14-year-olds to work in certain jobs in meatpacking plants.[91]

The decades ahead will likely be characterized by constant shortages of products and services, as the impact of labor shortages are felt. In the end, we will have to learn to adapt to this problem. This may result in consumers stocking up when goods are in stores, which would exacerbate the situation (as we saw in the early stages of the COVID-19 pandemic). Globalization has resulted in supply chains that cross borders, and any weak link in that chain—for example, a shortage of dockworkers in a dispatching or receiving port—has the potential to delay or disrupt the flow of goods. However, the knee-jerk reaction to bring back manufacturing to local markets may be fraught with its own problems, as we will see in the next chapter.

★ ★ ★

CHAPTER 12

REVERSE GLOBALIZATION WILL MAKE MATTERS WORSE

━━━

Eva recalls that there was a time when the government wanted to increase local manufacturing capacity. It made a lot of sense at the time—jobs were going to be created and it would have been good for economic growth. But it was not to last. After the initial fanfare of politicians cutting ribbons at groundbreaking ceremonies at factories had died down, the realities of local production set in. The local labor pool was not as pliant or as efficient as in distant lands; and the locals were not keen to sign up for these lower-skilled jobs, considering their higher educational qualifications. Local factories ended up having to rely on immigrant labor. Ultimately, though, the local products were of inferior quality and the prices were not competitive. Inevitably, the local factories started closing down and production shifted back to foreign lands. The "invisible hand" of the markets had once again prevailed.

As we noted in the previous chapter, globalized supply chains have drawbacks, and the shortage of life-saving gear such as personal protective equipment (PPE) during the pandemic perhaps hit home the most. The manufacturing of PPE products was concentrated in certain countries, and when these countries faced surges in COVID-19 infections, they halted exports to satisfy their own local demand. For instance, up until March 2020, around 50% of all face masks were produced in China alone, with a further 20% of world supply originating from Taiwan.[92] When life-saving equipment such as ventilators and PPE were in short supply, the countries that manufactured them would obviously address their own needs first. In March 2020, India—another of the world's major PPE manufacturers—banned all exports of PPE, accentuating the risk others were taking by being too dependent on imports. Even rich countries became just another customer having to wait in line for an allocation of the scarce stock.

This, understandably, provoked some reaction in those countries whose supply weaknesses had been exposed. Their response was a renewed focus on bringing back local manufacturing. This movement argues that a return to local supply will have several benefits, including reducing inequality in local markets, which has widened considerably during the era of globalization. The benefits of local production include lower transportation costs and a reduced carbon footprint, as goods are transported over shorter distances to the end consumer; support for the local economy by creating jobs and stimulating economic growth in the community; improved responsiveness to market demand; and increased resilience by reducing the reliance on global supply chains.

Some have argued that the reign of globalization has run its course and is now over, a case made in the book *Homecoming* by Rana Foroohar. Proponents of this view believe that technological advances will level the playing field between high and low labor cost countries and make it viable to have production closer to home. They also point to rising global tensions and conflicts as contributing to turning the tide on globalization—for instance, the global grain shortages caused by Russia's invasion of Ukraine in 2022, as well as the sanctions leveled against Russia, and their subsequent curtailing of natural gas exports to Western Europe.

But the move to onshoring production is fundamentally flawed. In the context of aging and declining population levels in developed countries in the decades ahead, it will only exacerbate an already dire labor situation. Supply chains have evolved to be highly complex and are globally integrated. One can take Apple's iPhone as an example. Apple designs the iPhone in California, but its components are sourced from suppliers in 43 countries spread across six continents. Parts of the iPhone camera and its glass screen are manufactured in Japan, elements of the battery are made in China, and the accelerometer is built in Germany.[93] The reason each of these components was sourced from those particular suppliers is that those suppliers are specialists in their fields and likely to be the best-quality provider of that component. To onshore production means that each of the new local suppliers must raise their standards of manufacture to a similar level. This is an unrealistic outcome, especially if the new manufacturing facilities start as greenfield operations. Specialist overseas suppliers have achieved their excellence in manufacture over many years of specialization and investment in research and development—they have hard-earned credibility in their respective fields. Specialist suppliers were able to invest in extensive research and development because they could exploit economies of scale by serving a global market. If manufacturing moves onshore to service a mainly local market, the local component suppliers will not have that scale advantage and will, therefore, be unable to invest in research and development to the same extent as the global specialists.

To achieve full supply independence, countries will have to shift 100% of component sourcing for a given item to their local market. Anything short of this could still expose the country to the risk of an offshore supply disruption, as the product is not complete and saleable until each component is delivered and assembled. For example, a jeans factory that is waiting only for zippers will not be able to ship the product despite it being 99% complete. In the jeans example, the Japanese company YKK is the market leader in zippers with a global market share of 40%. It will be very difficult for any local player to compete on price and quality against such a dominant category specialist.

To address some of these deficiencies in the local manufacturing drive, some countries have resolved to implement a hybrid form of "local" manufacturing—by getting foreign companies to set up local manufacturing plants. One such example is the Taiwanese chipmaker TSMC, who announced in 2022 that it would invest $12 billion in a new factory in Arizona. But TSMC soon found that setting up the facility in the United States was more costly than expected, and recruiting American engineers and technicians is more difficult than making equivalent hires in Taiwan.[94] Despite these challenges, TSMC subsequently announced it would triple its investment in the United States to $40 billion. These investments are probably only viable with the support of subsidies resulting from the country's CHIPS Act— and so, effectively, taxpayers must pay for the inefficiencies in local production.

A move to local manufacturing by developed countries will increase the demand for labor in those very countries that will be experiencing a pressing shortage of labor. In many cases, manufacturing jobs could require lower-skilled workers, which will be at odds with the steadily rising levels of tertiary educational attainment achieved in developed countries over the past few decades. Much like the shortage of agriculture workers in Italy, a growing manufacturing base in places like Europe and the United States may well result in factories scrambling to find more workers.

Instead of the pendulum swinging back completely against globalization, one alternative solution is to rebalance trade and diversify sourcing to other regions. This would result in shifting some production away from Asia to Africa, which will have an abundance of human capital well into the 22nd century. In this manner, the same products or components can be sourced from at least two different countries, which will allow for greater resilience in times of crisis. Comparative advantages will still be maintained, while a margin of safety can be built into the globalized supply chain.

Can Africa replicate China's path to prosperity?

The economic transformation of China since 1980 has been remarkable. China emerged from being a country in isolation with no major trading partners to a global economic superpower, second only to the United States in terms of GDP by 2010.[95] The reforms that China implemented, such as opening up the country for trade and investment, are not unique and some of these have already been implemented by many African countries. The key catalyst for China's explosive growth, however, was that the country was willing to be the "workshop of the world", where goods could be produced at unbeatably low prices.

China's ability to produce goods cheaply was *not* due to a skilled labor force, nor to advanced technology. In fact, during the first 20 years after opening its economy, its tertiary education enrolment rate remained below 5%. During this period, its exports as a percentage of GDP increased from 13% in 1992 to 36% by 2006. China was producing for the rest of the world using the brute power of its abundant low-cost labor.

It was only after 2000 that China's rate of tertiary education enrolment started rising rapidly. It was around this time that the first cohort of China's one-child policy children were finishing secondary school, and with their parents' dedication and resources focused on a single child, furthering their education was a natural progression. Tertiary enrolment spiked significantly after 2010, increasing from 25% to 67% in 2021, which was a consequence of the accumulated wealth built by single-child households over the past three decades.

Figure 23: Tertiary education enrolment (China)

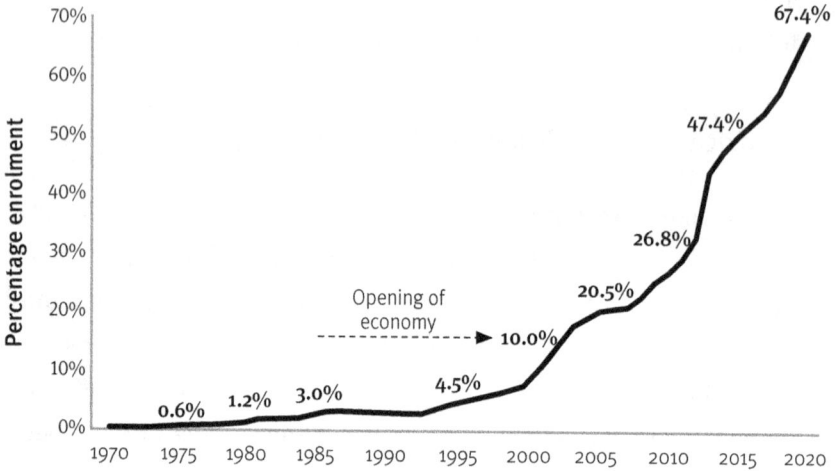

Source: UNESCO, Institute for Statistics, WITS, World Bank

Figure 24: Exports as a percentage of GDP (China)

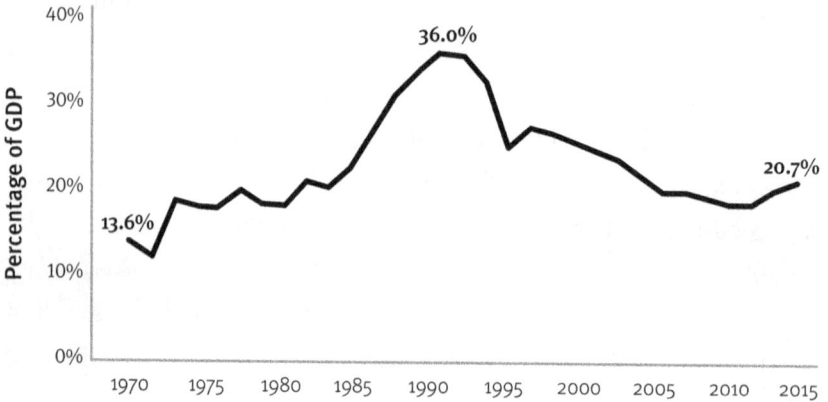

Source: WITS, World Bank

Africa can certainly emulate this path towards explosive growth. Although sub-Saharan Africa's education levels remain relatively low (it was only 9% in 2020), the experience of China shows that this should not be a limiting factor for growth in countries willing to be the "workshops of the world". China's capacity to be the global factory may already be waning. The Chinese Gen Zers had a tertiary enrolment rate of 67% in 2021 and many may not be as keen to work in factories as their parents have. Also, China's population has already started shrinking. In 2023, its population dropped by 2 million people, after experiencing its first decline in 2022. Between 2025 and 2030, its working-age population will reduce by 2.9 million people per year. By 2100, China's working-age population would have shrunk by a staggering 70%, from 983 million in 2023 to 293 million by 2100. Production has already started to shift to other low-cost hubs in Southeast Asia, such as Vietnam and Bangladesh. However, these countries' working-age populations will peak by mid-century and then drop as well. By 2100, Vietnam's working-age population will be 25% lower than it was in 2023 while Bangladesh's will be 22% lower than its peak in 2056. Countries in Africa, therefore, have a unique opportunity to use China's "factory of the world" playbook as a catalyst to develop their economies.

Figure 25: Tertiary education enrolment: China vs. Sub-Saharan Africa

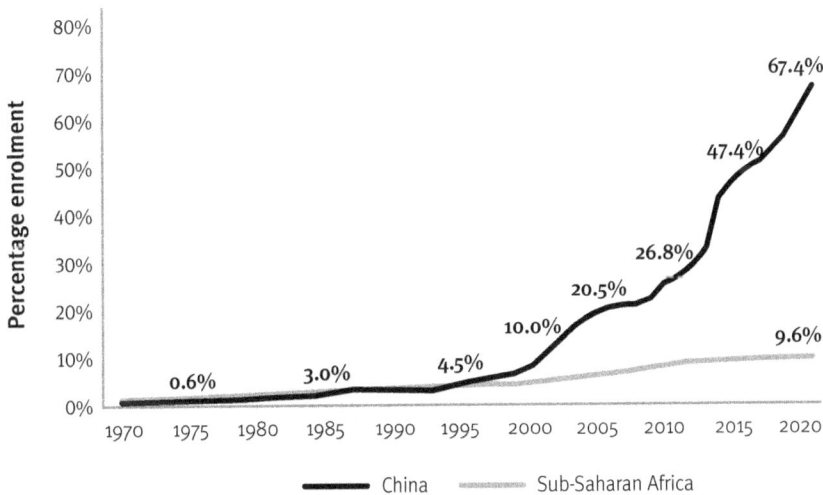

Source: UNESCO Institute for Statistics, World Bank

Figure 26: Exports as a percentage of GDP—Sub-Saharan Africa vs. world

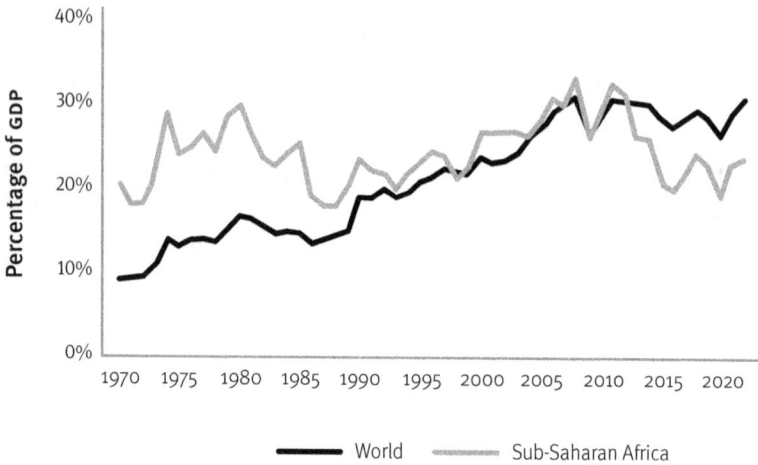

Source: WITS, World Bank

It is worth noting that Africa's exports as a percentage of GDP have previously been higher than the world average. But these exports were mainly basic resources and minerals with very little value enhancement (that is, additional refining or manufacturing). These resource exports did not do much to grow household wealth on the continent, although poor governance and corruption may have siphoned off many of the benefits that did exist. A strong manufacturing and industrial complex would do much better in creating more jobs and improving the living standards of Africa's population.

The vulnerability of globalized supply chains and distributed manufacture of goods to occasional breakdowns should not be exploited as an argument for increasing protectionist, inefficient economic policies. Similarly, politically driven discourse in some developed nations about insourcing labour-intensive jobs will have to square up to the demographic consequences of declining birth rates in those same countries. Globalization and immigrant labor should be viewed as positive forces. They are, after all, evidence of the "invisible hand" of the market at work, and will be all the more pronounced in a world where labor shortages become widespread.

★ ★ ★

CHAPTER 13

THE AFRICAN CENTURY

▬

Eva is looking forward to meeting up with her friend Nsayi on Sunday. Nsayi's parents were immigrants from the Democratic Republic of the Congo and moved here before she was born. Her father was a bus driver and her mother worked as a caregiver in an old-age home. They encouraged Nsayi to study hard at school and she eventually qualified as a lawyer when Eva had graduated. They have been best friends since their university days.

Nsayi confided in Eva that she often wondered how her life would have turned out had she been born and raised in the Democratic Republic of the Congo. Would she have had the opportunity to study law? Would her parents have been able to afford to send her to university? Did their moving here result in a better life for their child? And, was their migration a loss for their beloved home country?

Africa will buck the demographic trends of low fertility rates and shrinking workforce sizes observed in the rest of world, at least for the next century. With its population expected to almost triple from 1.4 billion in 2020 to 3.8 billion in 2100, the continent will have a vast pool of 2.5 billion working-age people by the end of the century. While many countries around the world will be grappling with labor shortages, the African continent will have a surplus of labor that can help to alleviate the shortages that will occur elsewhere. This places countries on the African continent in an ideal position to not only weather the effects of the coming demographic storm, but also to capitalize on it. As a result, the 22nd century could prove to be the "African Century".

The table below shows the countries that are projected to have the highest labor shortages by 2100, as well as those countries with the highest number of surplus workers. Of the 20 countries with the most surplus labor, sixteen are located in Africa.

Table 5: Countries with highest labor shortages and highest surplus labor (millions): 2100

Labor shortage		Surplus labor	
China	(72.7)	Nigeria	45.7
India	(22.3)	Democratic Republic of Congo	34.6
Bangladesh	(7.5)	Pakistan	32.5
Brazil	(6.1)	Ethiopia	20.7
Japan	(5.1)	Tanzania	15.2
Turkey	(4.3)	Angola	11.4
Iran	(4.1)	Afghanistan	9.1
Mexico	(3.8)	Mozambique	8.7
United States of America	(2.6)	Côte d'Ivoire	8.5
South Korea	(2.5)	Sudan	7.7
Colombia	(2.5)	Niger	7.5
Italy	(2.2)	Kenya	7.3
Vietnam	(2.2)	Yemen	7.3
Thailand	(2.1)	Mali	6.8
Germany	(1.9)	Egypt	6.8
France	(1.9)	Madagascar	6.3
Spain	(1.9)	Cameroon	6.0
United Kingdom	(1.9)	Chad	5.9
Argentina	(1.6)	Saudi Arabia	5.8
Poland	(1.4)	Somalia	5.7

Source: Author's calculations. Based on an essential worker-to-population ratio of 18.5% and a maximum essential worker-to-total workers' contribution of 32%

The numbers are intriguing. The forecasts show that China could have a labor shortage of 73 million workers by 2100, while its population is expected to decrease to 633 million (from the 1.4 billion in 2020). At that time, around 46% of the Chinese population will be older than 65 years, which will be the main cause of labor scarcity in that country. Nigeria, on the other hand, could have surplus labor of around 46 million workers by 2100. Nigeria's population is expected to grow from 214 million in 2020 to 477 million by 2100, of whom 67%—321 million—will be of working age. The global imbalances in labor availability will force countries to change their traditional migrant worker channels, and open up their borders to migrants from new locations.

Countries traditionally tried to fill workforce gaps with labor from within their own region. For instance, Japan mainly recruited foreign workers from neighbouring China and the Philippines. However, by 2100, many countries in East Asia may not have enough workers to satisfy the increased demand from China, Japan and South Korea. This is because at that stage, countries such as Bangladesh, Thailand, and Vietnam will also be in need of immigrant labor. Similarly, Western Europe will find it difficult to source labor from Eastern Europe, as those countries will themselves experience labor shortages. The dearth of workers will compel developed countries to look for immigrant labor from other regions, such as Africa.

The growing prominence and influence of Africa on the future world stage cannot be overstated. In 2020, the 1.3 billion people in Africa accounted for only 17.5% of the global population. But by 2050, the African population will comprise 25.5% of the global population, and by 2100, the continent is expected to account for around 37.5% of the world's inhabitants.

More importantly, from a labor perspective, Africa's share of the working-age population (those aged between 15 and 64 years) will increase from 15.2% in 2020 to 40.6% by 2100. In other words, people born in Africa will account for almost *half* of the total global workforce by the end of this century. We should not be too concerned that the continent might become overcrowded, as it is highly likely that with the significant demand for labor abroad, the levels of emigration from the continent will be high.

Figure 27: African population and working-aged persons, as a percentage of global totals

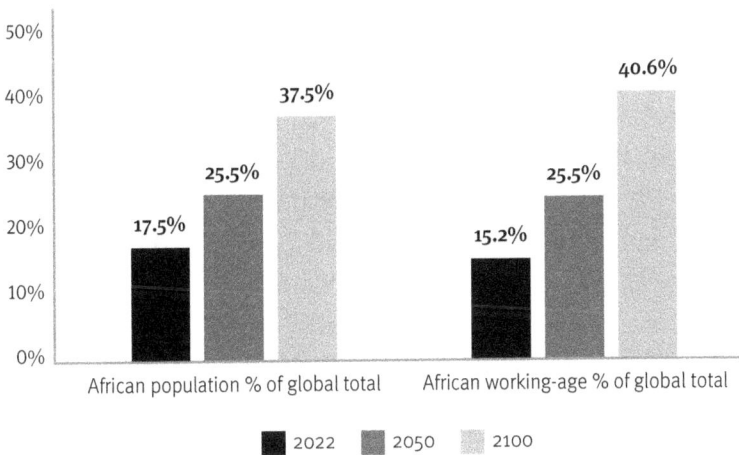

Source: United Nations, World Bank

In contrast to most developed nations, countries on the African continent will see their ratio of essential workers relative to their working-age population reduce, as more young people join the ranks of the workforce. This means that in Africa, more workers could be deployed in the higher-skilled, quaternary sectors (sectors that are based on new technologies and that require higher levels of education). This will include advanced jobs such as programming, technology development, financial planning, and design. The African continent could boost its human resources potential to drive innovation in the 22nd century, but this will require a significant improvement in educational levels on the continent over the next few decades. Presently, Africa is lagging in education provision.

According to the United Nations Educational, Scientific and Cultural Organization (UNESCO), sub-Saharan Africa has the highest rates of education exclusion.[96] In 2018, over 20% of African children between the ages of 6 and 11 did not attend school, as well as 33% of youth between the ages of 12 and 14. The UNESCO data also shows that almost 60% of youth between the ages of 15 and 17 did not attend school at all. Over the past two decades, there has been some improvement in Africa's tertiary education statistics, but the continent still trails other regions by a significant margin. Clearly, much more needs to be done if Africa is to reach its skilled labor potential.

We noted in the previous chapter that the current educational level in Africa is similar to that of China in the late 1990s, when that country experienced explosive growth. This means that the current

Figure 28: Tertiary gross enrolment ratio by region (2000–2020)

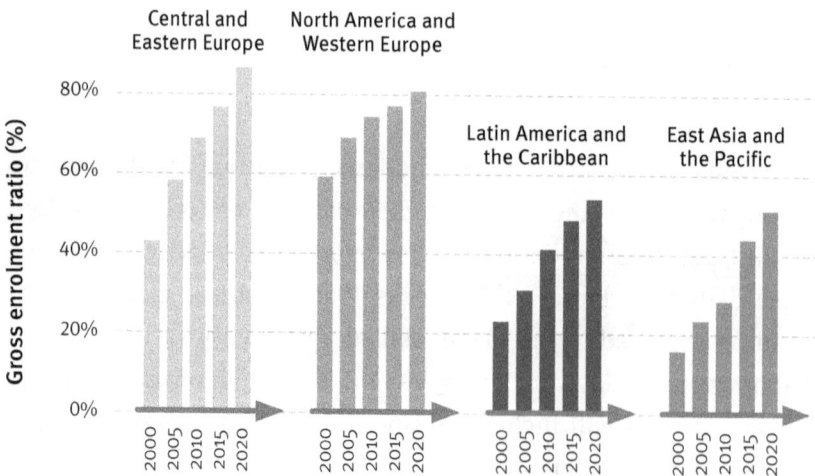

Source: UNESCO Institute for Statistics

low levels of educational attainment should not be a hindrance for Africa's development potential—that is, if it follows China's example and becomes the "factory of the world". This path to progress could unleash the promising potential of the continent.

As a future with a fast-shrinking labor pool in developed countries becomes a reality, there could be many catalysts that can improve the quality and provision of education in Africa. The first generation of emigrant workers from Africa would likely repatriate some savings to their families back home on the continent, providing an increase in household income in their home countries. This, in turn, will increase enrolment across primary, secondary and tertiary education in the home country. Subsequent generations will be better educated and could choose to either follow the migrant worker route (with higher-skilled jobs becoming a real prospect) or contribute to the development of their home economies by becoming locally employed.

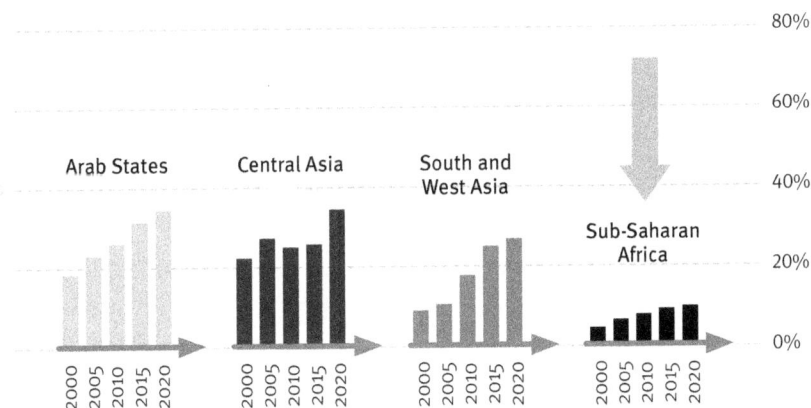

In the long run, it will be in the interest of developed countries to improve the quality and access to education in Africa, as well as other low-income countries where surplus labor is available. The developed countries will ultimately benefit from the influx of doctors, engineers, truck drivers and plumbers that will emanate from these countries. For instance, developed countries could fund and sponsor vocational training centres and universities in Africa. Scholarships could be provided to students with conditions attached, such as requiring recipients to work for a fixed period in their sponsor country. For example, an engineering student funded by the South Korean government for her four-year degree may have to work in that country for four years after graduating. And a plumber trained at an academy sponsored by Italy would have to work in that country for, say, three years.

Regardless what we think of historical colonialism today, it has forged many socio-cultural and institutional links between countries. Brazil, Angola and Mozambique, for example, are Portuguese-speaking countries, while Argentina and Colombia are Spanish-speaking. Africa's colonial past could frame the links for cooperation. For instance, French-speaking West Africa could provide surplus labor to France and other French-speaking countries. English-speaking Southern Africa would be well-positioned to provide labor to the United Kingdom and North America, while Portuguese-speaking Angola and Mozambique could supply workers to Portugal and Brazil.

The 22nd century will be an exciting time for Africa and it may well become known as the "African Century". This prestige will not be realized through the exploitation of the continent's abundant mineral resources, but rather because of the latent potential that its vast reservoir of human resources will hold.

Developed countries should not expect this to be a permanent one-way stream of migrant worker traffic, though. In the early stages of this transition, the workers' remittances to their families back home will drive those economies, fueling a virtuous cycle of growth. The money sent back home will increase retail sales and consumption, which in turn will boost tax revenue and the economic growth of the home country. And unlike the corporate profits from volatile mineral resource prices, the inflows from Africa's labor exports will provide consistent annuity income and deliver more equitable distribution of income as it flows directly to households. Countries in Africa may then follow the familiar pattern of development—with successive generations improving their education levels, incomes and living standards. Eventually, the living standards in the home countries will be on a par with the historically developed nations. Workers may then be less inclined to seek job opportunities abroad. Their own countries' economic growth could be much higher than the historically developed markets, whose growth will by then be weighed down by aging and shrinking populations. The pace of life in developed countries could slow down to match the older populace—such a state of affairs would hardly appeal to young people looking for an exciting journey through life.

Africa's population will reach 3.8 billion by the end of this century, quickly making up ground to Asia's projected population of 4.6 billion. But Asia's population will be in decline by then, and Africa could surpass it at some point in the 22nd century. With a massive pool of consumers, Africa will be a vibrant place with the potential for high economic growth. By contrast, the aging markets in Europe and elsewhere will be languid. Young African workers in future generations may find it more appealing to remain in their home countries and be a part of the vibrant, fast-growing local economies. As growth opportunities flourish in Africa, the younger workers may not want to go work in the former developed countries, which will have effectively evolved into retirement nations.

The aging developed countries will then have to find ways to incentivize foreign labor to come work in their economies. Moreover, the competition between countries for labor will see increasingly generous offers made to attract workers. Competition is likely to kickoff on financial terms—that is, by offering higher wages. Soon, other non-financial incentives will follow. For example, easy visa access, or even dropping visa requirements altogether (as Portugal did with its CPLP program) will become attractive options. The higher wages that must be offered will drive up inflation and increase the cost of living in the countries requiring that labor. This will not be good news for the labor-importing countries, because large parts of their population will be aged and on fixed pensions. These impacts are significant, and we will explore them in detail later in this book.

Short-term pain, long-term gain

While the long-term outlook for countries with surplus labor is optimistic, there is no doubt that the short-term impact will be massively disruptive to local communities in Africa. The immediate impact to be felt will be a "brain drain" as skills are poached by countries that can offer much higher salaries. The experience of Zimbabwe provides a sobering example of the first phase of this transition. In 2021 alone, Zimbabwe lost more than 4,000 doctors and nurses, with most moving to the United Kingdom and Ireland.[97] The United Kingdom has been actively recruiting medical professionals to plug its own staff shortages. This recruitment drive has now been extended to the teaching profession, and from 2023, the British government has allowed teachers who graduated in Zimbabwe to be eligible for "qualified status", meaning that successful candidates can go straight to teaching in classrooms without any further training.[98]

These foreign recruitment drives by developed nations have a devastating impact on service delivery in the target country. Health clinics in Zimbabwe are increasingly understaffed with many clinics operating at only 50% of their capacity. The local population must endure longer waits for healthcare services, while nurses are overworked and stressed. Many healthcare workers end up resigning, exacerbating an already bad situation. In financial terms, there is simply no contest. The lowest salary for nurses in Zimbabwe in 2023 was around $200 per month, whereas newly qualified nurses could earn $2,726 per month in the United Kingdom[99] (of course, the comparison should be tempered by a much higher cost of living in the developed country). With the recruitment drive now also targeting teachers, there are fears that Zimbabwe's education system could be similarly decimated. Zimbabwean teachers earned around $75 a month locally in 2023, but could expect to earn at least $2,800 a month in the UK (again, the cost of living is considerably higher there, so the difference in net income after expenses may not be as substantial).

The immediate impact on the home country will clearly be unsettling. But there is a silver lining: The Zimbabwean diaspora remitted more than $3 billion to their relatives back home in 2023. When one considers that Zimbabwe's GDP is $32 billion, the contribution of emigrant workers is a formidable economic injection for the country. To put that in perspective, Zimbabwe's agriculture sector contributes around 12% to its GDP, or around $3.9 billion—in other words, remittances from workers abroad fall only slightly short of matching the GDP contribution of Zimbabwe's entire agricultural industry. In time, the foundation provided by these remittances will increase standards of living and economic activity in the countries of origin, and the short-term pain will pay off handsomely. The appreciation that citizens living and working abroad are prized assets of a country are starting to be recognized.

★ ★ ★

CHAPTER 14

DIASPORA IS A STRATEGIC ASSET

Eva's friend Nsayi talks about her home country, the Democratic Republic of the Congo, a lot. Eva is fascinated by this, as Nsayi was born here and spent her formative years here. But her parents ingrained the importance of her roots and her home country in her upbringing, with their countless stories of life back home. Over the years, Nsayi enjoyed several holidays there, and she reconnected with her roots. She maintains relationships with her extended family back home, and regularly sends money to help them.

In the early phases of the migration transition, there is a risk that the home country of emigrants could lose many skilled workers, which may undermine economic growth and development. While this is a drawback, it is a temporary one. The net long-term impact is likely to be positive, and we can look to the examples of Ireland and India in this regard.

The Irish emigration experience is perhaps one of the greatest international migrations of a population in history. Since the 1700s, around 10 million people have emigrated from Ireland, which is double the current population of the country.[100] During the crisis of the Great Famine between 1846 and 1855, around 2.1 million people left the country, with most of them (around 1.5 million) setting up a new life in the United States. Almost two centuries later, Ireland's population has still not recovered to its 1845 peak of 8.5 million people. One might think that given this extent of loss of human capital, the country would be floundering. And up until the late 1980s, Ireland did experience sluggish growth, with high levels of indebtedness and high unemployment. But by the mid-1990s, the economy had transformed into the "Celtic Tiger", with high GDP growth, budget surpluses and full employment.[101] There were several reasons for this transformation, including the lowering of corporate tax rates and the opening up of the economy. But analysis by the European University Institute[102] contends that Ireland's transformation was mainly due to US multi-national companies who, because of the globalization phenomenon and closer ties between the United States and the European Union in the early 1990s, considered Ireland as its most closely aligned European partner in view of the 35 million US citizens of Irish extraction (the descendants of the Irish immigrants to the United States). Consequently, Ireland was a popular option for US multi-nationals when they had to choose a location for regional offices and manufacturing plants.

The Irish government has acknowledged that the diaspora is of enormous importance to Ireland, and that they have supported Ireland's economic growth and development for decades.[103] The Irish government even established an Emigrant Support Program in 2004 to provide support to organizations around the world who cater to the needs of the Irish diaspora.

India provides another remarkable example of the export of skilled labor. Perhaps the best-known cases are in the US technology sector where, in 2021, senior executives of several major technology firms were of Indian descent. These included the CEOs of Alphabet (the parent company of Google), Microsoft, IBM, Adobe and Twitter. Indian-born executives also served as CEOs of other large US companies including PepsiCo and Mastercard. But it is not just these celebrity CEOs that are making their home country proud. The Indian diaspora numbers around 18 million people across 136 countries. Collectively, they funneled $87 billion back to India in 2021 alone, the highest remittance level in the world. This inflow of money makes a significant impact in India: The remittances sent back home amount to 3.2% of India's GDP.[104]

The Indian government views their diaspora as a strategic asset, which they consider being a "brain gain" as opposed to a "brain drain".[105] Every two years since 2003, on the 9th of January, India celebrates *Pravasi Bharatiya Divas* (PBD, "Non-Resident Indian Day"), to mark the contribution of the overseas Indian community towards the development of the country. The date commemorates the return of Mahatma Gandhi, perhaps India's most iconic diaspora member, from South Africa to Mumbai in 1915. The PBD celebrations also serve to reconnect the diaspora with their roots in the home country, a reminder perhaps that they should not forget the origins of their achievements. The Indian diaspora has positively contributed to the perception of India in the world, as the achievements of Indian executives and innovators in Silicon Valley have strengthened the image of India as a technology powerhouse and a source of highly skilled human capital.

These two examples show that an exodus of skills and talent is not necessarily a negative development for a country, and it is possible to reap a "diaspora dividend" in future years. The immediate benefit from the diaspora dividend are the remittances sent by workers to their families back home. In 2023, remittances from migrant workers and expatriates globally totaled $857 billion, led by India ($120 billion) and Mexico ($66 billion).[106] In some countries, remittances are integral to the local economies. For instance, in Tajikistan, remittances from the diaspora abroad contribute 39% to the local economy. Other countries that are highly reliant on remittance inflow from migrant workers abroad include Lebanon, Nicaragua, Nepal and Honduras (see Figure 29).

Figure 29: Migrant remittance inflow as a percentage of GDP (2023)

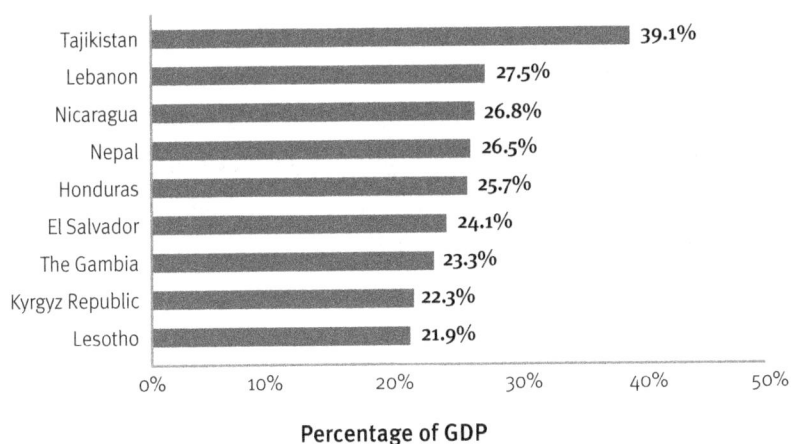

Source: World Bank

As labor shortages unfold across developed countries in the decades ahead, worker migration will increase and the level of remittances are likely to rise in tandem. This, effectively, represents increased exports from developing to developed countries, which would support the growth of the countries of origin of the workers.

India, a powerhouse of the next century

India overtook China as the world's most populous nation in 2023 and the United Nations projects that India will still have the largest population in the world by 2100, with 1.5 billion people. That means that at the end of the century, it would boast a population more than double that of China's projected 633 million. India's strong home base, combined with its "strategic assets" overseas, have the potential to make the country a formidable powerhouse over the next century. But there are some factors that could slow India's meteoric rise to the top of the economic world order.

As of 2020, India's urbanization level was still low at only 35.4%. As its economy develops, urbanization in India may well increase substantially, perhaps following a path similar to China, where urbanization increased threefold from 18% in 1979 to 64% in 2020. Over the ten years up to 2021, the annual increases in India's urbanization level have accelerated from 0.3% to 0.5% per year (at its peak, China's annual increase in urbanization level was around 1.4% per year). As has been observed in the developed world, a higher urbanization level will most likely lead to a lower fertility rate, and could therefore slow the upward trend in population growth.

Figure 30: Urbanization rate: India vs. China

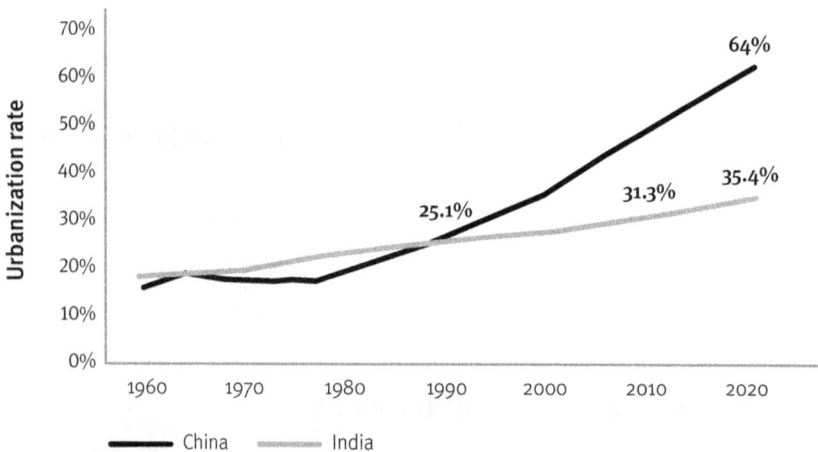

Source: United Nations

India also has a fast-aging population—aged persons, who only accounted for 7% of its population in 2023, will make up 30% of its population by 2100. The impact of this rapid aging on consumption and GDP growth will be explored in more detail in Chapter 18.

Furthermore, the United Nations population forecast for India is based on a fertility rate of 1.7 births per woman by 2100, whereas an alternative forecast by *The Lancet* projects a total fertility rate of only 1.04 in 2100.[107] This assumption is critical, and applying the lower fertility rate results in an Indian population count in 2100 that could be around 500 million lower than the United Nations projections—a very significant difference. India's fertility rate was already below the replacement rate at 2.0 in 2022, and if the urbanization level increases as expected, then its fertility rate could easily decline to 1.0 as projected by *The Lancet*. Nonetheless, even if the UN forecasts are taken as authoritative, India's population will peak at 1.7 billion in 2061, and then decrease by 196 million by the end of the century—a 12% decline that is only likely to accelerate in the 22nd century.

Figure 31: Fertility rate: India vs. China

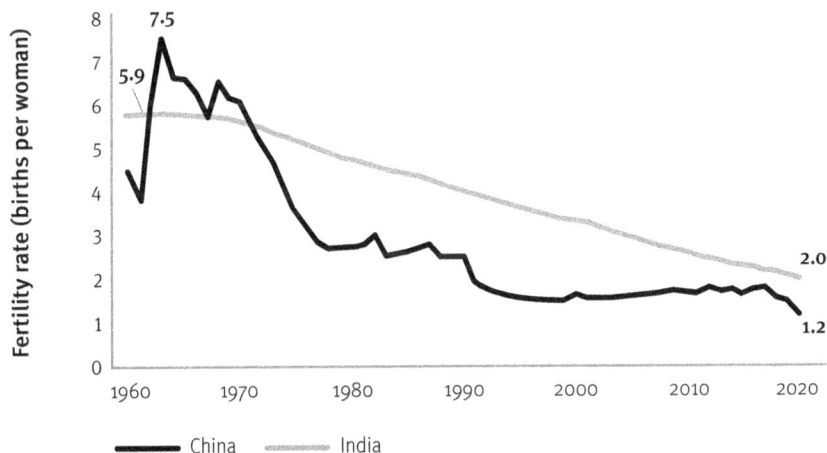

Source: United Nations

The Indian diaspora's high-profile achievements may result in a spike in demand for skilled Indian labor. Between 2010 and 2017, India had an outflow of 5.1 million migrants, the second-highest number of emigrants in the world after Syria (whose migrants were mostly refugees as a result of the civil war).[108] This outflow could accelerate in the years ahead. But, given its abundant supply of human resources, the loss of skilled workers is unlikely to cause a major short-term "brain drain" that would disrupt its economy.

Overall, India's ascendance in global prominence is all but assured, due to it being driven by its abundant skilled workforce. But despite India's future status as the most populous country in the world, it will not possess a significant supply of surplus labor that other countries with worker shortages can draw on. India may have its own shortage of labor towards the end of this century, as it will also track the familiar path to prosperity followed by other developed countries. As a result, the world will still have to turn to Africa to find the increasingly scarce resource that is labor.

* * *

CHAPTER 15

MIGRATION—GIVE ME YOUR HUDDLED MASSES

━━

The cashier at the store today was so friendly and chatty, Eva thought. "I think she is from Somalia," Eva muses to herself. There is a large Somali community living in the neighborhood, along with some people from Zambia. Store workers and other general workers come from all over the world, but in some neighborhoods, homogeneous communities tend to aggregate and their language becomes the de facto second language of that area. In the northern suburbs of the city there are large Pakistani and Congolese communities as well.

Immigration is a hot-button topic in many developed nations. Anti-immigrant rhetoric has fueled a number of recent political movements in developed countries, and policy responses to foreign workers, asylum seekers, and refugees regularly make headline news. But as we have already seen, the size of the working-age population in many developed countries is falling. More and more young people in these countries have attained high levels of education, and most of them do not want the basic types of jobs that are associated with essential services. A new economic reality is being born.

The worsening shortage of, and increased demand for, labor will upend the debate on immigration in many developed countries. The only viable solution for countries experiencing chronic labor shortages in the short term is to allow more foreign workers into the country to fill the void. If these workers are not allowed to enter the local labor market, the effects of the worker shortages will be felt as service levels decline. There is already evidence of this trend in countries such as Japan and Italy. Foreign workers play a vital role in taking up lower-skilled, often menial jobs that the local, more educated population find less appealing.

The recent shift to more conservative attitudes toward immigration in many countries is not sustainable and will ultimately prove to be damaging for those economies and the societies they support. Slogans such as "Make America Great Again" in the US, or the Brexit movement in the United Kingdom, fostered strong anti-immigration sentiment. But in the face of the hard economic realities of having insufficient workers to produce and deliver services in the economy, this move to the right will ultimately backfire. As countries such as the United States and Italy become more unwelcoming to foreigners (or are even perceived as being less welcoming), migrant workers may seek opportunities in lands that are less hostile to them. This may not happen over the short term, while there are only a handful of countries with severe labor shortages and job opportunities are limited. But in time, as more countries experience labor shortages, the bargaining power will shift from those countries to the immigrant workers themselves.

In a few decades, when the impact of severe labor shortages affects multiple countries, and the systems supporting developed societies start to falter, there will have to be a change of attitude. The alternative is to risk a decline in economic growth and quality of life. By then, however, it may be too late, as more and more countries join the list of eager recruiters of labor. Also, after having cultivated the perception of being an immigrant-unfriendly country, it may not be as easy as simply relaxing border controls and expecting immigrants to queue up to move in.

As we noted in an earlier chapter, when countries needed to fill gaps in their job markets in the past, the tendency was to recruit lower-skilled labor from within the region. Japan's foreign workers, for example, originated mainly from China, the Philippines and Vietnam. In the US, lower-skilled labor comes mostly from Mexico and Central America, while Western Europe has sourced labor mainly from Eastern Europe or North Africa. But the global shortage of labor will remove the luxury of choice for recruiting countries. Poland is expected to have a shortage of labor as early as 2050, and will therefore be unable to provide surplus labor to Western Europe. China will have a shortage of 43 million workers by 2060, while Vietnam and the Philippines won't have much surplus labor at all—this will force Japan to look elsewhere for lower-skilled workers. This trend will repeat around the world.

The demand for labor will have a dramatic impact on the demographic composition of countries. Places that were previously fairly homogeneous, will transform into multicultural melting pots. This could lead to some social friction, especially because a large part of the population will be aged and may have more conservative attitudes. Take Austria, for example. Around 20% of Austria's 8.9 million population are older than 65 years, and this is forecast to increase to 33% by 2100. In 2017, the country elected a conservative government who campaigned on a hard-line position on immigration. However, the country is already suffering from labor shortages, with the healthcare sector especially impacted. The labor situation prompted the Austrian health minister in 2022 to warn that immigration is "the only solution" because the country needed thousands of nurses and doctors to avoid a collapse in the health sector.[109]

The need to deliver the goods and services required for the functioning of society is a survival instinct, and will trump any reactionary attitudes. Protectionist policies will have to square off against the economic reality of labor shortages, and the self-interest of maintaining an existing standard of living will prevail.

The chart below shows the countries that could have the largest worker shortages by 2100. The data shows the absolute numbers of workers required, as well as what those immigrant workers would constitute as a percentage of the country's population. China leads the list with a shortage of 73 million workers, which would amount to 11% of its population at that time—if these jobs are filled by immigrant workers, China's demographic composition would change considerably. South Korea will need 2.5 million workers by the end of the century, which will be equivalent to 12% of its projected population, while Japan's requirement of 5.1 million workers will be equivalent to 7% of its population.

Figure 32: Countries with the largest shortage of workers (2100)

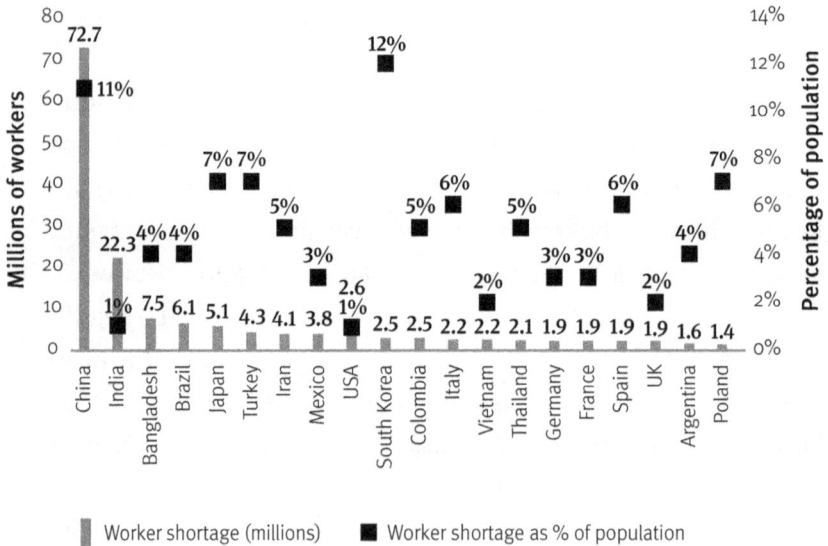

Source: Author's calculations based on United Nations population forecasts

Although these estimates of the changes in the demographic mix brought about by labor shortages may seem startling, it is even more unnerving if we consider the labor shortage in relation to the country's *working-age population.* This figure will not only reflect what proportion of the total workforce will need to be sourced from other countries, but it will also indicate how the population mix in the key consumer demographic age group of 15–64 years could change.

Figure 33 shows the labor shortages that will probably need to be filled by immigrants as a percentage of the total population and the working-age population. At the top of the list is South Korea, which will need to attract 2.5 million workers. That would not only account for 12% of its total population, but also amounts to a massive 25% of its working-age demographic (ages 15–64 years) in 2100. Similarly, China's working-age population will need to be supplemented by foreign workers to the tune of 25% of that cohort by the end of this century.

Filling labor shortages with immigrants will be highly transformative for many countries, especially in the working-age segment of the population. The impact is even more pronounced in some smaller countries, which are not shown in the chart below. For instance, Puerto Rico could see its total population drop from 3.3 million in 2020 to 995,000 by 2100, with the workforce dropping to only 401,000. The foreign workers needed by Puerto Rico will amount to 18% of its total population, but a staggering 43% of its working-age cohort. Such significant changes in the population mix will undoubtedly have a profound impact on the social fabric of many countries.

The problem can be ratcheted up one more notch: The impact may be even more pronounced than the estimates above, which are based on immigrant workers alone. In an environment where countries will need to work hard to attract scarce labor, they will have to somehow sweeten the deal for labor migrants in order to maintain a competitive advantage. Whereas currently low-skilled labor visas are granted for limited periods to workers only (with no visas granted to family or

Figure 33: Projected labor shortage as a percentage of working-age population (2100)

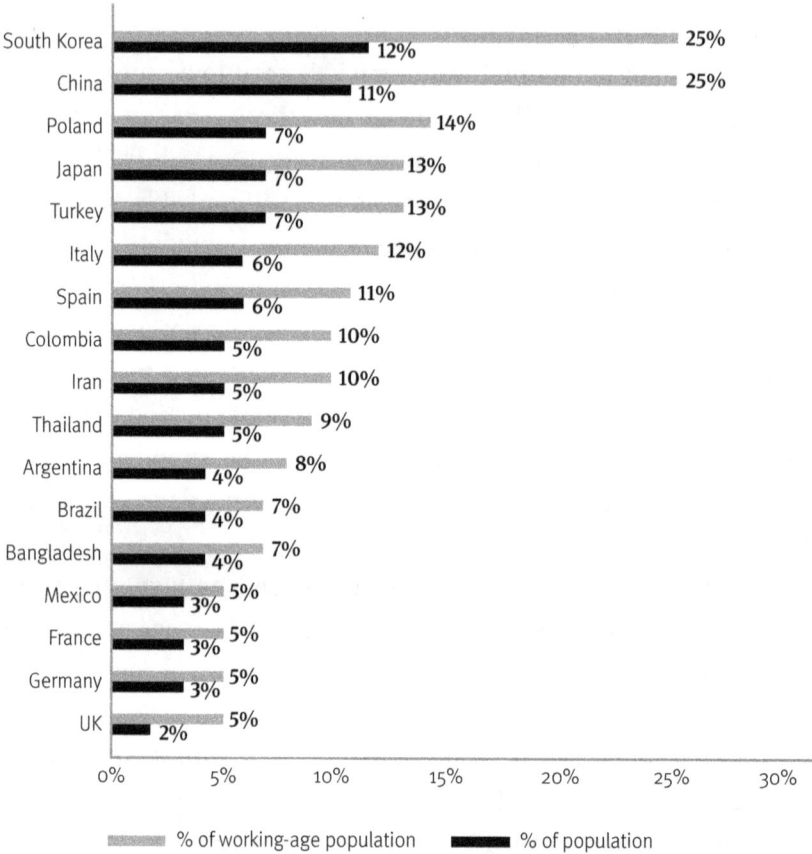

South Korea	12%	25%
China	11%	25%
Poland	7%	14%
Japan	7%	13%
Turkey	7%	13%
Italy	6%	12%
Spain	6%	11%
Colombia	5%	10%
Iran	5%	10%
Thailand	5%	9%
Argentina	4%	8%
Brazil	4%	7%
Bangladesh	4%	7%
Mexico	3%	5%
France	3%	5%
Germany	3%	5%
UK	2%	5%

% of working-age population   % of population

Source: Author's calculations based on United Nations population forecasts

dependants), countries could be compelled to allow family members to join the workers, so as to make it more appealing for them to migrate and work in that country. With two or more dependants accompanying each worker, the demographic and ethnic transformation of the labor-importing countries could be much more profound than indicated by the calculations above.

148

In an era where stronger border control has become a political rallying point, the likelihood of these scenarios being allowed to play out may seem unrealistic. But the alternative is even more menacing: The prospect of inexorable decay of developed economies and societies, should the widening labor gaps in these markets not be filled. In the end, the economic argument is bound to prevail, as it affects the daily lives of citizens in a very direct way.

The bronze tablet at the base of the Statue of Liberty in New York harbor that bears the text of Emma Lazarus's sonnet "The New Colossus" is prescient for the age to come. The sonnet reads:

"Keep, ancient lands, your storied pomp!" cries she
With silent lips. "Give me your tired, your poor,
Your huddled masses yearning to breathe free,
The wretched refuse of your teeming shore.
Send these, the homeless, tempest-tost to me,
I lift my lamp beside the golden door!"

The motivation to take in the "huddled masses" will be anything but altruistic. Rather, it will be the result of a struggle for the survival of those nations.

★ ★ ★

It is worthwhile at this point to pause and reflect on the evolution of communities and nations over time, to frame migration as a long-term evolutionary force. Humans started out as nomadic hunter-gatherers who, at some point, set down roots. Our ancestors found a nice patch of land close to a river, with some grazing for the animals that they had domesticated. They started to grow edible plants and over time, places with abundant resources attracted more settlers, and small settlements grew into villages.

Villages were often surrounded by thick walls with gates. The formation of villages may also have been motivated by security, and these walls could be considered to be the first form of "border control", and the concrete formalization of the "us versus them" mindset that persists today.

In time, nearby villages banded together into political entities with shared interests, and eventually kingdoms and empires would be forged. Early villages were largely informally governed, through councils of elders in the community, for example. The rise of kingdoms and empires sought to assert control over multiple settlements, and also initiated taxation and public services (which in those days mostly amounted to providing protection from outsiders). This was the start of the expansion of borders, either through alliance or conquest.

In earlier times, the expansion of borders was often achieved by force. Empires and kingdoms would expand by rulers conquering other lands. Invariably though, such expansion strategies tended to unravel eventually, and the conquered people would seek independence. A striking example is the British Empire, which spanned the globe during the 19th century. By the mid-20th century, however, the vast majority of its former colonial territories had regained their independence.

In contrast, voluntary mergers of populations are usually more long-lasting, as mutual cooperation has benefits for all parties. Unification allows for free trade, security and stability of the group at large. There are many examples of states merging and unifying into new countries. For example, Britain in the 6th century consisted of at least seven kingdoms,[110] but by the 16th century, these kingdoms had morphed into modern-day England. Similarly, the 19th century saw the rise of the modern nation-state, where populations formed country-level groupings often based on a perceived shared culture or language. Italy was formed between 1860 and 1870 by the unification of the Kingdom of Sardinia, the Kingdom of Lombardy–Venetia, the Papal States and the Kingdom of the Two Sicilies.[111] The German Empire came into being in 1871, after the formalization of alliances between a group of

German-speaking states and kingdoms.[112] Australia was formed in 1901 when the former British colonies of New South Wales, Queensland, South Australia, Tasmania, Victoria and Western Australia agreed to merge.[113] New Zealand was also invited to join, but in the end they decided to remain outside the federation.

Over thousands of years, small settlements developed into villages; collections of villages became kingdoms and then empires; and eventually, the world came to have the 195 countries that exist as of 2024. But there is no reason to think that this long-term evolutionary process of change in human communities is final or complete. Borders will continue to change in future, but the motivation for the changing of the lines drawn in the sand will not be empire building or the pursuit of power. Instead, geopolitical change will be driven by the need to gain access to increasingly scarce resources, namely labor and consumers.

A millennium from now, we are likely to see a world map that is very different to the one we have today. Alliances may be a first step towards changing borders. One might think of the alliances as an engagement period that happens before the marriage. Allied countries work closely together and share common interests. Over time, they may decide to formalize the alliance by merging as a single country. The European Union is a good example: It may well serve as a precursor to the "United States of Europe" as a country. The Brexit split by the United Kingdom, or similar movements for greater self-determination by some other countries, are but a temporary spasm of an antiquated yearning for a romanticized view of the past. Brexit, and other moves toward isolationism, cannot last. The crippling economic impact of labor shortages will sway opinions and attitudes, and eventually force a return to unification. The 10-country Association of Southeast Asian Nations (ASEAN) could similarly precede the "United States of Southeast Asia", while the African Union could in time evolve into the "United States of Africa". In the fullness of time, the 195 countries we have today might perhaps evolve into a one-country world. It may take centuries, but the rationale of separate countries will become increasingly obsolete and economically detrimental, and borders will inevitably fall. Labor will then be able to move freely, and respond flexibly to demand wherever it may arise.

In the context of the current geopolitical situation, it is almost impossible to imagine any country embracing radical change with regard to immigration, let alone a world without borders. And so it should be, as the time is not right yet—doing so now will only result in a deluge of migrants, which could overwhelm their systems. But the time will come when several countries will be ready (or more likely, compelled) to take this step—probably from around 2040. There is simply no other way: Developed countries will have to change their attitudes toward immigration and accept a world with fluid borders that is organized along more rational, economic lines.

* * *

CHAPTER 16

DEMAND DRIES UP

It has been a while since Eva visited clothing stores. There is no need really, considering she has almost everything she needs. Occasionally, she goes to buy some basic apparel, such as underwear. She is way past the fashion-conscious stage of her life—when she was younger, she loved shopping for new clothes and keeping up with the latest trends. It went hand-in-hand with her social life: dressing up to go to restaurants and bars with friends. But now that she is older, her social life has almost ceased, and she mostly stays home. Besides, she has other, more important things to worry about—such as her healthcare spending.

It's not just her, either. She notices that many clothing retailers have closed down over the years, as have many restaurants. The once-ubiquitous fastfood outlets that lined her route from work have thinned out. The city seems to have lost just as much interest in clothes and entertainment as she has.

As people age, their spending patterns change. Younger people spend proportionately more on clothing, dining out and transportation than older folk. On the other hand, older people are thriftier and spend more on healthcare. Data from the United States Consumer Expenditure Survey,[114] detailed in the chart below, shows that young adults' spending on clothing is proportionately more than double that of aged persons (that is, pensioners). Young people also spend considerably more on dining out than aged persons. Pensioners have different priorities—as a percentage of their total expenses, their spend on healthcare is four times higher than that of young adults.

Figure 34: Spending patterns: Pensioners vs. young adults (percentage of total expenses)

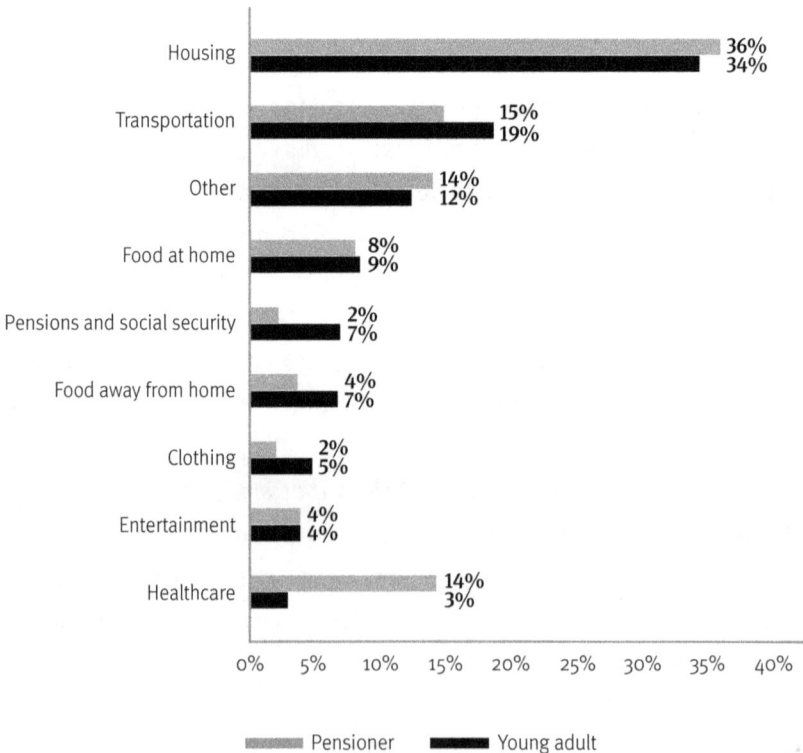

Source: Consumer Expenditure Survey, US Bureau of Labor Statistics

So, as a country's population ages, the changes in spending patterns will have a profound impact on the economy. Spending at discretionary retailers such as clothing and furniture retailers could decline considerably over time, putting these companies under immense pressure. Even attempts by the retailers to offer more merchandise targeting older customers could be futile. Whereas young people buy clothes to keep pace with the latest fashion trends, older consumers tend to maintain their wardrobe. Older customers often only buy replacements for worn-out or ill-fitting clothing, which may mean buying only a few garments a year. Younger people also need a wardrobe of work attire, and a shrinking workforce will lessen demand for these types of garments as well.

Other retail categories will also come under strain. When young people are setting up their first home, they need to buy everything from kettles to fridges and furniture. As they progress through their careers, these items are constantly replaced and upgraded, fueling a constant cycle of demand for consumer products. When they reach pension age, having spent a lifetime accumulating things, they now need to get rid of some their possessions, especially if they are scaling down to a smaller dwelling in their retirement. For pensioners, there is very little incentive to buy discretionary items such as clothing or appliances, unless something important breaks. The aging customer base will have a devastating impact across the retail landscape, as demand for consumer products drops.

Similarly, restaurants and fast-food outlets could see their target market shrink. Aged persons eat out less frequently than younger people, and when they do dine out, it is unlikely to be at fast-food outlets. Businesses in the quick-service restaurant sector, which typically target younger customers, could come under significant pressure due to the projected decline in demand.

Commuting patterns will also change which, in turn, will have a dramatic effect on several sectors. Older people spend much less on transport than young people, because retirees do not have to commute to work daily. As they get older, some pensioners may give up driving completely. Consequently, ride-hailing apps such as Uber are well positioned to cater for the transport requirements of the older generation. However, a major shift to vehicle sharing will lessen their need for owned vehicles. Demand for motor vehicles will drop significantly as the population ages and the entire automotive sector in developed markets—from manufacturers, to dealers, service centers and spare parts—could see an unending decline in demand due to the shifts in demographics.

Healthcare spending, on the other hand, is likely to increase substantially as aged persons spend more on this category. Hospitals, pharmacies, pharmaceutical companies and other healthcare service providers stand to benefit from the projected demographic changes. However, as a large part of the core market will be on fixed pension income, there will be pressure to regulate the pricing of healthcare products and services. With such price caps, these companies may not be in line for windfall profits despite the surge in demand.

Household consumption varies from country to country, but can typically account for about two-thirds of GDP. A decline in household consumption can therefore lead to lower GDP growth. Which countries would be most vulnerable to this changing dynamic? The chart below shows consumption as a percentage of GDP, as well as the expected rate of aging for a group of countries. The countries that have high consumption-to-GDP ratios and are expected to have a fast-aging population may be particularly vulnerable to a sharp decline in economic activity. The chart shows that there are some large emerging market countries that fall in this category, including the Philippines, Brazil, Mexico and India. These countries will see their proportion of aged people increase by more than 20 percentage points by 2100, and as their consumption as a percentage to GDP exceeds 70%, these countries may be at risk of rapidly slowing economic growth.

Figure 35: Consumption as a percentage of GDP compared to the change in the percentage of aged persons

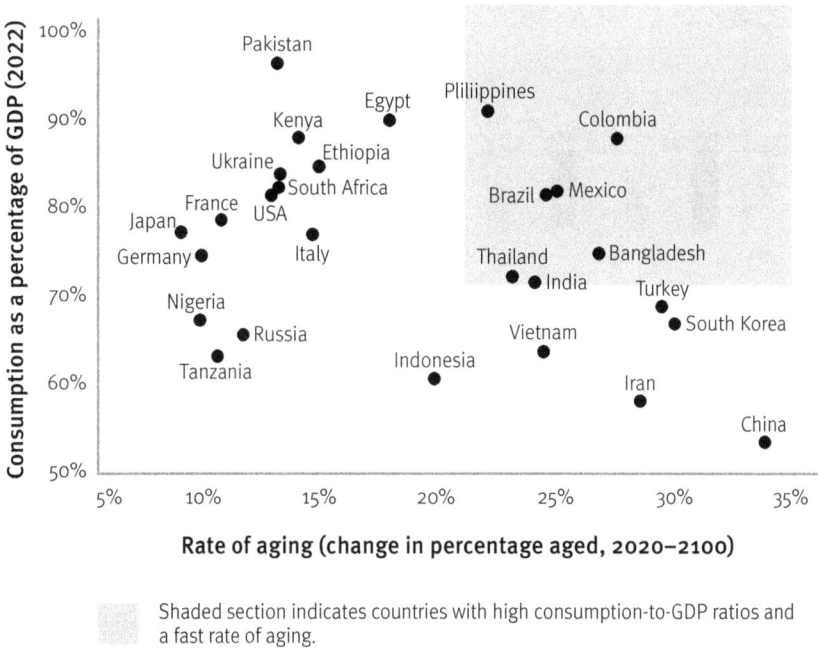

Rate of aging (change in percentage aged, 2020–2100)

Shaded section indicates countries with high consumption-to-GDP ratios and a fast rate of aging.

Source: World Bank

By examining the spending patterns per age group and applying them to population profiles for the different continents, we can build a picture of how consumer spending could change as the age profile of the population changes. This estimation is merely illustrative, and serves to highlight the impact that changing demographics could have on consumer spending—that is, what effect an older, and smaller, population of consumers may have on spending. This estimation does not take into account the effect of market conditions and fiscal policy, which could influence spending levels (for instance, poor policies could lead to higher unemployment and dampen consumer demand, even with positive population dynamics).

Figure 36: Total consumer expenditure (indexed to 100)

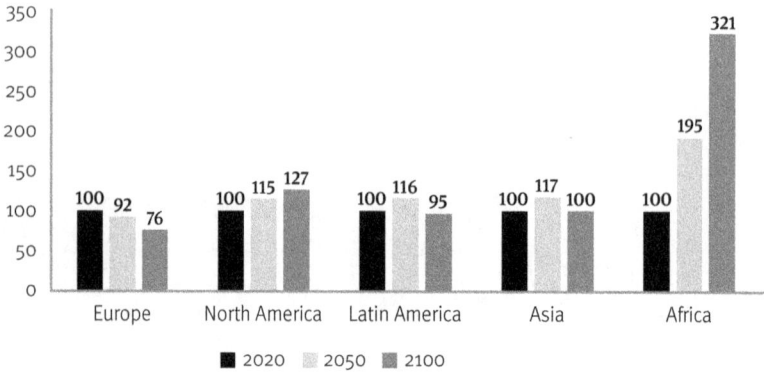

Indexed to 100 in 2020 and inflation adjusted. Based on current per capita spending using the US BLS survey, not adjusting for economic impacts which may occur over time (e.g. government policies).

Source: Author's calculations

The analysis shows that Europe could face a steep decline in consumer expenditure, brought about by its changing demographic profile. By 2100, European consumer spending is projected to contract by 24%. This is mainly due to the expected 21% drop in its population over this period, as well as the aging of its populace. This reduction in consumer spending will have a significant negative impact on Europe's GDP, which may shrink by a similar magnitude. Latin America and Asia are expected to follow similar patterns of initial growth in consumer spending up until 2050, but will then experience declines over the next 50 years as their populations also reduce and age. North America could show an increase in consumer spending of 27% by the end of this century, driven by its projected 29% increase in population. Note, however, that the growth forecast for the North American population hinges on past immigration patterns continuing, which seems increasingly doubtful considering the recent political discourse in the US. The demographic anomalies that will characterize the United States and Canada will be dealt with in Chapter 21.

In contrast to other regions, Africa's consumer spending could skyrocket and increase threefold by the end of the century. This is mainly because the African population will increase from 1.3 billion in 2020 to 3.8 billion by 2100, and a large part of that population would be of working age—the "sweet spot" for consumer spending. This is yet another reason why the African continent is set to play such a pivotal role in the world economy over the next two centuries.

But the aggregate continent-wide data hides significant variations at a country level. The table below shows selected countries along with their expected changes in consumer spending between 2024 and 2100, as well as their expected population levels. Understandably, there is a high correlation between the change in consumer spending and the change in population. South Korea, Taiwan, China and Poland could see a more than 50% decline in consumer spending, which is mainly driven by a similar decrease in population.

Table 6: Change in consumer spending 2020 to 2100 for selected countries

	Population in millions (2024)	Population in millions (2100)	Change in population (percentage)	Change in consumer spending (percentage, 2024-2100)
South Korea	52	22	-58%	-61%
Taiwan	23	10	-57%	-60%
China	1 419	633	-55%	-56%
Poland	39	19	-50%	-51%
Italy	59	35	-40%	-43%
Japan	124	77	-38%	-41%
Thailand	72	46	-36%	-38%
Spain	48	33	-31%	-35%
Turkey	87	65	-25%	-20%
Brazil	212	163	-23%	-20%
Argentina	46	38	-16%	-9%
Germany	85	71	-16%	-20%
Portugal	10	9	-16%	-21%
Russia	145	126	-13%	-14%
Iran	92	80	-13%	-8%
Colombia	53	47	-11%	-6%
Vietnam	101	92	-9%	-3%

	Population in millions (2024)	Population in millions (2100)	Change in population (percentage)	Change in consumer spending (percentage, 2024-2100)
Netherlands	18	18	-4%	-6%
Philippines	116	114	-1%	19%
Morocco	38	38	-1%	12%
Mexico	131	130	0%	11%
France	67	68	3%	2%
India	1 451	1 505	4%	17%
Indonesia	283	296	4%	15%
United Kingdom	69	74	7%	8%
Peru	34	38	12%	23%
Bangladesh	174	209	20%	43%
United States of America	345	421	22%	22%
Malaysia	36	44	24%	32%
Canada	40	54	35%	32%
Algeria	47	64	38%	61%
South Africa	64	94	47%	62%
Australia	27	43	62%	61%
Egypt	117	202	73%	113%
Kenya	56	104	85%	153%
Ghana	34	68	96%	156%
Pakistan	251	511	103%	173%
Uzbekistan	36	74	104%	139%
Nigeria	233	477	105%	198%
Saudi Arabia	34	71	109%	122%
Iraq	46	101	119%	194%
Uganda	50	121	142%	284%
Sudan	50	137	171%	283%
Ethiopia	132	367	178%	292%
Mozambique	35	104	201%	365%
Cameroon	29	89	205%	333%
Côte d'Ivoire	32	104	226%	338%
Tanzania	69	263	283%	444%
Democratic Republic of the Congo	109	431	294%	503%
Angola	38	150	296%	483%

Based on the 2019 United Nations forecasts, as the 2021 update did not feature detailed age groups. The later forecasts have substantially lower figures for China.

Source: Author's calculations

The difference between the change in consumer spending and the change in population reflects the impact of the evolving age profile of the consumer body. Consider the case of South Korea. By 2100, its population is expected to decrease by 58%, while its consumer spending may decline by as much as 61%. The additional 3% decrease is due to a greater proportion of older consumers, who spend proportionately less than younger people do.

These demographic shifts should be considered by corporations, to ensure that their deployment of capital is aligned with structural changes in their markets. For instance, without taking these shifts into account, companies might invest in factories in markets where the target consumer body will decline, or where the size of the workforce will shrink.

Similarly, investors should be aware of the impact that these changes in demographics could have on the performance of their investment portfolios. The companies they invest in may be vulnerable to a substantial decline in demand as the age profile of their consumer market changes. Investors should also be mindful of where future high-growth opportunities could lie (for instance, in African markets), and which markets and sectors to avoid.

There are many African countries that could have triple-digit increases in consumer spending, driven by their higher population numbers as well as a still-growing proportion of younger people in the population. Some of these markets may have short-term challenges— for example, governance problems and associated political risks—but what is undeniable is the long-term opportunity of its surplus labor resources in a world starved of workers.

Many countries may need to "import" consumers

Countries will have to find ways to stimulate demand within their economies. One solution is to replenish their ailing populations with more young consumers. But with the birth rates in developed countries trapped in a downward trend that is unlikely to reverse within the next few decades, the only option for these countries would be to attract more immigrants to boost consumption and consequently GDP growth. To stimulate demand, countries that experience workforce shortages should not just import labor—for example, by issuing limited-period visas of 3 to 5 years to workers only. By issuing working visas only, foreign workers are not encouraged to settle in the country with their families, and they will probably either save (as opposed to spend) or remit a large part of their earnings to their families in their countries of origin. As we noted earlier, remittances from migrant workers and expatriates totaled $857bn in 2023,[115] which is effectively siphoned out of the host economies and instead stimulates consumer spending in their home countries.

It will be in their economic interest for labor-importing countries to encourage the immigration of workers with their families. This will have dual benefits—the workers themselves will be the solution to the looming labor shortage situation, while their dependents will drive consumer spending in the host country. The level of remittances would reduce substantially with such strategies, and these earnings would stimulate the economy of the host nations.

In conclusion, over the next few decades, developed nations will start to experience a structural decline in consumer spending due to their aging populations. For these countries, encouraging permanent immigration will become a necessity, so that these younger, new citizens and their dependents can refill the ranks of their own dwindling consumer market. By the end of this century, there will be only one region that will have the capacity to supply the labor and the consumers in meaningful numbers. That region is Africa.

* * *

CHAPTER 17

A SHRINKING TAX BASE

The roads are in a terrible state, thinks Eva, as she goes for a stroll through the neighborhood. Some of the potholes have been there for years and have not been repaired. After every winter, the size of the potholes increases, and they deepen. Some good Samaritans occasionally fill the holes with sand and stones in a feeble attempt to lessen the impact for road users. But this does not always suffice— soon the temporary fillings are washed away by the rain and vehicles are once again vulnerable to the concealed road traps.

It's the same all across the city. Roads, parks and other amenities are neglected and left to decay. Only when something is life-threateningly dangerous, does the city act. The mayor says the budget cuts are necessary because the city's income has been in decline for years. The city is unable to borrow its way out of the situation, as the economic outlook is unlikely to improve considering the declining population. As a result, the city only spends on things that are absolutely necessary, and routine maintenance is often not considered essential.

"I hate paying taxes. But I love the civilization they give me," quipped the American physician and writer Oliver Wendell Holmes Sr. This probably sums up the attitude of most taxpayers. We loathe parting with our hard-earned money to hand it over to a government that seems to thrive on our contributions. But despite its near-universal unpopularity, taxation is a vital part of modern societies, as it pays for a host of public goods and services that we take for granted.

The business of government has as its main source of revenue tax collections from individuals and companies. Tax revenue is used to fund public services and social spending, including services such as infrastructure (roads, sanitation), healthcare, welfare, education, defense, and policing. So, when tax revenue declines, spending on these public services will have to be trimmed. Some of the cutbacks could be commensurate with the decline in population and the change in demographics. For example, an aging population with a lower fertility rate would need fewer educational facilities, and therefore spending cuts could be made in these areas without much disruption. But in other areas, costs are largely fixed and spending cuts become more difficult. For example, the cost to maintain road and transport infrastructure is mostly fixed, as is the cost of maintaining water and sewage systems.

In the case of personal taxes on individuals, these are collected from workers earning wages, investment income, or sales taxes. Accordingly, as the population declines and the number of workers and consumers decreases, the taxpayer base in the country shrinks. In the case of corporates, they pay taxes on the profits they generate. When the number of consumers declines, corporates' sales and profits will also reduce, resulting in lower corporate tax collections. In short, government revenue—be it federal or local—will decline as the population ages and shrinks in size.

Figure 37 shows the potential for personal tax collections based on the size and age of populations (adjusted for inflation and keeping all other factors unchanged). In Europe, income tax collections from individuals may drop by 26% by the end of the century, compared to the 2020 level. This is due to the population falling by 21% over this period, while the aging of the population accounts for the remaining 5% decline (pensioners have lower incomes and pay less tax). Individual tax collections in Asia and Latin America will increase until mid-century, but are then projected to decline rapidly in line with their decreasing population. Based on its demographic forecast, North America could avoid this scenario, because its population is expected to rise by 29% between 2020 and 2100. This is due to expectations of continuing immigration trends in the US and Canada, which we will challenge in a later chapter.

Figure 37: Personal income tax revenue (indexed 2020 = 100; inflation adjusted)

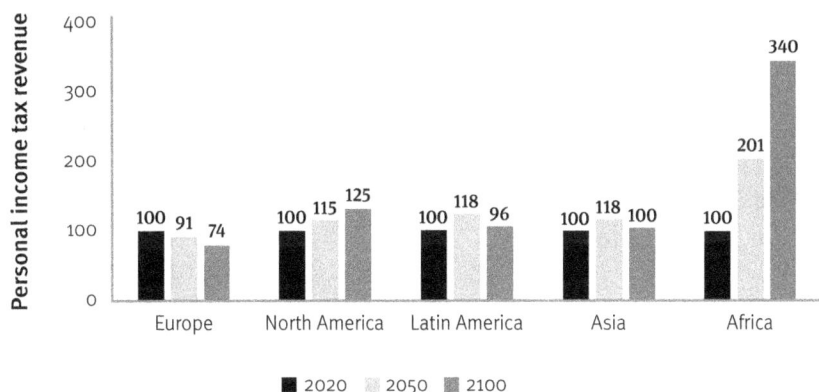

Source: Author's calculations

Japan, which is leading the world in terms of its aging profile, is an extreme example of what could happen to countries with a declining tax base. By 2100, Japan's personal income tax revenue is forecast to decrease by 44%, which is due to its population declining by 39%, and the remainder due to the aging of its population. In Japan, tax revenue collected from individuals accounts for 61% of total income tax revenue,[116] which means that the substantial drop in tax revenues will compel the government to make major cuts in public spending.

Africa once again stands out. The continent has the potential to generate significant increases in tax revenue, mainly because its population is expected to triple to 3.8 billion people between 2020 and 2100. Around 65% of Africa's projected 2100 population will be of working age (15–64 years) and would therefore be in the prime tax-paying segment of society. The tax windfall will be significant and would allow countries on the continent to develop more infrastructure and improve their public service delivery. This could start a virtuous cycle in which better infrastructure leads to more economic activity, which then further drives higher tax revenue. This is another boon supporting the case for the 22nd century becoming the "African Century".

In countries where a decrease in population will lead to lower tax revenue, governments will be forced to trim their spending. Major spending cuts will naturally lead to a decline in infrastructure maintenance and development, social welfare and other public spending. While some developed countries such as Japan may have excellent infrastructure today, this will need to be maintained, otherwise it will fall into disrepair. However, as we noted in Chapter 10, we can expect a scarcity of labor to do such maintenance work. A suitable analogy to comprehend the effects of oversized systems supporting a shrinking population is to think of a family of five living in a large house. While the kids are at home, the home is fully utilized. The family may even make extensions to the home to make it more comfortable. As time goes by, the children, one by one, start to leave—to pursue studies, careers, or to start their own families. When the parents retire and the children have moved out, the house may be too big and costly to maintain for the two elderly parents. Plumbing issues occur in parts of the house that are not even used, timber must be routinely treated, and the large lawn must be mowed regularly. "Empty-nester" parents solve this problem by downsizing and moving to a smaller home with lower maintenance requirements and costs— often in a retirement community. Unfortunately, cities and countries can't downsize and move somewhere else. They will have to deal with excess infrastructure (the "big house") that must still be maintained. To make matters worse, the cost of this maintenance will fall on a smaller population of working-age people. The surplus facilities built to support a population at its peak will inevitably be abandoned, deteriorate and decay. Under-utilized public facilities such as schools and public swimming pools will close and wither away. Parks and recreation facilities are unlikely to be public spending priorities and will become neglected. Even essential infrastructure such as roads, railways, water and sewage systems, and the electricity grid will become too costly to maintain by virtue of their oversized scale relative to an ever-decreasing population.

Higher taxes to fund social spending

To compensate for falling tax revenues, governments will be forced to increase tax rates. Spending cuts in some areas will be negated by increased healthcare and social service spending, required by a growing aged population. As an illustration of the impact that the aging of the population could have on taxes, a country with an average 35% tax rate, which spends 10% of its national budget on social services, could find it necessary to increase its average tax rate to 45% if the number of workers (that is, taxpayers) is reduced by 20%, and a commensurately larger number of pensioners must be supported.

The younger, working-aged people may resist the burden of such higher taxes placed on them. They could become disincentivized to work hard if tax rates are too high and they feel that they are not benefiting from the system. Workers could choose to adopt a more sedate lifestyle, generating only the minimum income needed to sustain themselves. As we saw earlier, this is already a growing trend with Gen Z workers, who desire a better quality of life. With more plodders and fewer highly ambitious workers, a country's total income (and also its tax revenue) will steadily decline.

In countries where workers consider the tax burden to be too onerous, they could even choose to emigrate to countries with lower tax rates, which would effectively offer a better return for their work efforts. Indeed, some countries with labor shortages could offer lower tax rates as part of a package of incentives to attract scarce labor. However, this is a double-edged sword. By making tax concessions, the tax revenue of these countries will be under more pressure, and negatively impact the state's ability to deliver public services. It will be very difficult for these countries to find a balance between attracting foreign labor to plug the growing gap in the local workforce (which may well entail lower tax rates), and maximizing tax revenue to support an aging population.

* * *

CHAPTER 18

A DECLINE IN INVESTMENTS

Eva is reviewing her annual pension statement. Her pension has hardly increased. It is becoming more and more difficult to make ends meet: Her pension simply does not keep up with inflation. She never thought she would face this situation—she had always planned ahead and saved consistently. It was a discipline instilled by her prudent parents. She was not extravagant in her spending habits and thought that she would retire comfortably. But the pension fund returns have been poor for many years, affecting everyone: not just Eva's pension fund, but the entire market delivered poor investment returns. Most pensioners are struggling, and some of her friends have tried to do some part-time work to supplement their pension income. But Eva feels her body won't allow her to work. The chronic medication she takes saps her energy and makes her lethargic. She just doesn't have the energy to go work again.

The advent of modern banking and investment was one of the most significant economic developments in human history. This allowed governments and corporates to tap public savings for their investment programs. Governments could borrow from the public by issuing bonds, allowing it to develop public infrastructure. Private enterprises could either borrow from public savings, or invite the public to invest in their ventures. This pool of capital is vital for the expansion of private enterprise. Investment fuels economic growth and allows businesses to expand while delivering returns to investors. Unfortunately, investment markets too could be extensively disrupted by the changes in demographics that will unfold over the next few decades.

To understand why this is the case, let's consider how the investment market works. The investment cycle starts when people save money. Most savings are made by workers who contribute to their pension funds over the course of their working lives. As an example, in the United States, workers' contributions to pension funds average about 7% of their income.[117] Their monthly contributions to pension funds, or 401(k)s, are intended to build a nest egg for their retirement years. To achieve that goal, though, the savings must be invested in assets that can deliver a satisfactory return. The pension funds invest the workers' savings in assets that yield a return for the investors. The contributions collected from workers are invested in the stock market, property funds, bonds, and other asset classes. This pool of capital, in turn, funds the growth of businesses, and can also finance countries through sovereign bonds. In the past, we almost always had a growing pool of savings, fueled by an expanding worker base. Other than the occasional market meltdown—which typically recovered after a period—we have not had a long-term structural net decline in the savings pool. This will change in the decades ahead. The aging population and the decline in the number of workers will have a widespread impact across the entire investment industry— affecting everything from the size of the investment pool to the return on investments, and even the conventional finance theories underpinning investment strategy.

With the number of workers in the population decreasing, the size of the total investment pool will shrink considerably. Besides the lower number of pension fund contributors, there will also be increasing drawdowns that will drain the savings pool. When the workers retire, they start drawing on their savings, which reduces the size of the investment pool. In the past, it has almost always been the case that workers outnumbered pensioners by a considerable margin. This meant that the drawdowns of pensioners were more than offset by the contributions of active fund members, and the savings and investments pool continued to grow. However, as the number of pensioners increases, this dynamic will change. The escalating drawdowns on savings could come to exceed the contributions of active fund members, whose numbers are set to decline in line with the reduction in the number of working-aged people in the population. The net effect is a reduction in investment capital that will impact the financing of corporations and governments.

Another consequence of the aging population is that the composition of investment asset classes could change dramatically. Investment managers must consider the age profile of their clients in their investment decisions. The savings of younger clients can be invested in higher-risk equity investments, because there is a longer timeframe before those clients cash out their savings. Short-term setbacks can be remedied, as there is still a long investment road ahead. As clients approach retirement age, their risk profile changes. Higher-risk equity investments are no longer appropriate, and their portfolios shift to lower-risk bonds and income-yielding assets, which provide more predictable cashflow streams. When they reach pension age, clients start drawing down on their savings, and their investments need to be in more liquid, money-market assets. Therefore, as the population ages and the proportion of aged people relative to working-aged people increases, a larger share of the savings pool will shift from equity investments to bond and money-market investments. Overall, the capital available for investment in most developed countries is likely to decrease, but the reduction in risk capital available for equity investments will be much more severe.

Equity investments are vital to support the growth and expansion of businesses. Equity investments range from venture capital startup funding to investments in listed stocks and are a critical source of funding for businesses. As the pool of funding shrinks in future due to the older investor profile, the equity capital available to grow businesses will dry up. The growth ambitions of companies will be constrained, and in turn, they will deliver lower returns to their shareholders (which include pension funds).

The reduction in pension fund contributions could be immense in some regions. In Europe, pension fund contributions by workers, adjusted for inflation, could be 31% lower by the end of this century, compared to the contributions made in 2020. Contributions made by workers in Asia could be 8% lower, and in Latin America, 13% down. At country level, Japan's pension fund contributions by active members could halve over the next 80 years. With such massive reductions in savings, economies would be starved of investment capital.

Figure 38: Pension and social security contributions (indexed 2020 = 100; inflation adjusted)

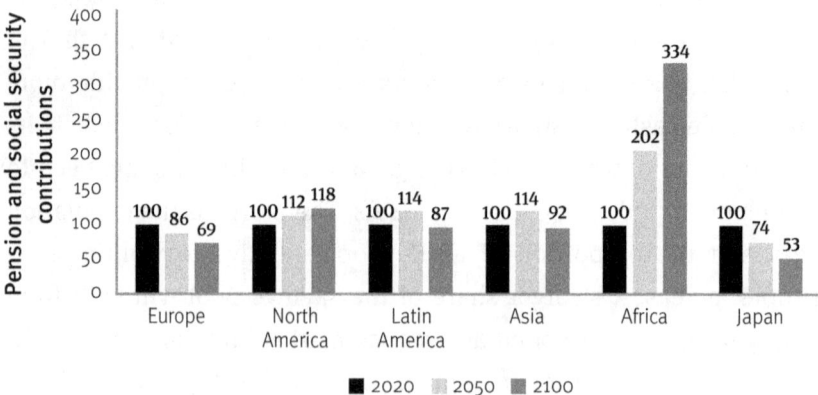

Source: Author's calculations

Africa, with its burgeoning working-age population, has the potential to build a considerable pool of pension capital, which could fuel economic growth on the continent. However, countries on the African continent must develop their financial sectors and encourage more pension fund savings for this latent potential to be realized.

Besides a shrinking investment pool, investors will also suffer declining investment returns. Investors look for assets that can provide growth and positive returns over time. They want to maximize the returns on their investments. However, it will become increasingly difficult to find companies that can deliver *any* growth in a market that is in a state of structural decline.

Since the advent of the modern professional investor in the early 20th century, the basic premise has been that the future expected cashflow should be greater than your initial investment, and the extent of the excess is determined by the return required by the investor. Yet, as we discussed in Chapter 16, in countries where the consumer base is aging and shrinking, consumption could be in a perpetual cycle of decline, and the underlying premise will no longer hold. Most companies in these markets face a future where their sales and profits will drop year after year. The best that company management may be able to do, is to slow the rate of decline. This would usher in a post-growth era, which traditional investment approaches have never dealt with before on a macro scale.

One of the fundamental conventions on which modern finance was developed is that long-term growth is positive. Markets may have some temporary setbacks (such as recessions), but the cycle will eventually turn and things will always get better. The conventional view is that a downturn will be followed by an upturn—the only debate is whether it will be a v-shaped or u-shaped recovery. But recovery it will be. This was certainly the case when the global consumer base exploded from 2.5 billion in 1950 to 8 billion in 2022. Not only did the number of consumers increase as the population grew, but household incomes rose, which expanded the middle class and drove higher consumption per capita. The rising middle class had aspirations that fueled demand for a growing list of consumer products, from clothing and televisions to mobile phones and automobiles. This virtuous cycle ensured that growth was always on an upward trajectory over the long term.

This upward trend is likely to peak somewhere around 2080, around the time when the global population reaches its high-water mark. In some countries, the upward growth trend may turn much earlier. In the short term, companies in these countries can diversify into other regions. Japanese companies, for example, could set up offshore subsidiaries in Vietnam and Indonesia and use local labor for their factories in those countries. Increasingly, though, such diversification opportunities will run out of road. As competition intensifies for the ever-shrinking pool of growth segments, countries might seek to become more protectionist and block outside competition. Governments could, for example, restrict foreign ownership to safeguard their own resources. Some countries already have restrictions in place in certain sectors (for example, in Canada there is a cap on foreign ownership in telecommunication and mining companies), but the scope of sectors affected by restrictions could expand significantly in future.

Ultimately, corporations' profits will trend down and their returns to shareholders—both dividends and capital—will decline. Figure 39 shows the long-term trend between the S&P 500 average price and the volumes traded (the demand)—there is a strong positive correlation between demand for stocks and the price of stocks. In other words, a higher demand for stocks will push up the price of stocks. The converse also holds: With a lower population and declining pension contributions in future, trading volumes on stock exchanges will decline and drag down the price of stocks.

How then would we assess opportunities for investment in a post-growth world? In the past, if an investor had, say, one million dollars to invest, they would select an asset that they believe holds the potential to grow to a value of, say, $1.2 million after a given period. If you invest in a company, you expect it to grow its revenue and profit, and so you would be able to exit your investment at a higher price. But in an era of population decline, the investor in this example is almost guaranteed to get less than one million dollars back. Why is this? Well, let's say that the company in which they are investing had $500 million in sales in the first year of investment. Over time, the company's sales would almost certainly decline due to the lower demand from a smaller and older customer base. As the company's sales fall, its profits will drop, and the value of the company will also decline. Faced with the outcome, the investor may well question if they should even bother to invest at all.

Figure 39: Demand for stocks drive up the price (S&P 500 vs. NYSE Volume)

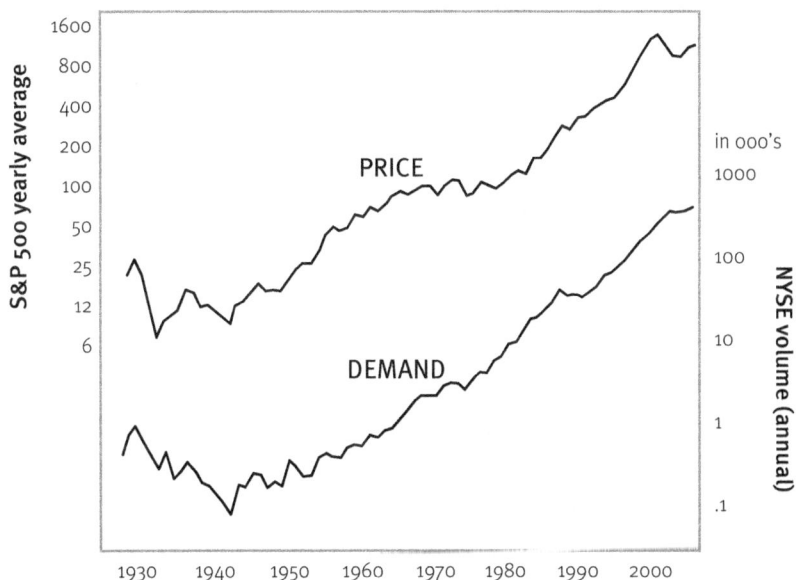

Source: The Journal of Behavioral Finance *2007, Vol. 8, No. 2, 84–108*

The alternative to investing in assets such as stocks or bonds, is to hold cash. This strategy, however, will have several negative consequences. First, it will accelerate the decline of investment capital available in the market, which will further curb economic growth. Second, cash could lose its value over time due to inflation. This may seem counterintuitive, considering a decline in demand would normally result in lower prices and therefore lower inflation. However, supply will also be reduced in the face of lower demand, restoring some price equilibrium.

Critically, though, the supply of money in the market must also be adjusted. Think about it this way: Let's say in a simple one-product market there is one million dollars of cash and one million widgets available for consumption. This means that the price of the widgets is one dollar each. If the market shrinks and the demand drops to 800,000 widgets, the price will rise to $1.25 each if the amount of money in the market remains unchanged. The excess supply of cash can therefore drive inflation, and those holding cash will be worse off. Governments will have to adjust their monetary and fiscal policies to soak up excess cash as the market shrinks. Also, inflation could be driven by higher wage inflation caused by the lack of workers.

The very foundation of capital markets could be rattled as the theoretical underpinning of the investment process will need to be revisited. Modern economics and financial systems are based on the premise of growth. For investors, negative growth is an anathema that is to be avoided at all costs, so much so that the traditional tools of financial analysis have not even catered for sustained negative growth scenarios. Yet, negative growth is a looming reality in an era of constant population decline in most developed countries. The current theoretical valuation tools deal with distressed companies as individual underperformers, which are either to be avoided or valued on a salvage basis. This approach is adequate when there are many alternative investment opportunities around for investors to choose from. But when most companies in a market are in decline, there may not be alternative opportunities at all. The current finance theories will then become ineffective—modern finance theory will need a major overhaul.

Many fundamental financial analysis concepts will need to be reassessed. For example, the concept of the time value of money holds that a sum of money is worth more now than the same sum will be at a future date, due to the earnings potential of the money in the interim. But as we can see above, in a world of declining demand, the earnings potential may be negative. Does this mean that a sum of money is worth less now than at a future date? Academics and financial analysts will have to start thinking about new frameworks that can deal with these situations.

Another example is the discounted cash flow (DCF) model, which is one of the primary tools used in investment valuations. The DCF uses as inputs the concepts of a risk-free rate of return, the equity risk premium and the cost of debt. The risk-free return is the return an investor can get on a "safe" investment such as government bonds. The high demand for such low-risk investments, due to the increase in the number of pensioners, will drive down the yields on these bonds and could lower the risk-free rate of return. The equity risk premium is the excess return over a risk-free rate required by investors when they invest in the stock market. This return compensates investors for taking on the higher risk of stock investing. The lower demand for risky stocks will drive down the price of those assets and increase the yield on them—thereby raising the cost of capital for companies. On the other hand, the cost of debt could drop, driven by the higher demand for more predictable interest income by pensioners. Investors will also favor cash dividends instead of capital growth (as there is a risk that the latter may not happen in such an environment).

These dynamics will encourage companies who need capital to take on more debt, and as a result their capital structures could change drastically. Traditionally, gearing ratios (that is, debt to equity) of 25% to 50% are considered optimal. With an excessively high equity risk premium, gearing ratios of 100% to 200% may become the norm, which substantially increases the risk of these investments.

All these factors come together in the weighted average cost of capital (WACC), which is the average rate a company is expected to pay to all its security holders to finance its assets. Companies should not invest in projects if the expected returns from such initiatives are lower than their WACC rate. The problem is that in a market that is experiencing constant decline, most projects will not pass this hurdle, meaning companies will cut back on investments, and when companies don't invest, innovation slows. Developments in artificial intelligence (AI) and robotics, which could soften the impact of a shrinking workforce, will be starved of capital and may not achieve their potential. In Chapter 5 we looked at the limitations of technology and AI in addressing the looming problem of a shortage of essential workers. We can now add a complication to that—the potential lack of funding to achieve these technology advances.

Sometime between now and 2080, the scenario sketched above could become a reality. So, when should investors start getting worried and factor these trends into their valuations? Investment managers typically have an investment horizon of about three to five years and assume perpetual terminal growth thereafter (this is because businesses are deemed to operate on a "going concern" basis, meaning they will operate indefinitely). Investors would usually pay for 10 to 20 years' worth of annual earnings, so if a company has earnings of, say, $1 per share, the share price could be $10 to $20 (if the price-to-earnings ratio is 10x and 20x, respectively). Given these time frames—a five-year investment holding period and purchasing the equivalent of 20 years' earnings—it means that from around 2050, the approach to investment management will have to fundamentally change. Those who prepare earlier for the changing dynamics of an aging and declining population will be in a better position to navigate the challenges ahead.

Markets are constantly changing, and over the long term, the changes can be astounding. Consider, for example, how the composition of the stock market has changed over the past century. In 1917, the list of the most valuable companies in the United States was dominated by resources companies, with 40% of the country's 50 largest companies being steel, oil or mining companies. This was a time of infrastructure expansion for a fast-growing nation and economy, and the stock market reflected those investment themes.

Table 7: Largest US companies (1917)

Rank	Company	Industry	Value ($bn; inflation adjusted)
1	U.S. Steel	Steel	$48
2	AT&T	Telecom	$15
3	Standard Oil	Oil and gas	$11
4	Bethlehem Steel	Steel	$7
5	Armour & Co.	Food	$6
6	Swift & Co.	Food	$6
7	International Harvester	Heavy equipment	$5
8	E.I. du Pont de Nemours	Chemicals	$5
9	Midvale Steel & Ordnance	Steel	$5
10	U.S. Rubber	Rubber	$4
11	General Electric	Conglomerate	$4

Source: Forbes

One hundred years later, those old giants have been replaced by new companies and industries. In 2017, technology, financial services, and pharmaceutical companies dominated the list of the 50 largest companies in the US. That year's list was led by consumer-focused companies—those that make smartphones, provide social media platforms, online shopping, and apps. The prospects of companies are inextricably linked to the populations they serve.

Table 8: Largest US companies (2017)

Rank	Company	Industry	Value ($bn)
1	Apple	Technology	$768
2	Alphabet	Technology	$605
3	Microsoft	Technology	$600
4	Amazon	Technology	$475
5	Berkshire Hathaway	Conglomerate	$432
6	Facebook	Technology	$401
7	Johnson & Johnson	Pharmaceutical	$358
8	Exxon Mobil	Oil and gas	$339
9	JPMorgan Chase	Financial services	$326
10	Wells Fargo & Co.	Financial services	$268
11	Walmart	Retail	$241

Source: Forbes

One hundred years from now, the list will again be very different. It is impossible to forecast who will lead the ranking tables then, but one thing we can be reasonably sure of is this: The market value of the leaders will be much lower than current valuations (adjusted for inflation). Why would this be the case? The reason is that current investment views are premised on a population that will continue to grow, from 8 billion in 2022 to around 10 billion by 2080. But after 2080, the global population will decline, and with that decline will come lower earnings prospects and lower company valuations.

There will still be some growth investment opportunities, but these will be related to companies linked to markets where the consumer base is still growing. These opportunities will mostly be in Africa. Already, more than 70% of the 50 largest packaged goods producers in the world are tapping into Africa's fast-growing consumer market.[118]

These investments are still relatively small, but they will ramp up significantly when other markets show signs of structural decline.

The pension funds of developed nations could seek investment opportunities in these developing regions, which in turn will boost the economic growth of the target countries. The combination of healthy population growth and access to investment capital will be one of the key catalysts in unlocking the potential of these regions.

Investors typically categorize investment opportunities as either *growth* stocks or *value* stocks. The growth style of investing focuses on finding companies with high growth prospects even if they may not be profitable in the short term. These companies concentrate on building up their revenue initially, and later shift focus to maximizing profits. Young technology company valuations, for example, often have very high valuation multiples. They may burn through cash and be loss-making in the early years of their existence, but the expectation is that once they have scale, the business will be profitable. In the past, this has turned out to be true in many cases. However, in future, that profitability tipping point may not materialize because of the declining population. Opportunities for growth investing will mostly be found in those countries with stronger population growth, and a stronger consumer body—again, most likely countries in Africa.

Developed countries, on the other hand, will mostly offer *value* investing opportunities due to their aging and declining populations. Value stocks do not have high growth characteristics but do have steady, proven business models that generate modest gains in revenue and earnings over time. Companies that are in decline could still offer value investing opportunities provided their share price is lower than their future profit potential. However, this will be a difficult hurdle to overcome, given the impact that the overall decline in demand for stocks will have on the price of these assets.

Most critically, in addition to the challenge of declining returns on investments, pension funds will be under immense pressure to honor obligations as they experience a net decline in contributing members. As the ratio of worker-to-aged people drops, there will be fewer new members joining pension funds. The number of retired people drawing down on their pensions will outstrip those making monthly contributions, and with the lower investment returns, the financial situation of most pension funds could be precarious, with many becoming underfunded. Most developed countries' public pension systems are "defined benefit" plans[119], which means that workers are guaranteed a certain pension on retirement—in these plans, the employer shoulders the investment risks. The burden of the underfunded pension plans falls on the employer, which in most cases, are government or public enterprises (the private sector has largely moved to "defined contribution" plans—or 401(k)s—which shifts the investment risks to the worker).

Governments have no alternative but to try and push ahead with pension reform. In the United Kingdom, the retirement age has increased from 65 years in 2018, and will reach 67 by 2028.[120] Australia has also increased its retirement age from 65 to 67 years, but did this on a faster timeline, between 2017 and 2023.[121] And in France in 2023, despite widespread unpopularity, the government proceeded with plans to increase the retirement age from the current 62 years to 64.[122] Underfunded social welfare systems are perhaps the only area related to the aging demographic environment that is receiving some attention from governments presently. While some governments may be able to raise the retirement age, recall that in Chapter 6 we dealt with the challenges and limitations of extending the retirement age— at best, it may only provide some temporary reprieve.

In the public sector, the government can try to fund social welfare programs by increasing taxes, although higher taxes on a smaller pool of workers may not necessarily yield a windfall. Private pension funds do not have the option of levying additional charges on active members. Defined contribution pension plans, which are prevalent in the private sector, shift the investment risk to the workers. This means that lower investment returns will reduce their pension payments. Pensioners will be hard-pressed to balance their budgets, given that their lower income will come into conflict with the high inflationary increases in their living expenses.

In summary, in a few decades, the overall investment environment could be bleak for all stakeholders—for investors, corporates and governments. The decline in the investment markets will come to mirror the decay that will be seen across the rest of society. For now, investment managers must be careful not to be too focused only on short-term earnings and forecasts, and thus potentially miss the seismic shifts that await on the horizon.

* * *

CHAPTER 19

THE DEBTS OF MY FATHER

Eva's son called earlier today. He seemed stressed. Matthew has a good job and works long hours, but always seems to be under financial pressure. Lately he has been saying things that make her very uneasy for his future. He says that the high tax rates make him wonder if it is worth working at all. He toys with the idea of living "off the grid" and adopting a subsistence lifestyle. Eva is aware that things have changed since her young days, but this sort of thinking is alien to her.

She remembered how her late husband used to complain about taxes. Every pothole, every instance of poor service delivery, and any corruption scandal would set him off on a tirade against having to fund the government. "They are wasting my hard-earned money," he would rant. What would he think now, given the poor state of the city's infrastructure? How can taxes increase year after year, but all the while service delivery gets worse? This morning Eva saw a news report on the country's mounting debt crisis—she feels sorry for Matthew and his generation, as they are shouldering this burden.

In 2023, the value of government debt worldwide was $98 trillion, or about 94% of global gross domestic product (GDP).[123] Government debt accounted for almost 38% of all debt (which amounted to

$250 trillion in 2023). The remaining debt consists of corporate and household debt. Since 2007, government debt has risen rapidly due to the responses to the global financial crisis of 2008 and the COVID-19 pandemic in 2020.

Governments accumulate debt when their public expenditure is not covered by tax or other revenues. This deficit spending can sometimes be beneficial as it can support national economies during temporary adverse episodes—for example, during wars, financial crises and pandemics. Governments generally aim to maintain debt in relation to the country's GDP, and a ratio of around 60% debt to GDP is considered reasonable. Debt levels that are excessive could lead to higher interest payments and may make governments vulnerable to a debt crisis—that is, when a country is unable to make debt repayments and cannot borrow more. One such example is Argentina's debt crisis of 2001, which resulted in the collapse of its currency and a sharp increase in inflation. A few years later, in 2009, Greece faced a sovereign debt crisis, which necessitated austerity measures, including several rounds of tax increases and spending cuts.[124]

Government debt must be serviced. Rising debt levels mean the service costs of the debt increase. The higher interest payments take up a larger share of the country's national budget, which means there is less money available for other public spending programs. In the case of Argentina's debt crisis, the country's debt service cost as a percentage of gross national income increased from 2.3% in 1994 to 11.7% in 2003, which forced the government to implement several rounds of austerity measures, including pay cuts for civil servants.

Because governments hardly ever fully repay their debt, the debt burden is continually rolled and carried forward. This means that the government debt results in an inter-generational transfer of liabilities, because the beneficiaries of the government's expenditure on goods and services when the debt is created could differ from the individuals responsible for repaying the debt in the future. With a shrinking population, this means that current debt obligations will fall on a smaller cohort in future, who will therefore have to carry a greater individual debt burden. This is yet another blow to the dwindling working-aged population, as they will be saddled with more government debt per capita, despite a significant reduction in their potential to generate wealth in future.

The chart below shows the countries with the highest debt per capita as of 2023. The debt burden on Singaporean citizens in 2023 was $137,382 per person, which was the highest in the world. The United States ($99,712) and Japan ($85,314) filled out the rest of the top three spots.

Figure 40: Debt per capita (US$, 2023)

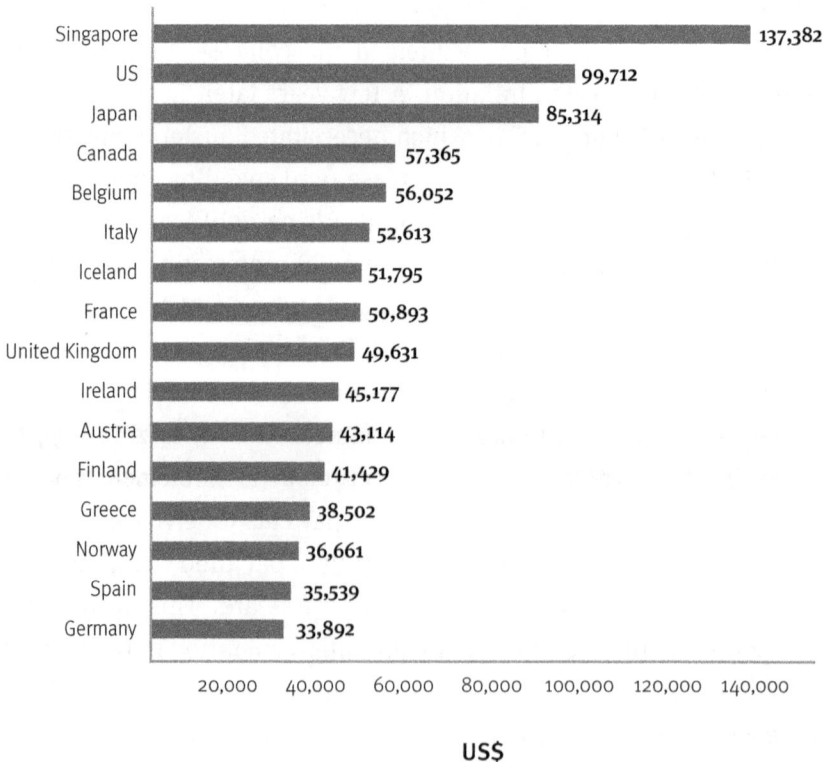

US$

Source: UNCTAD

Advanced economies not only generate most of the global GDP, they are also accountable for most of the global debt. Seven countries—the United States, Japan, China, France, Italy, the United Kingdom and Germany—account for 74% of the world's total debt. However, most of these developed nations are due to experience some of the biggest changes in demographics. These countries with the highest debt levels will see that burden transferring to a fast-shrinking population—in other words, the debt per capita could rise sharply in those countries.

In the chart below, we can see the impact that a smaller population may have on debt per capita ratios. Singapore's already high burden of $137,382 could increase to $195,297 by 2100, by virtue of its population decreasing by 28%. Similarly, Japan's debt burden per person could increase from $85,314 to $138,353, and Italy's from $52,613 to $87,525 by 2100. All of these future values are expressed in today's money— that is, adjusted for inflation.

Figure 41: Debt per capita (US$): Impact of declining population

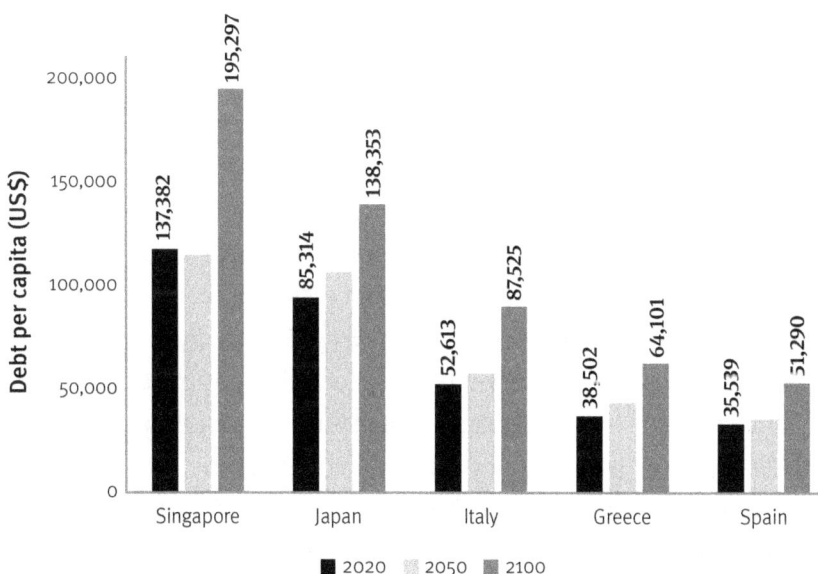

Source: UNCTAD, UN population forecasts

187

A full list of countries' debt per capita ratios is shown in Appendix 5. These calculations also assume the total debt remains stable at current levels, which is highly unlikely. Most of these countries run budget deficits—this means that the current year's spending is more than the income, therefore more debt must be raised to balance annual budgets. As an example, in the 50 years between 1970 and 2020, the US had budget surpluses in only 4 years. The total debt could therefore be substantially higher in future (the United States, for example, is on track to add $19 trillion to its national debt over the next decade).[125]

The situation may be even more dire than suggested by Figure 41, which calculated the debt per capita on the *total population* of each country. Besides the projected decline in total population in some countries, the demographic composition will change substantially as the proportion of people over 65 years of age increases. Pensioners have lower economic activity, pay less tax, and are unlikely to make meaningful contributions to discharging national debt. Therefore, a more appropriate measure is to calculate the debt burden per capita based only on the *working-age* population. Figure 42 reveals a much more striking picture of the debt burden to be borne by future generations.

Singapore's per capita debt based on its working-age population is set to more than double from $186,963 in 2023 to $397,065 by 2100. Japan's individual debt burden will increase from $145,411 to $270,642, while Italy's debt per working-age person increases from $81,777 to $170,071 by the end of the century. To put these numbers in context— the average annual wage in Japan was $37,362 in 2023, which means that its debt burden per worker by the end of the century is equivalent to almost 7 years' worth of wage income (adjusted for inflation).

Clearly, this trend is not sustainable. Presently, there are no immediate plans for most of these governments to consolidate and reduce debt. In fact, as the US projected budgeted deficits show, there are no short-term plans to even balance budgets, so the debt levels will continue to rise (this situation is the same in most developed countries). The can continues to be kicked down the road. To make matters worse, the occasional crisis leads to step-change increases in debt levels. For instance, the COVID-19 pandemic resulted in record levels of government lending.[126]

Figure 42: Debt per capita (US$), calculated on the working-age population

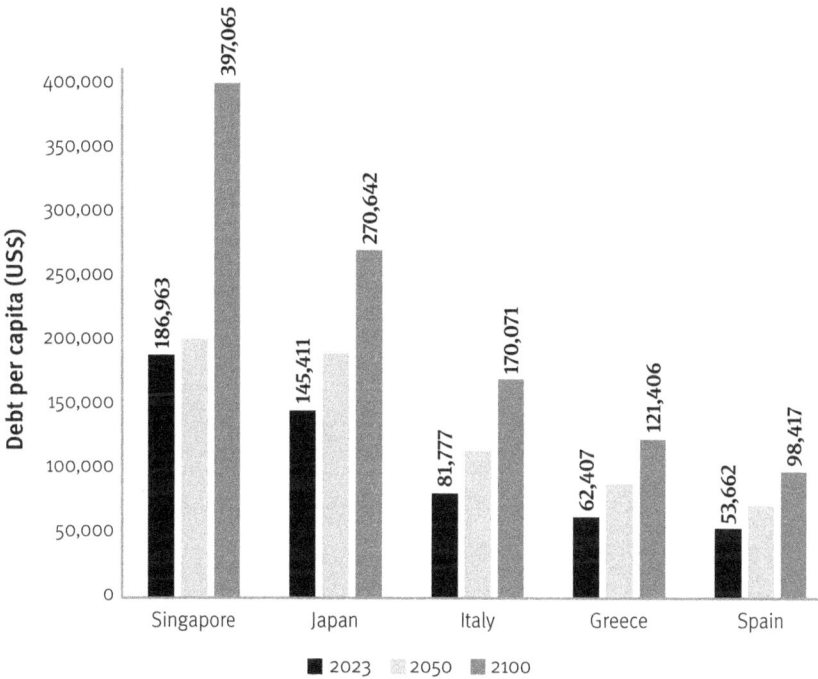

Source: UNCTAD, UN population forecasts

The inter-generational shifting of the debt burden to smaller and older future generations seems likely to end in an inevitable debt crisis, with the risk of currency collapse and very high inflation. Future generations may have to pay the price through prolonged austerity measures, which could be met with widespread public resistance and anger. Public reaction to the European sovereign debt crises after

2008 had major political and social consequences. Austerity is never a popular policy with the public. But faced with unserviceable debt levels being handed down to a smaller number of future taxpayers, governments will have no other option but to take a tough stance.

★ ★ ★

CHAPTER 20

A DECLINE IN LIVING STANDARDS —THE POVERTY OF NATIONS

Eva is stressed about her household finances. The cost of living is rising but her pension is not. She is finding it increasingly difficult to pay her bills. Prices are constantly rising due to high inflation. Her friends say it is because of the foreign workers who must be paid high wages to come work here. And with the expense of those high wages, everything becomes more expensive.

Supermarket prices have increased relentlessly over the last few years, making many of her favorite products unaffordable. Goods such as cheese, meat and seafood are now luxuries for her. When she was young, she was very particular about her diet, preferring lots of grains, fish, and fresh fruit. But now, her wallet dictates what she eats. Tonight, it is spaghetti with canned sauce.

A shortage of workers will naturally lead to higher wages which, in turn, will push up inflation. In the near term, countries that face a labor shortage can recruit workers from countries where surplus labor is available. This will alleviate shortages and keep wages in check. However, the scale of such activity is still low and because the surplus labor supply in poorer countries is still abundant, it is generally not a problem to fill the gaps when they arise. Also, the recruiting countries currently have the luxury of setting the terms and conditions for immigration, which are often quite onerous. Aspiring immigrants must jump through several hoops for the privilege to move to these countries. But, in time, this situation will flip, and the roles will be reversed. Presently, the most significant stumbling block is the political climate, where the rising influence of right-wing and conservative parties is often fueled by anti-immigration sentiment. This can lead to some baffling developments. For example, Italy, which has one of the fastest aging populations and lowest birth rates in the world, elected a conservative government in 2022 who had campaigned on anti-immigration policies.

But the relevance of anti-immigration policies will soon reach its expiry date. Within the next three decades, the volume of demand for labor will increase exponentially as thirteen countries join the ranks of those with a worker-to-aged ratio of less than 2 (which we showed earlier could be the tipping point when problems will start to manifest). The labor market will change from a buyers' market, where receiving countries can dictate the terms for foreign workers to enter the local labor market, to a sellers' market—where immigrant workers will be able to choose the countries that offer them the best deal.

As more and more countries clamor for their share of a shrinking labor pool, bidding wars could develop for both high and low-skilled workers. Initially, the competition may involve simple price bidding, with recruiting countries offering increasingly higher wages. But other sweeteners will soon follow, where recruiting countries have to add perks to the package. These may include financial benefits such as free housing, tax exemptions, or paid flights to return home for holidays; as well as non-financial incentives, such as allowing families to join the workers, visa-free access and longer holidays. The cost of these incentives will ultimately be passed on to the consumer.

The impact of higher wages was evident in the United Kingdom with its shortage of heavy goods vehicle drivers during and after the COVID-19 pandemic.[127] In some cases, high double-digit percentage wage increases were reported during this time, with truck drivers commanding earnings of £50,000 per year (at a time when the median average salary for full-time workers in the United Kingdom was £31,285). Curiously, despite the generous wages, some British truck drivers were still walking away from the job, complaining of very long working hours, living away from family, sleeping in trucks, poor food, and not being able to exercise regularly.

As the standard of living and quality of life rises in developed countries, tolerance for poor working conditions drops. Local workers may not find the remuneration or the working conditions of some jobs appealing, and will instead explore other options. This was the case with the British truck drivers. Foreign workers from poorer countries, on the other hand, may be more than willing to put up with less favourable working conditions. Foreign workers may initially take the less-desirable jobs at a lower wage than would be acceptable to the local workforce. However, as more options become available to them in future, and several countries compete aggressively for their share of the global labor pool, the attitudes of these workers towards poor working conditions may change. For instance, foreign truck drivers may develop the same loathing of the working conditions as those cited by the British truck drivers earlier. They may then choose countries that offer better working conditions (for example, countries with more rest-stop facilities) or demand better compensation for the inconveniences associated with the job.

There are many knock-on effects of labor shortages that will also start to manifest themselves. As an example, Australia experienced a workforce crisis in its childcare sector in 2022, resulting in parents being unable to place their children in childcare programs because there were not enough staff in those facilities. Parents were forced to find alternative options for childcare during and after school hours, which resulted in a spike in fees for babysitters. The hourly rates for babysitters rose to AU$ 45 per hour, almost double the minimum wage of a qualified childcare worker (AU$ 24 per hour) at the time.[128] There will be countless other instances where there are consequential disruptions in the labor market.

With the supply of labor falling, and demand rising, higher wages are inevitable. The higher cost of labor will be passed on to consumers, and the most vulnerable to the effects of higher wages on inflation will be older people who survive on fixed pension income. The buying power of pensioners—who will form a larger part of the total population in future—and their quality of life will wane as inflation rises.

* * *

All the issues we have dealt with in the previous chapters coalesce to produce one overarching outcome—a decline in our standards of living. Developed countries with low birth rates and who are slow to respond filling their labor gaps through immigration, will be the first to experience this transformation.

Developed countries should not be over-confident that their progress and developmental achievements are an immutable baseline, a floor below which they cannot fall or regress. The wealth of nations is constantly changing. Fortunes rise and fall, and with them, the influence of these countries. As recently as the 1800s, Portugal was one of the richest countries in the world, but by the early 2000s it was ranked as one of the poorest nations in Europe. A few centuries ago, Britain, Spain and the Netherlands dispatched fleets around the world, usurping distant lands and resources, and boosting their wealth and influence on the global stage. But by the mid-20th century, most of their colonized lands regained independence, and the wealth and influence of the former colonizers diminished. India, which was under British rule until 1947, is now the fifth largest economy in the world, surpassing its former colonial master. Over the next century, these patterns will be repeated and the rich countries of today will by no means be guaranteed to be the leaders in the decades to come.

Countries with aging populations like Japan, South Korea, and Italy could find that their standards of living deteriorate over time, while countries with younger, growing populations are likely to overtake them due to their booming economies. The widespread impact of a smaller workforce can be summarized in the diagram below.

Figure 43: Impact of fewer workers

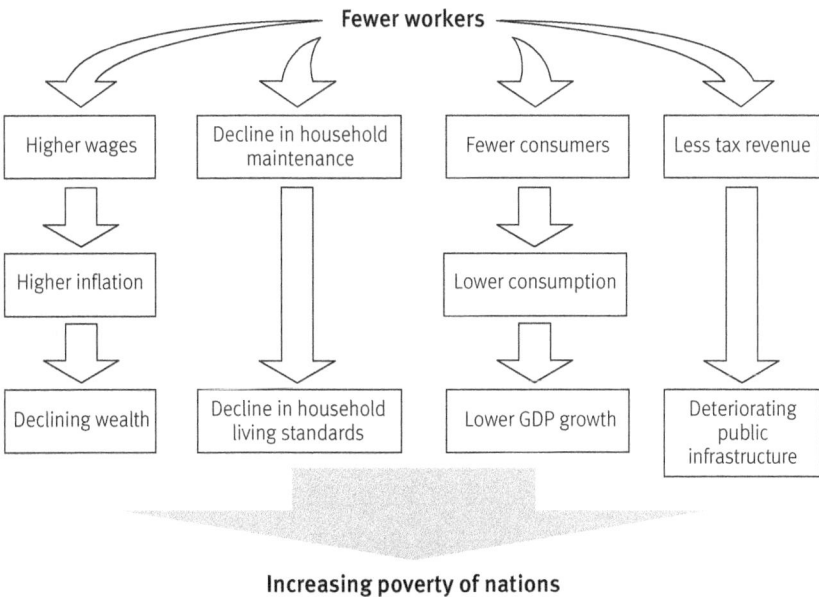

Increasing poverty of nations

The higher wages needed to attract scarce labor resources will drive inflation and eat into the real wealth of individuals. With fewer workers, maintenance will decline, resulting in a deterioration of infrastructure and living conditions. Also, with more vacant units in residential areas (apartment buildings and suburbs), malls and offices, the entire property spectrum will become more decrepit. Fewer workers and fewer younger people mean that there will be fewer consumers, and consumption will be lower. As consumption is a key driver of GDP growth, the latter will also be dragged down. Tax revenue will also decline and governments will have less money to spend on public goods and services—they may also have to implement austerity measures as high debt levels must be serviced. This potent mix of interrelated consequences could culminate in a general decline in the wealth of a country.

This changing wealth of nations could be one of the most important trends in future. These changes in the economic order are likely to happen at the same time that the world contends with the challenges of global warming and climate change. Consider the damages wrought by natural disasters—floods, hurricanes, earthquakes, and wildfires brought about by droughts. After such catastrophic events, massive rebuilding efforts are required. Many countries may find that they do not have enough essential workers—nor the funds—to undertake such reconstruction projects. Developed countries may suffer the most, as they are the ones that will be experiencing the most rapid population declines.

To avoid this scenario, countries with declining populations have only two options—either find a way to increase the fertility rate to at least the replacement rate of 2.1; or replenish their declining worker and consumer populations with immigrants. We will consider the effectiveness of the measures taken by some countries to increase fertility rates in Chapter 24. With the immigrant option, short-term fixes such as contract labor will not be sustainable, as this will become increasingly costly and will drive up inflation. Countries will have to embrace an open society approach to immigration, failing which they will wither in terms of wealth and global influence. With the rising nationalist sentiment in some countries, this may be difficult to accept for populist politicians and their followers. Ultimately, politics will have to submit to the relentless pressure that will be exerted on the economies and societies.

We have not yet witnessed such a structural decline in any of the modern developed societies. Recessions and depressions do result in a decline in wealth, but this situation is typically transient and the economies recover. The events set in motion by a decline in population are structural and will not be easy to reverse. Japan has a fast-aging population, but has not yet shown any significant change in its living standards or wealth. However, Japan's GDP per capita has been stagnant for the past three decades. Japan's population peaked at 128 million people in 2009, and by 2030 its population will decline by more than 700,000 per year. It may only be a matter of time before the decline in society described here will become a reality—this will likely begin around 2040 when more countries experience labor shortages and competition for human resources intensifies.

Adam Smith, the father of modern economics, argued in his 1776 book *The Wealth of Nations* that humans are self-serving by nature, but that as long as every individual seeks the fulfillment of her or his own self-interest, the material needs of the whole society will be met. This may have been true at a time when working-aged people outnumbered the aged by 10 to 1, but in a world where there are fewer than two working-aged people for every aged person, the increasing self-interest of the aged may not contribute much to the material needs of society. In fact, their demands for healthcare and other social services could steer governments away from more productive, growth-enhancing economic activities. *The Wealth of Nations* described the forces that built a country's wealth at the dawn of the Industrial Revolution. But given the prospect of a structural decline in wealth, a treatise with the title *The Poverty of Nations* may be a more apt tome to describe the principal forces that will drive decay at the dusk of this age.

★ ★ ★

CHAPTER 21

THE ANOMALIES—NORTH AMERICA, NORWAY AND AUSTRALIA

———

Clearing out the clutter from her old cupboard, Eva comes across some long-forgotten brochures. "Canada wants you!" shouts the heading. She sighs. She remembers the cultural fair she attended in her early thirties, where a bright-eyed young man at the Canadian stall had handed her the brochures. For weeks her head had swirled with ideas of moving to Canada, finding a job, and enjoying all the wonderful benefits of the country detailed in that brochure. But she was hesitant about the harsh winters there. Besides, she had a good job and Matthew was on the way. Years later, Matthew's college roommate emigrated to Canada. He is walking the path she has not taken.

While most of the developed world will be experiencing significant declines in their working-age populations, four developed countries are conspicuous in apparently bucking this trend—the US, Canada, Norway and Australia. According to UN forecasts, Australia's working-age population is projected to grow by 44% by the end of this century, Canada's by 18%, Norway's by 12%, and that of the United States by 8%. Considering that Europe's working-age population will drop by 32% over the same period, the fact that these four developed countries defy the demographic trends seems peculiar. Let's take a closer look at why this may be the case.

The fertility rates of these four countries are well below the replacement rate of 2.1, and not much different from Europe. The fertility rate in Canada in 2022 was 1.33, Norway was at 1.41, Australia at 1.63, and the United States at 1.67. Moreover, the fertility rates of these countries have dropped consistently over the past six decades, as shown in the chart below—and there is little evidence that the fertility rate is likely to rise, let alone surpass the replacement rate anytime soon. So how is it that their working-aged population levels will reverse the trends of other developed countries, and actually grow strongly over the next few decades?

Figure 44: Fertility rates—Norway, Canada, Australia, and the United States

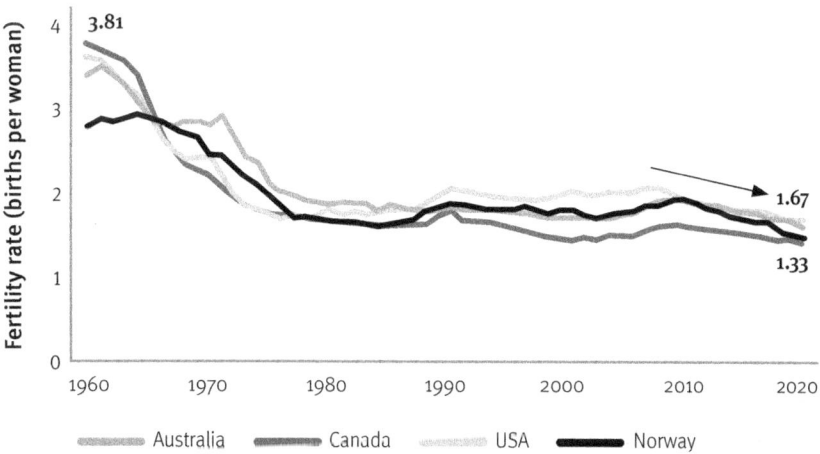

Source: United Nations

The reason for the projected growth in their workforces is almost entirely due to past immigration patterns, which the projections assume will persist into the decades ahead. There are, however, considerable risks that these projections will not be realized, simply because immigration patterns may not hold in the future. Unlike fertility rates, immigration trends are not a long-term structural development that follows a fairly fixed course—rather, they can be highly volatile and sensitive to the vagaries of changes in policy or public sentiment. Recent developments and trends in these countries suggest that forecasts of high immigration may be questionable, and therefore their projected strong population increases could be overstated. Let us look at the situation in each country individually.

United States of America

In the US, there has been a sharp decline in immigration since 2016. Net annual international migration to the United States dropped from more than one million people in 2016 to fewer than 600,000 in 2019, according to the US Census Bureau.[129] The political discourse during and after the 2016 presidential elections (with Donald Trump prevailing) may have painted the United States as becoming a less welcoming place for immigrants. While the situation improved somewhat after the COVID-19 pandemic, the resumption of hardline anti-immigration policies after the 2024 US elections could discourage legal migration. Waning interest in the United States as a preferred destination is evident in student visa applications, which dropped by 43% between 2015 and 2019. Foreign students often remain in the United States if they can find jobs there after graduating, and many have excelled at the highest levels. In 2020, the CEOs of Microsoft, Alphabet, IBM and Adobe were all Indian-born, and the CEO of Tesla and SpaceX was born in South Africa. If the next generation of star CEOs view the United States as unwelcoming, they will hone their skills and ingenuity in another country. The United States will not only lose out on a pool of highly talented workers, but the loss will also strengthen the ranks of competitor countries. The effect of forecasting a lower immigration rate in the US population is substantial—if the net migration in the US continues at the 2019 rate (which was about 600,000 immigrants), its population growth will peak by 2050, and by 2100 the country could have 60 million fewer people than projected in the UN forecasts.[130]

The recent immigration pattern in the United States is more concerning where lower-skilled labor is concerned. As we noted in earlier chapters, many of these workers function in essential areas such as agriculture, manufacturing and the supply chain; a shortage of these essential workers could push up inflation. This is already evident in the economic data—in 2022, the Federal Reserve noted that immigration policies had directly led to a shortfall in workers, with significant economic side effects.[131] Immigrant labor shortages of around 2 million people were cited as contributing factors for the spike in inflation.[132] The prevailing populist political sentiment against immigration could cause the United States to lose its current advantage in worker-aged population, which had been earned by more than a century of immigration-friendly policies. In time to come, the US may be no different to other developed countries, struggling with the impact of a declining workforce.

Norway

Another developed country that is projected to buck the trend is Norway. But while the UN forecasts that Norway's population will grow by 6% between 2020 and 2050, this is entirely attributable to very optimistic immigration assumptions. Here too, though, are signs that past trends could change and that the declining local population may not be sufficiently offset by immigrants. Norway's net migration (that is, the difference between those immigrating and those emigrating) peaked at 47,343 people in 2012, and since then there has been a continuous decline (there was a short-lived spike after the pandemic, which may have been due to a backlog of applications). In 2019, just

Figure 45: Norway—net migration

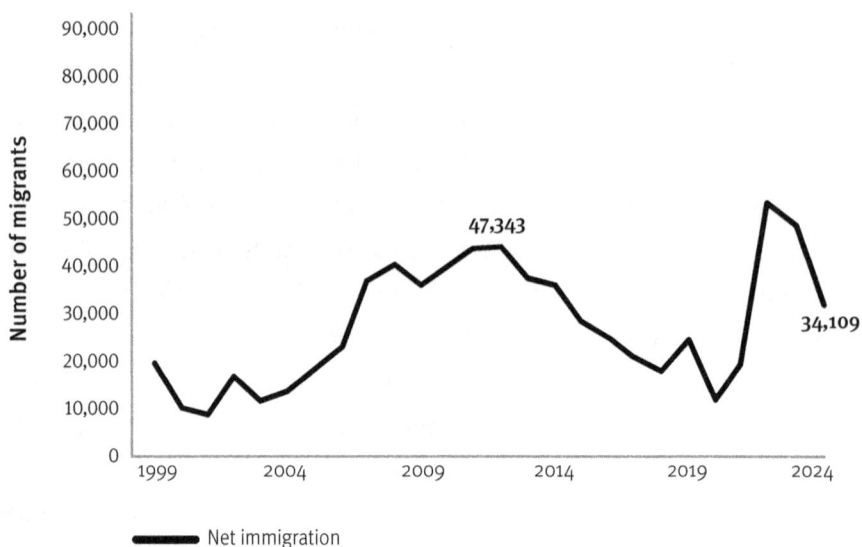

Figure 46: Norway—immigration vs. emigration

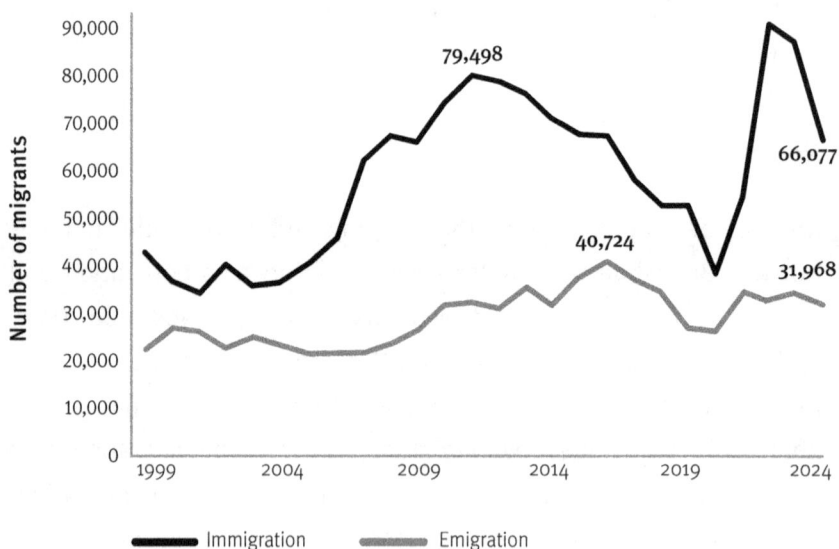

Source: Statistics Norway

before the COVID-19 pandemic, net migration was at 25,327—a 47% drop from its peak level.

Immigration to Norway has dropped from 79,498 in 2011 to 66,077 in 2024. More interestingly, *emigration* from Norway has risen consistently since 2006. This is surprising as Norway, along with other Scandinavian countries, is frequently ranked among the best countries in the world for quality of life. So why would an increasing number of people want to leave such a pleasant place? The answer to this question is the focus of a research study that commenced in 2022 and will run through to 2025.[133] However, the researchers have already found one factor that stands out. Most of those leaving Norway originally came to the country as immigrants. For some reason, many of those who sought a better life in Norway, have changed their minds. About three out of four people who leave Norway are European citizens, with half of them originally from Eastern European countries.[134] The Norwegian Central Statistics Bureau's research noted that changes in economic conditions in the home countries of immigrants have made it relatively less attractive to work in Norway. So, given the chance, immigrants seemed ready to move back to their home country when conditions improved. Norway's political climate has also become less immigrant-friendly in recent years, and a hard-line approach could deter future immigrants, despite the high quality of life on offer.[135] Norway, therefore, may end up following the same path of a declining population as other European countries (the latest UN forecasts in 2024 revised Norway's population in 2100 down by 25% from the previous 2022 estimates).

Canada

Canada's projected 35% increase in its population by the end of the century can also be questioned. In 2023, Canada saw a record-low fertility rate of 1.26, and the country has had a fertility rate below the replacement requirement of 2.1 since 1971.[136] Consequently, the country has become reliant on immigration to fill the gaps in its labor force. Immigration accounted for a massive 92% of its population growth in

2024 and it is forecast that by 2034, Canada's population growth will be entirely due to immigration.[137] Immigrants already accounted for 23% of the Canadian population in 2021, a ratio that will almost certainly rise in the years ahead.[138]

Canada has built a reputation for welcoming immigrants and valuing multiculturalism. The Canadian public has also held favorable views of immigration in the past, and although a 2021 survey found that a majority of respondents felt the number of immigrants should be reduced because of the impacts of COVID-19,[139] this may have been a sentiment specific to that crisis. With its very low fertility rate, the government had no other option but to push ahead with its aggressive immigration targets of up to 500,000 newcomers per year to support economic growth. However, rising concern over the growing numbers and their impact on housing and social services forced the government to reduce its immigration targets in 2024, setting a goal of 365,000 permanent residents by 2027. The measure was described as a short-term pause in population growth, as the government acknowledged the country's reliance on immigration for economic growth.[140]

Canada's success in attracting immigrants may have been relatively easy in a world where most countries are less welcoming of migrants. But in a future where competition intensifies for workers, Canada may find it more difficult to attract the more than 400,000 immigrants it needs to draw annually. Like Norway, it is conceivable that Canada may face a rise in emigration when the economic conditions improve in the home countries of imported workers. If immigrants have more choices, those from warmer climes (such as Africa), may become more selective in their choice of country, and may be averse to adapting to the harsh Canadian winters. Already, around 4 million Canadian citizens (which is about 11% of the population) live abroad.[141]

Australia

Lastly, let's look at Australia, where immigration numbers seem to be strong. The country welcomed about 500,000 migrant arrivals a year prior to the COVID-19 pandemic.[142] However, most of these migrants are only temporary visa holders. Temporary visas are issued to international students, working holiday-makers and temporary skilled migrants, and account for about 62% of all migrant arrivals. As the name reflects, these visa holders leave the country after a period and, on average, about 300,000 people emigrate from Australia each year (mostly temporary visa holders). In total, Australia had about a million temporary visa holders in 2021, or about 4% of the population.[143] With the number of permanent visas issued annually at only 160,000, most of these temporary visa holders will have little chance of settling permanently in the country.

There is growing opposition to immigration from conservatives in Australia, which could slow immigration in future.[144] In 2024, the Australian government introduced several reforms to their immigration policy, largely targeting temporary skilled migration and international students.[145] These changes may also make Australia less appealing to migrants. Following the implementation of the more stringent visa requirements, Australian student visas dropped by 40%. The level of student visas was well below the government caps, leaving universities with a shortage of international students.[146] As we saw from the example of Griffith in Australia in Chapter 9, there are already acute labor shortages in some areas of the country, and adding more obstacles for immigrants will only worsen the economic and social consequences in the decades ahead.

In summary, the apparently anomalous countries that seem to be bucking the depopulation trend are actually not immune to the demographic crisis. Even though these countries are forecast to grow their populations through immigration, they may find it increasingly difficult to attract workers in the numbers they will need to keep the ranks of their labor forces full. They too will have to brace themselves for an Age of Decay.

* * *

CHAPTER 22

THE PLANET GETS A BREATHER

━━━

The air is so much fresher these days, Eva thinks to herself. And the extreme weather patterns from her youth have settled down. There are fewer extremely hot days, and the massive bush fires that used to be an annual occurrence have now returned to their normal cycle of every five to seven years. Rainfall has also reverted to its normal patterns, and now floods and droughts are less frequent. In her youth, concern about global warming and climate change was the issue of the day. And for good reason, as the world seemed to be on a one-way path to an ever-warmer climate. Predictions of climate change reaching a tipping point, fortunately, did not come to pass.

One of the rare positive aspects of the declining population trend is that it could lower carbon emissions and ease the pressure on the environment. A smaller population means there are fewer consumers, which reduces the demand for products and services. Consider, for example, that the production of one t-shirt generates around 15 pounds of carbon emissions, while a pair of sneakers produces nearly 30 pounds. Jeans are even worse, spewing out around 44 pounds of carbon emissions for every pair produced.[147]

Having fewer consumers buying such products will obviously reduce production and lower the impact on the environment.

In addition, as we discussed in Chapter 16, older people consume considerably less than younger people. Therefore, because people over the age of 65 will form a significantly greater proportion of the total population in the future, the aggregate level of consumption will be lower. Older people also make fewer trips than younger folk, as they are less active and stay home more often. These factors mean that the aging of the population over the next few decades will contribute to lower carbon emissions. Research conducted in South Korea on the impact of aging and low fertility rates concluded that a 1% increase in the proportion of the elderly results in a 0.4% decrease in CO_2 emissions.[148] Consequently, if a country's proportion of aged persons in the population increases from, say, 20% to 30%, then its carbon emissions should drop by around 4%. The study also found that a 1% increase in the proportion of young people results in an increase in carbon emissions of around 0.25%. The surge in carbon emissions in the post-Second World War baby-boom era may be partly attributable to the higher proportion of young people in the population (along with rapidly rising population numbers, of course). Now that the population trends are reversing, we should see a commensurate decline in our carbon footprint.

Carbon emissions vary significantly across countries. Figure 47 shows that developed countries and oil-exporting nations have the highest per capita CO_2 emissions, while emerging markets have relatively low per capita emissions. The carbon footprint per capita in the United States is among the highest in the world at 14 tons of CO_2 per person per year, whereas the average for countries in Africa is only 1.2 tons of CO_2 per person per year.[149]

Many countries with high per capita CO_2 emissions will experience aging and declining populations in the decades ahead, whereas the carbon impact of Africa's strong population growth is softened by the low per capita emissions in the region (it is likely, though, that as

Africa develops, its per capita emissions could also rise). From Figure 48, we can assess the impact of the change in population composition on CO_2 emissions—that is, the impact of having a greater proportion of older people in the population.

Figure 47: CO_2 emissions per capita (tons p.a.)

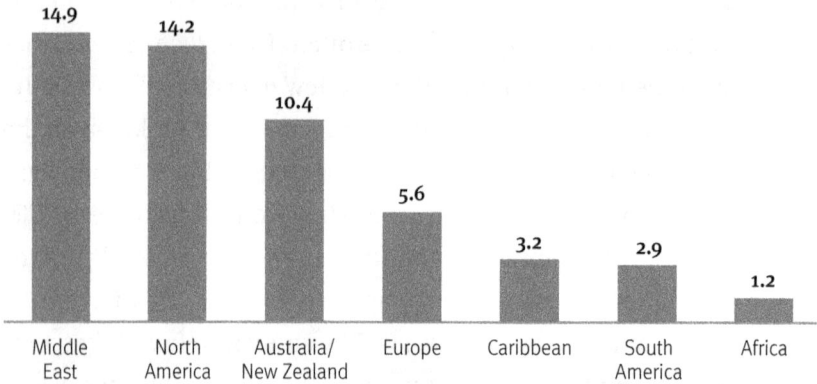

Source: World Bank

Figure 48: CO_2 emissions (millions of tons), based on the expected change in population numbers (black line) and increased aging (grey line)

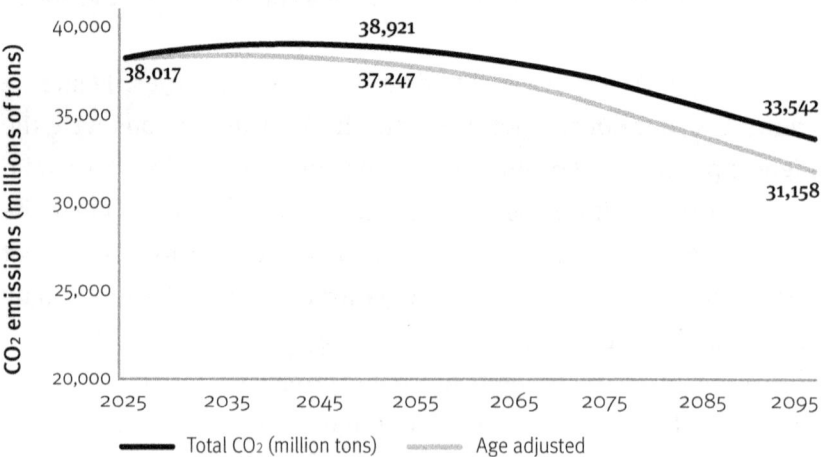

Source: Author's calculations based on World Bank data

In 2024, total global CO_2 emissions amounted to 38 billion tons. If the per capita emissions remain constant, then the increase in the global population from 7.8 billion in 2020 to 9.7 billion in 2050 should result in CO_2 emissions increasing to 39 billion tons (the black line in Figure 48). Thereafter, the carbon emissions may drop, even though the global population will go on to grow to 10.3 billion people by 2080. The reason for this trend is that the populations of some countries with higher per capita CO_2 emissions will drop (for example, Germany with per capita emissions of 7.0 tons), while developing countries with low emissions will see their populations increase (for example, Nigeria, with per capita emissions of 0.56 tons). It is likely that the per capita emissions of developing countries will increase as their consumption patterns increase, but with the increased emphasis on environmental sustainability, their per capita emissions could still remain lower than those of developed nations. Note that this analysis does not consider any improvements in lowering the per capita carbon footprint, and merely serves to illustrate how the change in demographics can impact CO_2 emissions.

If we add the impact of the aging population (the grey line in Figure 48), total global emissions could drop to 31 billion tons by the end of the century. The reduction is mainly due to the carbon footprint of aged persons being less than that of younger people. The analysis above assumes that the carbon footprint per capita will remain unchanged at current levels over the coming decades. However, with the increased attention to environmental sustainability and efforts to reduce emissions, the footprint per capita is likely to also decline. If the footprint per capita was reduced by 10%, global CO_2 emissions could drop to 28 billion tons by 2100. This is a remarkable 20% reduction from the expected peak in emissions of 35 billion tons by 2050.

Figure 49: CO$_2$ emissions (millions of tons), forecast based on the change in population

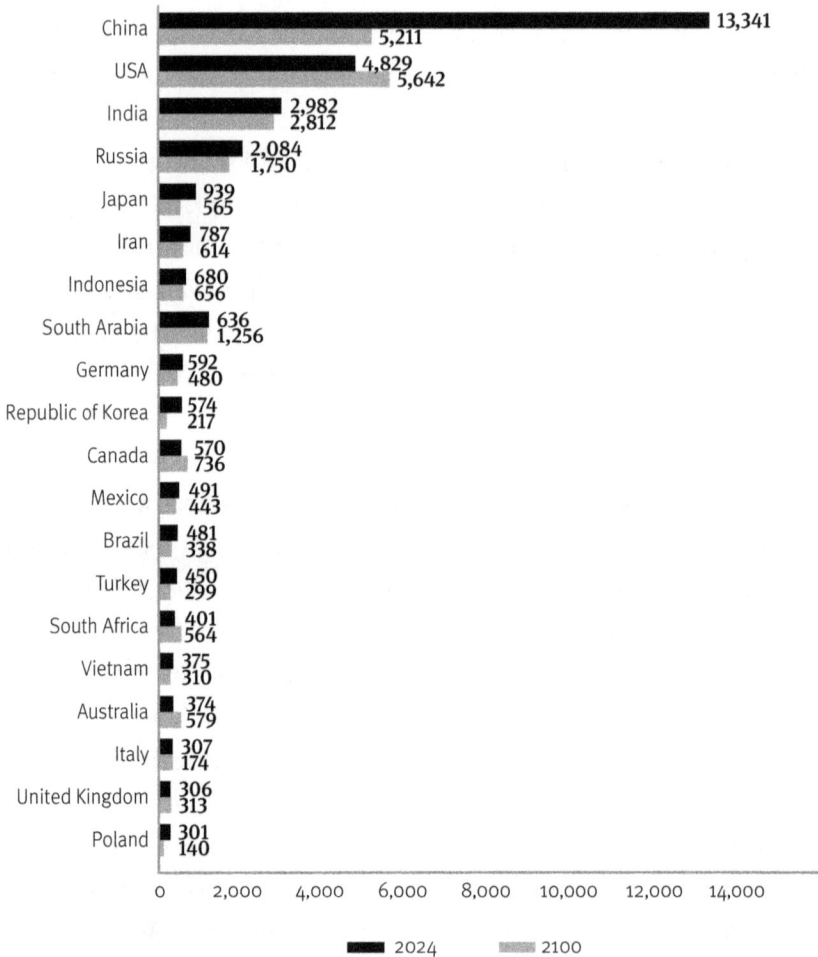

Country	2024	2100
China	13,341	5,211
USA	4,829	5,642
India	2,982	2,812
Russia	2,084	1,750
Japan	939	565
Iran	787	614
Indonesia	680	656
South Arabia	636	1,256
Germany	592	480
Republic of Korea	574	217
Canada	570	736
Mexico	491	443
Brazil	481	338
Turkey	450	299
South Africa	401	564
Vietnam	375	310
Australia	374	579
Italy	307	174
United Kingdom	306	313
Poland	301	140

Source: Author's calculations based on World Bank data

Changing demographics will also impact the country profile of the largest polluters in the world. China could drop to the second biggest polluter by the end of the century, and their total CO$_2$ emissions are likely to fall by 55% by virtue of its aging and declining population.

Similarly, by the end of the century, Japan's total carbon footprint could drop by 38%. The United States could become the largest CO_2 emitter due to its forecast 22% growth in population by the end of century, followed by India in third place. Again, these estimates are based on demographic changes only, and do not take into account any measures implemented by countries and individuals to lower per capita emissions, neither do they account for a potential rise in per capita emissions in developing countries such as India.

Combined with current efforts to reduce carbon emissions that should result in lower emissions, the impact of a smaller, aging population will be amplified and could significantly relieve the pressure on the environment.

The current focus on the environment and sustainability is commendable. However, as we can see above, this problem will be lessened by the changing demographics over the next few decades. The real challenge is how we navigate the environmental transition as the planet rejuvenates itself with fewer people to support. There is, however, one glaring omission in the current environmental campaigns that focus on the sustainability of natural resources— and that is the sustainability of human resources. This is arguably the most important resource we need to protect; yet, we take it for granted because it is currently abundant. But the tide has turned. Our numbers are already dwindling in some countries, and in a few years, the decline will accelerate around the world. Some of the consequences of a depletion of human resources have been shown and discussed at length in this book. We should make every effort to ensure the sustainability of this resource too.

* * *

CHAPTER 23

IS THIS AS GOOD AS IT GETS?

———

Eva recalls how her parents would tell her stories about when they were children. They seemed to have lived in a golden age, when everything worked well and life was good. They spoke of the advent of the internet and how it profoundly impacted and improved their lives. The advances in technology that followed lifted living standards for everyone. Countries were at peace with one another, and there was no global strife. Everything and anything seemed possible—how is it that things went downhill so quickly during her lifetime?

For those who live in developed countries, the modern world is one of convenience. We have access to good healthcare, infrastructure, education and economic opportunities. Everything needed to support society generally works well—minor irritations aside. Infrastructure is supplied and maintained by governments to whom we pay taxes, and the world's political order is mostly stable. Efficient trade makes goods cheaper. Supply chains work and we can procure everything we need to live comfortable lives. But with the demographic changes looming on the horizon, and the first cracks already beginning to show, it seems reasonable to ask if we have peaked as a civilization.

We assume that technological advancement will continue indefinitely. After all, look at what we have achieved so far. We may expect that at some point in future we will have flying cars, an army of robots to serve us, and we will be able to travel to distant planets. But such future progress presupposes that there will be an ever-growing supply of new talent and technological innovators.

The future may well be decidedly different. As the working-age population shrinks and a greater proportion of jobs are taken up by essential services workers, the creative and innovative occupations (which underpin the industries providing technology, research and development) could be elbowed out. As proportionately more workers are needed to keep society functioning, the pool of innovators and inventors is set to shrink. Fewer workers will be available to drive innovation and make sci-fi dreams a reality.

As populations grow older, society's priorities will tilt toward issues more relevant to the older population. Aged persons may not be as enthused by driving cutting-edge technological advancement, or adventures such as space travel. They would probably prefer developments that are more meaningful to their stage of life, such as spending on healthcare and services for the aged.

The rapid technological advances that we enjoyed after the Second World War were fueled by a global population that increased threefold between 1950 and 2020. More people meant that there was a larger pool of innovators and inventors who could advance and propel society forward. The new innovators pushed society forward across a wide array of sectors, like the branches spreading out from a growing tree. But with a smaller population, and an even smaller working-age cohort, there will be fewer innovators and the pace of innovation may slow in future. And, to continue the tree metaphor, when some branches are not fed the resources they need to grow, those branches will wither away. This could happen in the next few decades. The few countries whose worker-to-aged ratio drops below 2 will be the first to experience this new dynamic, but many other countries are sure to follow soon thereafter.

Politicians win elections by speaking to the issues that are important to the majority of the voters. In future, a large block of voters will be aged people. Politicians that campaign on the issues that address the concerns relevant to the aged electorate are more likely to get voted in. Besides the greater number of aged persons in the population, older people are also more active participants in elections. Over the past nine US presidential elections, voters aged 60 and above have had a turnout rate of 70%, while those aged 18 to 29 only achieved a turnout of 42%. Put differently, to politicians the older voter is around 1.7 times more important than the younger voter, as that segment of society is more likely to turn up at the polls. Consequently, the needs and concerns of older voters are far more likely to gain attention from politicians. And conversely, the issues important to younger people may be hamstrung by their declining share of the population and their lower propensity to participate in elections.

Figure 50: Voter turnout rate by age in US presidential elections (1988–2020)

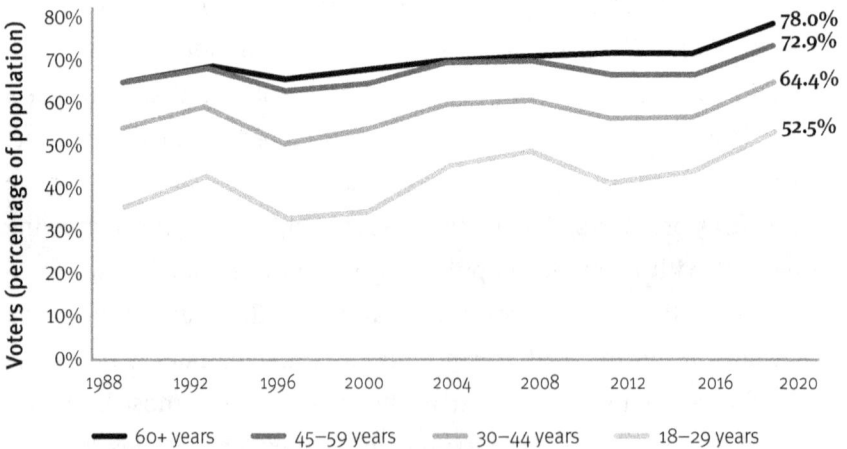

Source: University of Florida Election Lab

Would sending spaceships to Mars, or any other audacious goals, resonate with an electorate that is more worried about their well-being in their twilight years? Probably not. Even perennially safe budgetary allocations such as defense spending could come under immense political pressure. Why would countries need to maintain a vast and expensive defense capability if their main adversaries are also dealing with aging and declining populations? Besides, the size of standing armies will reduce considerably, in line with the lower working-aged population. This is already starting to happen, albeit for different reasons. The US Army fell 25% short of its recruitment goal of around 60,000 in 2022 and 2023, and the overall size of the force is projected to decline in the near term.[150] It seems that Gen Z do not find enlisting in the military appealing, apparently for "fear of death" and leaving friends and family.[151]

Innovation could slow in developed countries as the focus shifts to healthcare, welfare and other issues more relevant to the older population. We could enter a period of perpetual decline, retreating from the high-water mark of our civilization. At some point in the future, we may look back to the three decades between 1990 and 2020 as the peak of our civilization. Before 1990, the world was compartmentalized along different ideologies and a decades-long Cold War, with the constant threat of nuclear annihilation clouding sentiment. Many countries had to deal with internal strife—The Troubles in the United Kingdom as well as civil wars in several countries in Latin America, Africa and Asia. But around 1990, a confluence of events ushered the world into a period that, in hindsight, now seems like a Golden Age of Prosperity: the fall of the Berlin Wall and the subsequent thawing of the Cold War, China opening up to the rest of the world and embracing elements of the free market economy, and the rise of the internet and social media that democratized news and information. The opening of economies encouraged cross-border trade and the globalization that followed. Production shifted to low-cost countries, making consumer goods more affordable and propelling large swathes of the global population into the middle class. Life was generally good but, unfortunately, it was not to last. Three decades later, in 2020, the COVID-19 pandemic was the bell that rang out the end of this golden age.

There is some evidence that we may have peaked in terms of scientific and technological progress. Several studies have examined the relationship between population and technological advancement, and one such study differentiates between macro-inventions and micro-inventions.[152] Macro-inventions are revolutionary inventions and discoveries that are radically different from former iterations, and can trigger further technological inventions—examples include the steam engine and power supply systems. Micro-inventions are extensions and improvements emanating from macro-inventions. A macro-invention may lead to several micro-inventions that extend the reach of that technology within society. The macro-invention of bringing power supply into homes led to a multitude of micro-inventions including the television, air conditioning and microwave ovens.

While both types of inventions are required for society to progress, without macro-inventions society cannot leap forward. Worryingly, the study concluded that macro scientific advancement may have peaked around the 1920s and plateaued during the 20th century. Figure 51 shows how macro scientific and technological advances and the world's population superimposed on one another, with a clear flatlining in macro-inventions in the 20th century. This plateau may be due to the low-hanging fruits of science and technology having been already picked.[153] This suggests that future macro-inventions could be much more difficult to achieve.

This finding is surprising considering the rapid rise in education levels, as well as the increase in research and development spending over the past century. However, much of the research and development funding may have focused on micro-inventions (as opposed to macro-inventions) that are easier to commercialize and profit from. This explains the progress we enjoyed as consumers over the past century—from flat-screen televisions to mobile phones. But without significant macro-inventions, the number of micro-inventions will eventually reduce and the marginal returns on investment in research and development will diminish. Budgets for research and development could be cut, and coupled with a smaller pool of talented innovators, the likelihood of a new wave of macro-inventions in future diminishes. We should note that there is some uncertainty regarding the nature of the causal relationship—do technological advances lead to greater

Figure 51: Macro scientific and technology accumulation and population from 8000 B.C. to 2000 A.D.

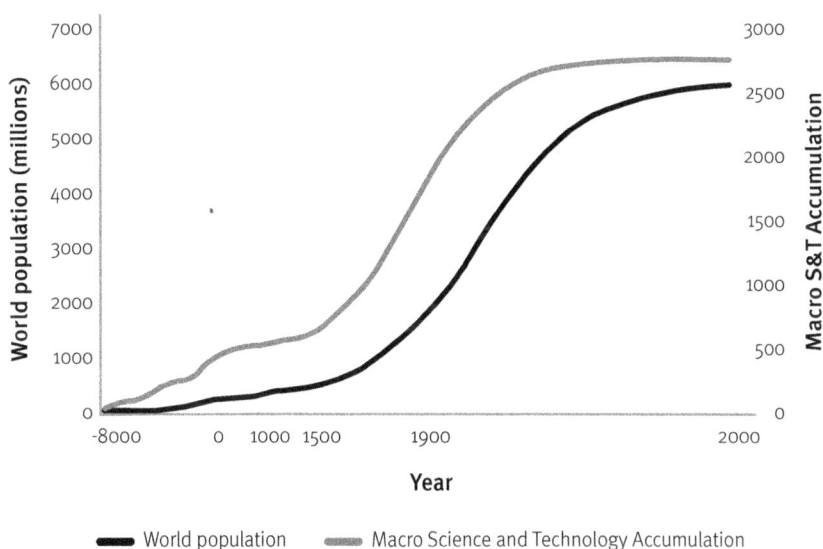

Source: *Jielin Dong, Wei Li, Yuhua Cao, Jianwen Fang*

population growth, or vice versa? However, intuitively at least, the larger the population, the higher the probability that some genius inventor will come up with an innovation that advances technology. Also, a larger population means that there will be more than enough human resources to provide essential goods and services to society, freeing up more people to participate in the tertiary and quaternary sectors, which often spawn technological advancement.

Throughout history, the advancement of human civilization has gone hand-in-hand with innovation and technological progress. But this aspect of human history, too, will not escape the coming demographic crisis.

* * *

.

CHAPTER 24

WHERE WILL IT END?

━━━

Eva is sometimes overcome with feelings of despair. Everything seems so bleak with no signs of better days in the future. Her daily struggles make her doubt her choices in life—the most important being the decision to have only one child. "Would life be easier if I had more children?" she wonders. Certainly, it would have been easier for two or three children to share the burden of taking care of her in old age. Alas, it is too late now...

Can we avoid this bleak future, where we will be in a continuous cycle of decline? Is there a way out of this mess? In the end, there is only one solution: The slide in fertility rates must be arrested and maintained at a level that will ensure a sustainable society. While this seems simple enough, how and if this can even be achieved once a population is in a seemingly permanent trend of decline is unclear.

Many countries have attempted to introduce pro-natalist policies, which are encouraging and supporting of increasing the birth rate. The measures are typically incentives that could include paying birth bonuses, providing childcare benefits, offering tax credits, and extended paid maternity and paternity leave. Such schemes are not new—in the 1970s and 1980s, former Communist Bloc countries

Bulgaria, Czechoslovakia, Hungary, Romania, and the Soviet Union implemented policies to encourage families to have more than one child.[154] These policies seemed to have had some positive results in the short term, but following the collapse of the Communist Bloc in 1990, the fertility rates in these countries dropped precipitously. The decline was possibly due to economic uncertainties at the time. Nonetheless, thirty years later, the fertility rates of those countries have still not recovered to the levels of the 1970s and 1980s.

In other countries, such programs have proved mostly fruitless. For example, Singapore implemented a package of pro-natalist incentives in 2001, which included paid maternity leave, childcare subsidies, tax relief and rebates, one-time cash gifts, and even grants for companies that implemented flexible work arrangements.[155] However, despite these measures, the fertility rate in Singapore still fell from 1.60 in 2000 to 0.97 in 2024.

Encouraging higher birth rates through financial incentives can be expensive and may not be sustainable in the long term. Also, it is not clear to what extent grant recipients may only bring forward planned births to benefit from such incentives, and still only have a single child by the end of their childbearing years.

Immigration will be essential to stave off the immediate impact of population decline and labor shortages, but this will become increasingly difficult when more countries start to compete for scarce labor. In any case, studies have shown that immigrants soon adopt smaller family sizes, similar to other citizens of the host countries, once they have settled.[156] Immigration, therefore, at best will only delay the inevitable decline in population.

The issue of declining populations could become one of national security for some countries. Can a country maintain its status as a global power if its population, economy and the size of its armed forces is shrinking? History is littered with once-powerful empires that faded to a shadow of their former selves—the Mongol, Ottoman, Spanish and British empires, to name but a few. To what lengths would the current global powers go to avoid that path and maintain their stature?

It is conceivable that government actions, which we now consider unthinkable and draconian, could be implemented to prop up birth rates. For instance, banning abortions and restricting the sale of contraceptives might be viewed as viable options by some governments in a desperate attempt to deal with this challenge. This is what happened in 1966 when the Romanian dictator, Nicolae Ceausescu, banned access to abortion and contraception to boost that country's population. This resulted in the average number of children born to Romanian women jumping from 1.9 to 3.7.[157] One might also imagine a future dystopian world where some women are coerced to produce children, as was envisaged in Margaret Atwood's novel *The Handmaid's Tale*. Such nightmarish scenarios must obviously be avoided at all costs, so viable solutions should be found.

Could we learn from history and replicate past periods of strong population growth? One of the most striking historical examples of strong population growth was the baby boom experienced by the United States between 1946 and 1964. During this period, around 4.2 million babies were born per year in the US. By 1964, the 76.4 million babies born during the boom accounted for 40% of the United States population of 192 million. The total fertility rate in the United States increased from 2.0 children before the Second World War to a peak of 3.6 children per woman in 1960.

Could we replicate the circumstances and initiate another baby boom to stem the projected population decline? Research by Doepke, Hazan and Maoz[158] argues that the US baby boom was mainly due to the exclusion of younger women from the labor force, mostly by older women who had gained work experience during the War. Before the War, young women normally worked until they got married and then started a family. During the War years, with many men shipped off to the battlefield, more women were needed to fill the void in the workplace, and older women returned to work. After the War ended, though, many of these older women stayed on in the workplace, which meant that the cohort of younger women reaching working age had fewer job opportunities. According to this research, these young women then got married earlier and started families earlier, which resulted in larger families.

Considering these unique circumstances, it is very unlikely such conditions can be replicated to incubate another baby boom in the 21st century. Improved education levels and urbanization are resulting in more employment opportunities for young women. In fact, females are thriving and out-performing males in tertiary attainment—in the US, women made up around 60% of college students, and men only 40% in 2021.[159] The situation is similar in most developed countries, to varying degrees, but nonetheless consistent in that women out-number men in tertiary enrolment. Furthermore, with growing labor shortages, the demand for their labor will increase and present females with even more opportunities.

Hamstrung by these constraints, governments do not have many options. One increasingly popular strategy is to improve maternity benefits and implement pro-natalist policies. Some European countries offer the most generous parental leave benefits in the world. In Norway, for instance, parents can opt for 49 weeks with full pay or 59 weeks with 80% pay. In addition, a lump sum grant of approximately $9,000 per child is paid. But despite these generous incentives, Norway's fertility rate has still dropped from 1.85 in 2012 to 1.40 in 2023.

So why are potential parents not incentivized by these generous concessions? This may be because the analytical approach of governments—trying to quantify and price the opportunity costs of having children—does not adequately deal with the social issues influencing the size of families. Singapore's experience, where fertility rates continue to fall despite considerable government efforts over the past two decades, can offer insights into why the decline is so difficult to stem.

A paper published by the International Monetary Fund pointed out four factors that are not being addressed by current pro-natalist incentives.[160] First, the policies do not address the rising age of childbearing. More and more women are choosing to have children later in life, which shortens the window for childbearing and also increases the risk of not achieving pregnancy (due to unexpected income shocks, partner breakups, health or fertility issues). And with the increase in female tertiary educational attainment noted above, more women will block off at least three years for college and perhaps another five to ten years to establish a career. This takes ten years out of a reproduction period of around 25 years. Therefore, policies need to encourage childbearing at peak childbearing ages (generally for females, in their twenties)—but as this would conflict with a woman's educational and early career aspirations, it is easier said than done.

Second, there is a misplaced belief in the effectiveness of repro-ductive technologies, which would supposedly allow childbearing later in life. Japan, for example, has the highest percentage of babies born through in vitro fertilization; yet, it still has one of the world's lowest fertility rates. It turns out the success rate of in vitro fertilization is very low for older women—at age 38, the success rate is about 25%, and this drops to only 12% by the age of 41.[161]

A third factor is that financial support and help with formal child-care cannot be a substitute for the parents' desire to spend quality time with their children. If parents believe they won't have the time available to dedicate to their offspring due to career commitments, they may opt to have fewer or no children.

Lastly, countries with very low fertility also tend to score very well in human capital rankings (that is, the citizens are high-achieving individuals). Parents in these countries invest considerably in their children to ensure they achieve success. The low fertility rate may therefore be linked to an economic and social system that rewards achievement and penalizes lack of ambition. Unless these social issues are addressed, parents will continue to focus their resources on fewer children to give them a greater chance to succeed. Any "baby bonus" or additional maternity benefits will be unable to convince parents otherwise.

To reverse the declining trend in fertility will be incredibly difficult, if not outright impossible. The "low-fertility trap" hypothesis[162] describes self-reinforcing mechanisms that would result in a continued decrease in births, as the normalization of small family sizes means that fertility rates become harder to raise through family policy or other means. The muted response to China's lifting of its three-decade one-child policy shows how family size ideals can be influenced by changing norms—parents in China now voluntarily choose to have just one child, even though state restrictions on the matter have been lifted.

As if this troubling issue was not enough, there are several other social trends that hamper any improvement in the situation in the near term. In Japan, for example, staying single has been growing in popularity. A 2022 survey found that one out of four single people in their thirties do not want to get married due to the financial implications, the loss of freedom, and housework-related issues.[163] In the West, the growing trend of gender fluidity could also weigh on fertility rates, as will the growing number of people openly identifying as LGBTQ+. A 2019 report noted that although LGBTQ+ people have similar rates of family-planning, they are more reliant on adoption, foster care, or assisted reproductive technology, all of which can be expensive.[164] However, the pool of babies available for adoption or foster care is likely to shrink with the overall decline in fertility rates.

How all this will play out in the very long run is anyone's guess. One scenario is that if global fertility rates converged to a level of 1.5 over the next few decades, then after peaking at 10.4 billion people around 2080, the world population may shrink to 4.0 billion by 2200. It will continue to fall and by 2300, the global population would be just over one billion. This would essentially return global population to pre-Industrial Revolution levels.

Figure 52: Global population, 1050 to 2500

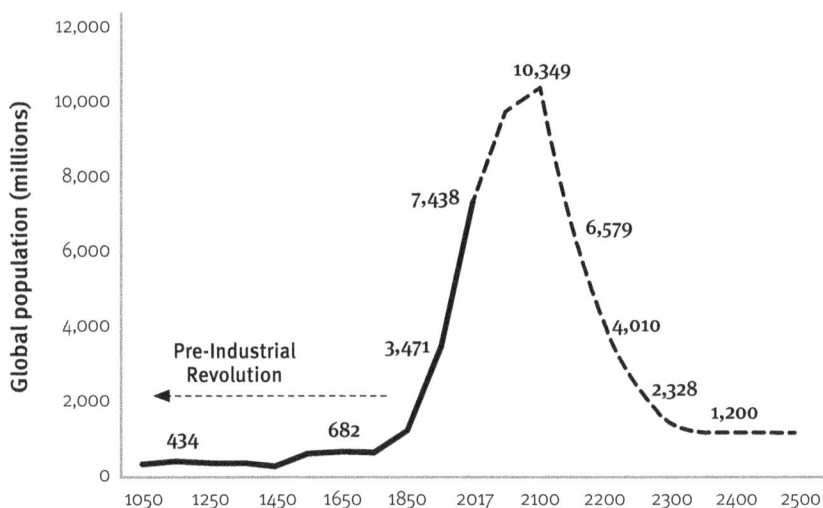

Source: Global population scenarios to 2300; Stuart Basten, Wolfgang Lutz, Sergei Scherbov

I don't believe that the global population will drop all the way down to one billion people. Somewhere on that downward slope, the norms for family sizes will once again change. As the population declines and the worker-to-aged ratio drops, living conditions will become more and more difficult, especially for the elderly, as was described in this book. Young people will see the older generation struggling and will realize that they cannot rely on their savings and pensions alone to provide them with funds for retirement. They will revert to the same rationale their forebears had in pre-Industrial times—that is, that they need more children to take care of them in their old age. They cannot take a risk by having only one child. It will make more sense to spread the burden over two or more children. And as in the pre-Industrial era, more pairs of hands will again be considered an asset for families. At this point, fertility rates will naturally start to rise again, and the decline in population will finally be arrested.

It is tempting to think that the world population will then return to an upward trajectory, followed by another 400-year cycle comprising a sharp rise and fall in population, as is the case for the period 1750 to 2150. But I think it will be different the next time around. The 200-year adjustment period that the world is about to experience will change our views on life. Our philosophy of life and economics could move from aspiration and growth, which fueled unbridled consumerism, to a more sedate way of life. It will be an Age of Contentment, and the global population could settle at a long-term stable and sustainable level, with considerable benefits for the environment and the planet. We will live in balance and harmony with what the earth can provide.

Getting to this point involves getting through the next two centuries, which will be incredibly challenging for the next few generations—as this book has tried to demonstrate. We have been fortunate to have enjoyed the exciting upward trajectory of the journey so far, but the path downward to the reversion of the mean will be stressful and very difficult for the next ten generations. For it is they who must navigate the Age of Decay.

★ ★ ★

APPENDICES

APPENDIX 1: Fertility rate (births per woman)

Country	1960	1980	2000	2020
Afghanistan	7.3	7.6	7.5	4.8
Albania	6.5	3.6	2.2	1.4
Algeria	7.5	7.0	2.6	2.9
Angola	6.7	7.5	6.6	5.4
Antigua and Barbuda	4.6	2.3	2.2	1.6
Argentina	3.1	3.3	2.6	1.9
Armenia	4.8	2.5	1.6	1.6
Aruba	4.8	2.4	1.9	1.3
Australia	3.5	1.9	1.8	1.6
Austria	2.7	1.7	1.4	1.4
Azerbaijan	5.9	3.5	2.0	1.7
Bahamas, The	4.8	2.9	2.1	1.4
Bahrain	7.2	4.8	2.8	1.8
Bangladesh	6.8	6.3	3.2	2.0
Barbados	4.3	2.0	1.8	1.6
Belarus	2.7	2.0	1.3	1.4
Belgium	2.5	1.7	1.7	1.6
Belize	6.5	5.8	3.6	2.0
Benin	6.3	7.0	5.9	5.0
Bermuda			1.7	1.3
Bhutan	6.7	6.5	3.4	1.4
Bolivia	6.4	5.5	4.0	2.7
Bosnia and Herzegovina	3.9	2.0	1.3	1.4
Botswana	6.6	6.3	3.3	2.8
Brazil	6.1	4.0	2.3	1.6
British Virgin Islands	5.2	2.9	1.9	1.0
Brunei Darussalam	6.8	4.1	2.3	1.8
Bulgaria	2.3	2.1	1.3	1.6
Burkina Faso	6.2	7.2	6.5	4.9
Burundi	7.0	7.4	6.9	5.2
Cabo Verde	6.9	6.4	3.5	1.9
Cambodia	6.3	5.8	3.8	2.4
Cameroon	5.6	6.7	5.5	4.5
Canada	3.8	1.7	1.5	1.4
Central African Republic	5.8	6.1	5.9	6.0

Country	1960	1980	2000	2020
Chad	6.3	6.9	7.2	6.3
Chile	4.7	2.7	2.0	1.5
China	4.5	2.7	1.6	1.3
Colombia	6.7	3.9	2.6	1.7
Comoros	6.8	7.1	5.3	4.1
Congo, Dem. Rep.	6.1	6.5	6.7	6.2
Congo, Rep.	6.1	6.1	4.8	4.2
Costa Rica	6.7	3.6	2.4	1.6
Cote d'Ivoire	7.7	7.6	5.8	4.5
Croatia	2.2	1.9	1.4	1.5
Cuba	4.1	1.6	1.6	1.5
Cyprus	3.5	2.3	1.6	1.3
Czechia	2.1	2.1	1.2	1.7
Denmark	2.6	1.6	1.8	1.7
Djibouti	6.8	6.6	4.6	2.8
Dominican Republic	7.6	4.3	2.9	2.3
Ecuador	6.7	4.7	3.1	2.1
Egypt	6.8	5.6	3.4	3.0
El Salvador	6.6	5.1	3.1	1.8
Equatorial Guinea	5.7	5.8	5.8	4.3
Eritrea	6.5	6.6	5.4	3.9
Estonia	2.0	2.0	1.4	1.6
Eswatini	6.8	6.5	4.0	2.9
Ethiopia	6.9	7.3	6.6	4.2
Faroe Islands		2.5	2.6	2.3
Fiji	6.5	4.0	3.0	2.5
Finland	2.7	1.6	1.7	1.4
France	2.9	1.9	1.9	1.8
French Polynesia	5.9	3.9	2.6	1.7
Gabon	4.4	5.7	4.5	3.5
Gambia, The	6.2	6.4	5.8	4.8
Georgia	2.9	2.3	1.6	2.0
Germany	2.4	1.4	1.4	1.5
Ghana	6.8	6.5	4.9	3.6
Greece	2.2	2.2	1.3	1.3
Greenland		2.4	2.3	2.0
Grenada	6.7	3.6	2.6	2.0

Country	1960	1980	2000	2020
Guatemala	7.0	6.2	4.6	2.5
Guinea	6.1	6.5	5.9	4.5
Guinea-Bissau	5.9	6.5	5.7	4.1
Guyana	6.4	3.8	3.0	2.4
Haiti	6.2	5.7	4.4	2.9
Honduras	7.5	6.4	4.2	2.4
Hong Kong	5.1	2.0	1.0	0.9
Hungary	2.0	1.9	1.3	1.6
Iceland	4.3	2.5	2.1	1.7
India	5.9	4.8	3.4	2.1
Indonesia	5.5	4.5	2.5	2.2
Iran	7.3	6.6	2.0	1.7
Iraq	5.3	6.6	4.9	3.6
Ireland	3.8	3.2	1.9	1.6
Israel	3.9	3.2	3.0	2.9
Italy	2.4	1.6	1.3	1.2
Jamaica	5.6	3.7	2.2	1.4
Japan	2.0	1.8	1.4	1.3
Jordan	7.7	7.3	3.9	2.9
Kazakhstan	4.5	2.9	1.8	3.1
Kenya	7.6	7.6	5.1	3.4
Kiribati	6.6	5.0	4.1	3.3
Kosovo	6.4	4.9	2.7	1.5
Kuwait	7.2	5.4	2.7	2.1
Kyrgyzstan	5.4	4.2	2.4	3.0
Laos	6.3	6.3	4.4	2.5
Latvia	1.9	1.9	1.3	1.6
Lebanon	5.8	4.0	2.5	2.1
Lesotho	5.8	5.7	3.7	3.0
Liberia	6.4	6.9	5.9	4.2
Libya	7.4	7.2	2.9	2.5
Lithuania	2.6	2.0	1.4	1.5
Luxembourg	2.3	1.5	1.8	1.4
Madagascar	7.3	6.7	5.4	3.9
Malawi	7.0	7.6	6.0	4.0
Malaysia	6.4	4.1	2.9	1.8
Maldives	6.8	7.2	2.7	1.7

Country	1960	1980	2000	2020
Mali	7.0	7.3	6.9	6.0
Malta	3.6	2.0	1.7	1.1
Mauritania	6.4	6.6	5.5	4.5
Mauritius	6.2	2.8	2.0	1.4
Mexico	6.8	4.8	2.7	1.9
Micronesia	6.7	6.2	4.3	2.8
Moldova	3.3	2.4	1.5	1.8
Mongolia	6.8	6.3	2.3	2.9
Montenegro	3.5	2.2	2.1	1.8
Morocco	7.0	5.7	2.8	2.4
Mozambique	6.3	6.5	5.8	4.7
Myanmar	6.0	4.8	2.8	2.2
Namibia	6.2	6.2	4.0	3.3
Nepal	6.0	5.6	3.9	2.1
Netherlands	3.1	1.6	1.7	1.6
New Caledonia	6.3	3.4	2.6	2.0
New Zealand	4.2	2.0	2.0	1.6
Nicaragua	7.2	6.0	3.1	2.3
Niger	7.5	7.8	7.7	6.9
Nigeria	6.4	6.8	6.1	5.3
North Korea	3.6	2.8	2.0	1.8
North Macedonia	4.0	2.4	1.9	1.3
Norway	2.9	1.7	1.9	1.5
Oman	7.2	8.1	3.9	2.7
Pakistan	6.8	6.7	5.3	3.6
Panama	5.8	3.8	2.7	2.3
Papua New Guinea	6.0	5.7	4.5	3.3
Paraguay	6.5	5.1	3.6	2.5
Peru	6.9	5.0	2.8	2.2
Philippines	7.1	5.1	3.7	2.8
Poland	3.0	2.3	1.4	1.4
Portugal	3.2	2.3	1.6	1.4
Puerto Rico	4.8	2.8	2.0	0.9
Qatar	6.6	5.5	3.2	1.8
Romania	2.3	2.4	1.3	1.6
Russia	2.5	1.9	1.2	1.5
Rwanda	8.2	8.2	5.9	3.9

Country	1960	1980	2000	2020
Samoa	7.6	5.9	4.5	4.0
Sao Tome and Principe	6.2	6.4	5.2	3.9
Saudi Arabia	7.6	7.2	4.1	2.5
Senegal	7.0	7.3	5.5	4.5
Serbia			1.5	1.5
Seychelles			2.1	2.3
Sierra Leone	6.2	6.6	6.4	4.1
Singapore	5.8	1.8	1.6	1.1
Slovak Republic	3.0	2.3	1.3	1.6
Slovenia	2.2	2.1	1.3	1.6
Solomon Islands	7.0	6.7	4.8	4.0
Somalia	7.3	7.2	7.6	6.4
South Africa	6.2	4.8	2.4	2.4
South Korea	5.9	2.8	1.5	0.8
South Sudan	6.7	6.9	7.5	4.5
Spain	2.9	2.2	1.2	1.2
Sri Lanka	5.5	3.6	2.2	2.0
Sudan	6.6	6.7	5.4	4.5
Suriname	6.6	3.9	2.9	2.4
Sweden	2.2	1.7	1.5	1.7
Switzerland	2.4	1.6	1.5	1.5
Syria	7.5	7.2	4.0	2.8
Tajikistan	6.5	6.1	4.0	3.2
Tanzania	6.7	6.9	5.7	4.8
Thailand	6.2	3.4	1.6	1.3
Togo	6.7	6.9	5.3	4.3
Tonga	6.9	5.6	4.1	3.3
Trinidad and Tobago	5.3	3.2	1.8	1.6
Tunisia	6.9	5.1	2.0	2.1
Turkey	6.4	4.4	2.5	1.9
Turkmenistan	6.6	5.3	2.9	2.7
Uganda	6.9	7.1	6.8	4.7
Ukraine	2.2	2.0	1.1	1.2
United Arab Emirates	6.7	5.9	2.7	1.5
United Kingdom	2.7	1.9	1.6	1.6
United States	3.7	1.8	2.1	1.6
Uruguay	2.8	2.6	2.2	1.5

Country	1960	1980	2000	2020
Uzbekistan	6.6	5.0	2.6	2.9
Vanuatu	6.9	5.7	4.5	3.8
Venezuela	6.4	4.2	2.8	2.2
Vietnam	6.3	4.9	2.1	2.0
West Bank and Gaza			5.4	3.6
Yemen	7.9	8.7	6.3	3.9
Zambia	7.1	7.2	5.9	4.4
Zimbabwe	7.2	6.6	4.0	3.5

Source: United Nations

APPENDIX 2: Determining the minimum level of essential workers

How can we determine the minimum number of essential workers needed for a functional society? And how will this minimum level impact the structure of the labor market when a population declines? We can answer these questions as follows:

- We can look at the occupational data of a developed country, where detailed data is available (I have selected the United Kingdom and its occupation data for 2021).
- By analysing the occupational data, we can identify the essential jobs and determine how many such workers were in that country to make it fully functional (on the reasonable assumption that the United Kingdom was a fully functional society in 2021).
- Finally, we can assess how the ratio of essential workers to all workers changes as the population ages.

Let's apply this reasoning to the United Kingdom, which in 2021 had 33.4 million people employed out of a total population of 68.2 million. The 33.4 million workers were employed across 319 different occupational groups, and of these, about 99 occupations can be considered essential (that is, they are needed to support the functioning of society). These essential workers encompass a wide range of occupations and include healthcare workers, transport workers, retail workers, maintenance workers and care workers, to name but a few. The occupations that can be considered essential employed around 12.5 million people in the United Kingdom in 2021. This amounts to about 185 essential workers per 1,000 people (or 18.5% of the population). This is a subjective estimation based on my assessment of which jobs constitute essential services, and different opinions on this classification may result in estimates varying from anything between 150 essential workers per 1,000 people, to 250 essential workers per 1,000 population (that is, 15% to 25% of the population). The accuracy of the number does not affect the trends that will unfold in future, but it could affect the timing at which the events occur by a decade or so. To nail down this figure more accurately, further academic research is needed in this area, as it will provide important insights for us to better understand the risks facing society as populations decline.

Now that we have an estimate of the minimum proportion of essential workers needed to support a society, we can make an assessment of how this might impact the labor market composition as the population ages and declines in number. In developed countries presently, children make up about 17% of the total population, meaning 83% of the population are adults. In Table 9, the adult population is split based on a target worker-to-aged ratio of 2, and then the workers are further split between essential workers (based on the requirement that there should be 185 essential workers per 1,000 population) and other, non-essential workers. In the example below, given a population of 1,000, there are about 170 children and 830 adults.

Table 9: Calculation of essential workers as a percentage of all workers

	Per 1,000 population	% of population
Population size	1,000	
Children (17%)	(170)	17%
Total adult population	830	83%
Target aged ratio:		2.0
– at a ratio of 2, the number of aged persons is	277	33%
– at a ratio of 2, the number of workers is	553	67%
– essential workers (18.5% of the population)	185	33%
– other workers (remainder)	368	67%

With a ratio of worker-to-aged people of 2, this implies that the adult population of 830 has 553 workers and 277 aged people. As the minimum number of essential workers needed is 185 per 1,000 people, the residual non-essential workers amount to a total of 368 (that is, 553 workers minus 185 essential workers). In this case of a worker-to-aged person ratio of 2, the essential workers amount to 33% of the total workers, while the non-essential workers account for 67% of the total workforce.

Using this methodology, we can now assess various scenarios, as detailed in the chart below. When the ratio of worker-to-aged people is 4, then essential workers comprise about 28% of all workers. But as the worker-to-aged ratio drops to 3 and 2, the proportion of essential workers increases slowly to 30% and 33%. However, once the ratio of worker-to-aged people drops below 2, the increase in essential workers relative to all workers accelerates. At the parity ratio of 1 (meaning the number of workers equals the number of aged people in the population), the essential workers needed to sustain a society would account for 45% of the labor force. And when the aged outnumber the workers in a population, most available workers would have to work in essential services, which will limit future progress and development, because the pool of talented (but non-essential) innovators will have shrunk dramatically.

Figure 53: Essential workers as a percentage of all workers

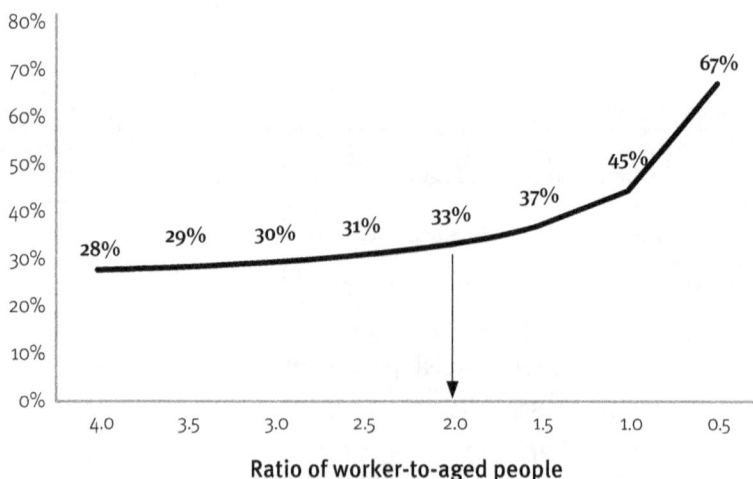

Source: Author's calculations

Regardless of the age of the population, essential services such as maintenance and supply chain services must still be provided. And as the number of workers decreases, a greater proportion of workers must work in essential jobs to sustain society. This leaves fewer surplus workers to focus on innovation, research, and development of ideas. In effect, the essential jobs could crowd out other, higher-skilled jobs, leading to a stagnation in innovation in both science and culture.

* * *

APPENDIX 3: Countries that will drop below a worker-to-aged ratio of 2 by 2100

	Countries	2020	2030	2040	2050	2060	2070	2080	2090	2100
1	China	5.5	3.8	2.4	1.9	1.5	1.3	1.0	0.9	1.0
2	South Korea	4.6	2.7	1.7	1.3	1.1	1.0	0.9	0.9	1.0
3	Albania	4.6	3.1	2.5	2.2	1.5	1.2	1.1	1.1	1.1
4	Chile	5.5	4.0	3.0	2.3	1.7	1.4	1.2	1.1	1.1
5	Taiwan	4.5	2.7	1.9	1.4	1.2	1.1	1.1	1.1	1.2
6	Ukraine	4.0	3.2	2.7	2.1	1.6	1.5	1.2	1.1	1.2
7	Singapore	6.6	4.2	3.1	2.4	1.6	1.1	1.1	1.2	1.2
8	Lithuania	3.3	2.8	2.3	2.1	1.7	1.5	1.4	1.3	1.3
9	Poland	3.7	2.9	2.5	1.8	1.4	1.5	1.4	1.3	1.3
10	Cuba	4.4	3.1	2.1	1.9	1.7	1.5	1.4	1.3	1.3
11	Turkey	7.6	5.4	4.0	2.8	2.2	1.8	1.5	1.4	1.4
12	Japan	2.0	1.9	1.5	1.4	1.4	1.4	1.4	1.3	1.4
13	North Macedonia	4.1	3.1	2.6	2.1	1.8	1.7	1.5	1.4	1.4
14	Bosnia and Herzegovina	3.3	2.4	2.0	1.6	1.5	1.4	1.4	1.4	1.4
15	Italy	2.7	2.2	1.6	1.4	1.4	1.5	1.4	1.4	1.4
16	Uruguay	4.2	3.8	3.2	2.7	2.2	1.8	1.5	1.4	1.4
17	Spain	3.4	2.6	1.9	1.5	1.4	1.5	1.4	1.4	1.4
18	Montenegro	3.9	3.1	2.7	2.2	2.0	1.9	1.7	1.5	1.4
19	Jamaica	10.1	6.9	5.0	3.5	2.3	1.7	1.5	1.5	1.4
20	Croatia	2.9	2.4	2.1	1.8	1.8	1.7	1.5	1.5	1.5
21	Latvia	3.1	2.6	2.3	2.0	1.7	1.8	1.6	1.4	1.5
22	Greece	2.8	2.4	1.9	1.5	1.6	1.7	1.5	1.5	1.5
23	Iceland	4.6	3.7	3.1	2.6	2.0	1.7	1.6	1.5	1.5
24	Colombia	8.3	5.5	4.1	3.2	2.3	1.8	1.6	1.5	1.5
25	Belarus	4.3	3.2	2.7	2.2	1.8	1.8	1.5	1.4	1.5
26	Thailand	5.5	3.5	2.4	2.0	1.8	1.6	1.5	1.5	1.5
27	Iran	9.5	6.8	4.6	2.8	1.9	1.9	1.7	1.5	1.5
28	Estonia	3.1	2.7	2.3	1.9	1.6	1.8	1.6	1.5	1.5
29	Serbia	3.0	2.5	2.3	2.0	1.8	1.7	1.7	1.6	1.5
30	Slovakia	4.0	3.0	2.5	1.9	1.6	1.7	1.7	1.6	1.5
31	Argentina	5.5	5.0	4.2	3.2	2.6	2.1	1.7	1.6	1.6
32	Finland	2.7	2.4	2.2	2.1	1.9	1.8	1.6	1.6	1.6
33	Tunisia	8.0	5.6	4.2	3.1	2.4	2.3	1.9	1.6	1.6

	Countries	2020	2030	2040	2050	2060	2070	2080	2090	2100
34	Brazil	7.3	5.0	3.8	2.8	2.3	1.9	1.8	1.7	1.6
35	Austria	3.5	2.6	2.1	1.8	1.7	1.7	1.7	1.6	1.6
36	Ireland	4.5	3.7	2.9	2.2	2.1	2.0	1.7	1.6	1.6
37	Norway	3.7	3.1	2.5	2.2	2.0	1.8	1.7	1.7	1.6
38	Ecuador	8.7	6.9	5.1	3.8	2.9	2.3	1.9	1.7	1.6
39	Sri Lanka	6.2	4.6	3.8	3.1	2.7	2.3	2.0	1.8	1.7
40	Luxembourg	4.8	3.7	2.8	2.3	2.0	1.9	1.8	1.7	1.7
41	Romania	3.4	3.2	2.4	2.1	1.9	2.0	1.9	1.7	1.7
42	El Salvador	8.6	7.4	5.8	4.6	3.3	2.3	1.9	1.8	1.7
43	Armenia	5.5	3.7	3.2	2.6	1.9	1.9	1.9	1.7	1.7
44	Slovenia	3.2	2.5	2.1	1.7	1.7	1.9	1.8	1.7	1.7
45	Belgium	3.3	2.7	2.3	2.1	2.0	2.0	1.8	1.7	1.7
46	Netherlands	3.4	2.7	2.3	2.3	2.1	1.9	1.8	1.7	1.7
47	Bulgaria	2.9	2.7	2.3	1.9	1.8	1.9	1.9	1.8	1.7
48	Bangladesh	11.1	8.8	6.9	4.9	3.6	2.7	2.2	1.9	1.7
49	Switzerland	3.5	2.7	2.2	1.9	1.7	1.8	1.8	1.7	1.7
50	Sweden	3.1	2.8	2.5	2.3	2.0	2.0	1.8	1.7	1.7
51	Peru	7.5	6.3	4.8	3.7	2.8	2.3	2.0	1.8	1.7
52	Mexico	8.9	6.8	5.0	3.9	3.0	2.5	2.1	1.8	1.7
53	Panama	7.9	5.8	4.3	3.4	2.8	2.4	2.1	1.9	1.8
54	Denmark	3.2	2.7	2.4	2.3	2.2	2.0	1.9	1.8	1.8
55	Viet Nam	9.0	5.8	4.2	3.2	2.5	2.4	2.0	1.9	1.8
56	United Kingdom	3.4	3.0	2.6	2.4	2.3	2.2	1.9	1.8	1.8
57	Germany	2.9	2.3	2.0	1.9	1.8	1.9	1.9	1.8	1.8
58	Portugal	2.8	2.2	1.8	1.6	1.7	1.8	1.8	1.8	1.8
59	France	3.0	2.5	2.1	2.1	2.1	2.1	1.9	1.8	1.8
60	New Zealand	4.2	3.2	2.7	2.5	2.2	2.1	1.9	1.8	1.8
61	Czechia	3.1	2.8	2.4	1.9	1.8	2.1	1.9	1.8	1.8
62	Dem. People's Republic of Korea	6.3	4.6	3.1	3.0	2.6	2.3	2.2	2.0	1.8
63	Morocco	9.5	6.7	5.2	3.9	3.1	2.7	2.3	2.0	1.8
64	Canada	3.7	2.8	2.5	2.4	2.2	2.0	1.9	1.9	1.9
65	Malaysia	10.3	7.5	5.7	4.0	2.9	2.3	2.0	1.9	1.9
66	India	10.5	8.1	6.2	4.6	3.4	2.6	2.2	2.0	1.9
67	Georgia	4.3	3.6	3.4	3.0	2.6	2.5	2.2	1.9	1.9
68	Hungary	3.3	3.0	2.5	2.1	2.0	2.2	2.1	2.0	1.9
69	Lebanon	6.9	5.4	4.4	3.9	3.7	3.0	2.3	2.1	1.9

APPENDIX 4: Estimated shortage of workers per country (2040 to 2100)

Countries	2040 (millions)	2050 (millions)	2060 (millions)	2070 (millions)
China	83.2	16.7	(43.1)	(53.0)
India	179.5	163.1	118.8	60.7
Bangladesh	19.5	19.7	14.7	7.8
Brazil	19.1	10.9	4.2	(0.8)
Japan	(4.0)	(6.9)	(6.0)	(5.0)
Turkey	8.7	4.7	1.7	(1.1)
Iran	11.6	4.8	(1.0)	(0.9)
Mexico	13.4	11.5	8.1	4.0
United States of America	15.6	12.1	9.5	6.4
South Korea	0.3	(2.4)	(3.6)	(4.0)
Colombia	5.5	4.2	1.6	(0.9)
Italy	(1.4)	(2.9)	(2.5)	(2.0)
Vietnam	9.6	5.7	2.6	2.6
Thailand	3.3	0.7	(0.5)	(1.5)
Germany	(0.0)	(1.0)	(1.7)	(0.8)
France	0.2	(0.6)	0.0	0.0
Spain	0.1	(2.4)	(2.3)	(1.6)
United Kingdom	2.9	1.9	1.1	0.8
Argentina	4.8	3.3	2.0	0.6
Poland	1.9	(0.4)	(1.6)	(1.2)
Chile	1.7	0.8	(0.3)	(1.0)
Peru	3.3	2.8	1.7	0.6
Ukraine	2.9	0.9	(0.6)	(0.8)
Taiwan	0.6	(0.9)	(1.5)	(1.4)
Canada	1.8	1.4	0.7	0.0
Sri Lanka	1.6	1.1	0.9	0.4
Morocco	3.7	3.0	2.2	1.6
Algeria	5.1	3.0	2.1	3.7
Ecuador	2.1	1.7	1.1	0.4

2080 (millions)	2090 (millions)	2100 (millions)	% of population	% of working age population
(98.0)	(99.9)	(72.7)	11.5%	24.8%
19.5	(2.9)	(22.3)	1.5%	2.6%
1.9	(3.4)	(7.5)	3.6%	6.6%
(3.6)	(5.5)	(6.1)	3.7%	6.9%
(5.9)	(5.8)	(5.1)	6.7%	13.1%
(3.5)	(4.5)	(4.3)	6.6%	12.9%
(2.7)	(4.3)	(4.1)	5.1%	9.6%
(0.1)	(2.4)	(3.8)	2.9%	5.3%
(0.1)	(1.3)	(2.6)	0.6%	1.1%
(4.3)	(3.4)	(2.5)	11.6%	25.2%
(1.9)	(2.3)	(2.5)	5.4%	10.3%
(2.6)	(2.5)	(2.2)	6.3%	12.3%
(0.3)	(1.7)	(2.2)	2.4%	4.4%
(2.5)	(2.4)	(2.1)	4.7%	8.8%
(0.8)	(1.7)	(1.9)	2.7%	4.8%
(1.5)	(1.9)	(1.9)	2.8%	5.0%
(2.1)	(2.1)	(1.9)	5.7%	10.9%
(1.0)	(1.8)	(1.9)	2.5%	4.5%
(1.3)	(1.7)	(1.6)	4.1%	7.6%
(1.5)	(1.7)	(1.4)	7.2%	14.1%
(1.5)	(1.5)	(1.3)	9.7%	20.2%
(0.3)	(0.8)	(1.2)	3.2%	5.9%
(1.7)	(1.6)	(1.2)	8.1%	16.2%
(1.3)	(1.2)	(0.9)	9.5%	19.6%
(0.5)	(0.7)	(0.8)	1.5%	2.7%
(0.2)	(0.6)	(0.8)	3.7%	6.8%
0.5	(0.3)	(0.7)	1.9%	3.3%
2.0	(0.5)	(0.7)	1.1%	1.9%
(0.3)	(0.6)	(0.7)	3.6%	6.7%

241

Countries	2040 (millions)	2050 (millions)	2060 (millions)	2070 (millions)
Netherlands	0.4	0.4	0.2	(0.3)
Malaysia	5.3	4.1	2.6	1.1
Hong Kong	(0.1)	(0.6)	(0.9)	(0.9)
Tunisia	1.2	0.6	0.3	0.3
Cuba	0.1	0.0	(0.2)	(0.3)
Australia	1.2	0.9	0.4	0.4
Romania	0.5	(0.0)	(0.2)	(0.0)
Singapore	0.6	0.4	(0.1)	(0.6)
Belgium	0.3	0.1	(0.0)	(0.0)
Sweden	0.4	0.2	(0.0)	0.0
Costa Rica	0.5	0.2	(0.0)	(0.2)
Greece	0.0	(0.4)	(0.3)	(0.2)
Switzerland	0.2	(0.1)	(0.3)	(0.2)
North Korea	1.5	1.4	0.8	0.5
Austria	0.1	(0.1)	(0.2)	(0.2)
Portugal	(0.2)	(0.4)	(0.3)	(0.2)
Norway	0.2	0.1	(0.0)	(0.1)
Ireland	0.3	0.0	0.0	0.0
Belarus	0.6	0.1	(0.1)	0.0
Serbia	0.2	0.0	(0.1)	(0.1)
Panama	0.4	0.3	0.2	0.1
Finland	0.2	0.0	(0.0)	(0.0)
Puerto Rico	0.0	(0.1)	(0.1)	(0.2)
El Salvador	0.7	0.7	0.5	0.1
Czechia	0.4	(0.1)	(0.2)	0.1
Denmark	0.1	0.1	0.1	(0.0)
Slovakia	0.2	(0.0)	(0.2)	(0.1)
New Zealand	0.2	0.2	0.1	0.0
Uruguay	0.2	0.2	0.1	(0.0)
Nepal	3.7	4.0	3.6	2.4
Albania	0.1	0.1	(0.1)	(0.2)
Croatia	0.1	(0.0)	(0.1)	(0.1)

Source: Author's calculations based on UN population forecasts

2080 (millions)	2090 (millions)	2100 (millions)	% of population	% of working age population
(0.4)	(0.5)	(0.6)	3.4%	6.2%
(0.2)	(0.5)	(0.6)	1.3%	2.3%
(0.8)	(0.7)	(0.5)	24.0%	71.0%
(0.2)	(0.5)	(0.4)	3.9%	7.2%
(0.4)	(0.4)	(0.4)	7.3%	14.5%
0.0	(0.2)	(0.4)	0.9%	1.6%
(0.2)	(0.3)	(0.4)	3.4%	6.2%
(0.5)	(0.4)	(0.4)	8.6%	17.5%
(0.3)	(0.4)	(0.3)	3.1%	5.7%
(0.3)	(0.4)	(0.3)	3.0%	5.5%
(0.4)	(0.4)	(0.3)	8.6%	17.6%
(0.3)	(0.4)	(0.3)	5.0%	9.5%
(0.2)	(0.3)	(0.3)	3.3%	6.0%
0.3	(0.2)	(0.3)	1.5%	2.6%
(0.2)	(0.3)	(0.3)	3.8%	7.1%
(0.2)	(0.2)	(0.2)	2.7%	5.0%
(0.2)	(0.2)	(0.2)	3.7%	6.9%
(0.2)	(0.2)	(0.2)	3.8%	7.0%
(0.2)	(0.3)	(0.2)	4.2%	7.7%
(0.1)	(0.2)	(0.2)	4.8%	9.1%
(0.0)	(0.1)	(0.2)	3.0%	5.5%
(0.2)	(0.2)	(0.2)	3.8%	7.0%
(0.3)	(0.2)	(0.2)	17.5%	43.3%
(0.1)	(0.1)	(0.2)	3.3%	6.0%
(0.1)	(0.2)	(0.2)	2.0%	3.6%
(0.1)	(0.1)	(0.2)	2.8%	5.1%
(0.1)	(0.2)	(0.2)	4.7%	8.8%
(0.1)	(0.1)	(0.1)	2.4%	4.4%
(0.1)	(0.2)	(0.1)	6.2%	12.1%
1.2	0.4	(0.1)	0.4%	0.7%
(0.2)	(0.2)	(0.1)	10.5%	22.3%
(0.1)	(0.1)	(0.1)	5.3%	10.0%

APPENDIX 5: Debt per capita (US$)

Based on 2023 government debt levels

Country	Debt per capita (US$)–on total population			Debt per capita (US$)–on working-age population		
	2023	2050	2100	2023	2050	2100
Albania	4,776	6,093	11,519	7,283	9,929	24,370
Algeria	2,635	2,033	1,878	4,166	3,235	3,311
Angola	2,167	1,073	531	4,123	1,787	812
Argentina	21,673	20,949	26,455	33,875	32,437	49,247
Armenia	4,113	4,885	7,202	6,158	7,954	13,196
Australia	32,312	26,461	19,937	50,350	43,777	35,046
Austria	43,114	44,995	53,052	65,606	79,036	98,277
Azerbaijan	1,382	1,254	1,405	1,959	1,918	2,419
Bahamas	28,655	27,286	30,072	41,300	42,368	52,552
Bahrain	35,207	26,017	18,012	45,833	34,972	26,477
Bangladesh	1,043	827	852	1,586	1,235	1,571
Barbados	25,297	27,765	37,679	39,120	45,733	69,365
Belarus	3,522	4,339	7,433	5,354	7,256	13,851
Belgium	56,052	55,448	59,508	88,408	95,142	108,757
Belize	4,539	3,962	4,575	7,304	5,746	8,299
Benin	765	430	266	1,353	693	405
Bhutan	4,320	3,755	4,799	5,838	5,409	8,667
Bolivia	3,204	2,412	2,188	4,936	3,583	3,532
Bosnia and Herzegovina	2,209	3,117	5,600	3,689	5,738	10,936
Botswana	1,484	1,155	1,034	2,510	1,679	1,668
Brazil	9,011	8,463	11,267	12,555	13,466	20,833
Brunei Darussalam	797	678	758	1,059	1,041	1,332
Bulgaria	3,496	4,147	6,345	5,181	7,306	11,601
Burkina Faso	539	338	253	997	520	385
Burundi	204	110	70	371	178	107
Côte d'Ivoire	1,468	1,891	1,205	6,396	3,064	1,842
Cabo Verde	5,039	5,136	6,973	8,302	7,565	13,279

Country	Debt per capita (US$)–on total population			Debt per capita (US$)–on working-age population		
	2023	2050	2100	2023	2050	2100
Cambodia	636	493	476	971	751	790
Cameroon	717	402	231	1,304	644	358
Canada	57,365	50,253	42,764	89,288	82,560	75,979
Central African Republic	286	138	78	583	230	117
Chad	343	158	88	621	268	133
Chile	6,627	6,510	9,850	9,764	10,525	20,476
China	10,467	11,722	23,325	15,030	19,822	50,339
Colombia	3,662	3,216	4,057	5,213	4,958	7,737
Comoros	449	341	233	901	536	365
Congo	2,369	1,321	726	4,185	2,150	1,130
Costa Rica	10,018	9,875	14,001	15,020	15,900	28,473
Croatia	13,560	16,113	24,335	21,216	28,495	46,320
Cyprus	27,053	16,517	19,536	26,608	27,013	36,839
Czechia	13,519	14,930	17,829	21,278	26,469	31,942
Democratic Republic of the Congo	96	44	22	179	74	34
Denmark	20,746	20,096	20,993	32,571	33,549	38,152
Djibouti	2,374	1,598	1,328	3,229	2,388	2,103
Dominica	8,645	10,124	13,026	13,910	15,223	22,509
Dominican Republic	6,816	5,624	6,261	9,848	8,588	10,864
Ecuador	3,598	3,079	3,441	5,461	4,684	6,349
Egypt	3,575	2,337	1,871	5,270	3,564	3,059
El Salvador	4,483	4,278	5,619	6,764	6,273	10,302
Equatorial Guinea	2,827	1,389	873	4,012	2,203	1,317
Estonia	6,188	7,199	10,240	9,796	12,609	19,301
Eswatini	1,583	1,223	1,373	2,406	1,799	2,134
Ethiopia	574	270	165	820	417	260
Fiji	4,959	4,546	5,171	7,425	6,704	8,282
Finland	41,429	43,073	50,100	66,932	73,456	92,733

Country	Debt per capita (US$)–on total population			Debt per capita (US$)–on working-age population		
	2023	2050	2100	2023	2050	2100
France	50,893	49,168	48,978	82,136	86,453	88,962
Gabon	6,549	3,542	2,095	9,818	5,609	3,265
Georgia	3,207	3,270	4,034	4,944	5,242	7,128
Germany	33,892	36,594	40,411	53,539	64,665	73,283
Ghana	1,995	1,299	972	3,228	2,019	1,521
Greece	38,502	45,650	64,101	62,407	85,788	121,406
Grenada	7,222	7,270	11,143	10,298	11,017	21,269
Guatemala	1,495	1,151	1,096	2,482	1,674	1,854
Guinea	617	396	290	1,164	614	442
Guinea Bissau	791	446	328	1,235	683	506
Guyana	5,806	4,901	5,186	8,690	7,360	8,634
Haiti	456	379	368	752	556	574
Honduras	1,482	1,046	912	2,253	1,547	1,539
Hungary	16,256	17,886	20,918	24,903	30,442	36,920
Iceland	51,795	46,413	55,425	77,864	74,339	105,340
India	2,069	1,760	1,964	3,022	2,606	3,486
Indonesia	1,972	1,706	1,851	2,860	2,597	3,122
Iran	1,321	1,122	1,428	1,822	1,796	2,708
Iraq	2,592	1,562	1,116	4,188	2,394	1,785
Ireland	45,177	39,607	44,732	69,531	68,035	82,790
Israel	32,344	24,104	15,981	56,851	39,673	27,220
Italy	52,613	59,670	87,525	81,777	114,144	170,071
Jamaica	4,932	5,519	12,701	6,536	8,099	24,062
Japan	85,314	101,138	138,353	145,411	197,257	270,642
Jordan	4,101	2,841	2,181	6,307	4,363	3,707
Kazakhstan	3,019	2,259	1,781	4,746	3,672	2,950
Kenya	1,548	955	766	2,418	1,444	1,182
Kuwait	1,038	808	536	1,355	1,067	746
Kyrgyzstan	912	656	539	1,444	1,009	879
Lao People's Democratic Republic	2,462	1,913	2,016	3,751	2,785	3,361

Country	Debt per capita (US$)–on total population			Debt per capita (US$)–on working-age population		
	2023	2050	2100	2023	2050	2100
Latvia	10,063	12,517	20,476	15,984	21,499	38,634
Lesotho	669	478	439	1,011	699	675
Liberia	451	275	193	785	425	292
Lithuania	9,631	12,293	22,973	14,909	20,479	45,310
Luxembourg	33,306	27,816	29,433	47,921	45,924	54,128
Madagascar	299	168	104	500	264	160
Malawi	469	285	180	901	442	283
Malaysia	8,461	6,316	6,353	11,334	9,423	11,248
Maldives	19,983	13,447	16,704	19,948	20,568	30,673
Mali	469	237	138	902	397	208
Malta	20,024	20,258	30,152	30,371	33,851	60,647
Mauritania	1,188	559	307	1,949	908	486
Mauritius	9,247	10,532	20,045	12,728	16,862	39,943
Mexico	7,243	6,377	7,292	10,911	9,726	13,282
Mongolia	2,722	2,119	1,728	4,447	3,304	2,876
Montenegro	7,195	8,540	13,970	11,197	14,591	26,857
Morocco	2,745	2,339	2,682	4,074	3,613	4,795
Mozambique	579	309	188	1,111	497	284
Myanmar	705	652	770	1,033	968	1,260
Namibia	3,136	1,837	1,405	4,730	2,803	2,210
Nepal	532	477	519	857	687	905
Netherlands	29,587	27,796	30,100	45,037	46,390	55,271
New Zealand	21,822	19,864	19,669	34,092	32,693	35,521
Nicaragua	1,078	822	836	1,613	1,228	1,470
Niger	316	163	94	649	265	143
Nigeria	781	483	364	1,372	748	540
North Macedonia	3,902	5,322	9,328	6,716	8,971	18,073
Norway	36,661	34,388	37,476	56,588	57,964	69,266
Oman	7,865	5,072	3,282	10,902	6,902	4,908
Pakistan	1,126	701	510	1,793	1,084	795
Palau	12,690	14,719	20,530	18,248	23,244	33,675

Country	Debt per capita (US$)–on total population			Debt per capita (US$)–on working-age population		
	2023	2050	2100	2023	2050	2100
Panama	9,773	7,729	7,370	14,864	12,257	13,444
Papua New Guinea	1,316	1,084	867	2,474	1,628	1,324
Paraguay	2,342	2,048	1,956	3,987	3,096	3,320
Peru	2,545	2,116	2,250	3,806	3,269	4,123
Philippines	2,189	1,839	2,164	3,253	2,657	3,624
Poland	11,179	12,522	21,257	16,222	22,089	41,958
Portugal	27,602	29,124	32,505	43,305	54,464	59,018
Qatar	31,017	22,166	12,693	37,212	27,978	17,749
Republic of Korea	18,316	20,937	43,260	25,836	39,891	93,704
Republic of Moldova	2,369	2,515	3,975	2,994	4,079	6,787
Republic of The Gambia	641	720	1,139	858	1,169	1,944
Romania	9,207	10,932	16,271	14,237	18,920	29,880
Russian Federation	2,683	2,884	3,106	4,097	4,766	5,254
Rwanda	644	383	265	1,067	594	420
Samoa	1,494	1,145	814	2,593	1,927	1,283
Sao Tome and Principe	1,400	890	608	2,432	1,410	974
Saudi Arabia	8,531	5,871	3,943	11,517	8,185	5,979
Senegal	1,376	823	532	2,393	1,282	852
Serbia	5,540	6,647	9,935	8,576	11,496	18,743
Seychelles	12,204	8,610	10,524	13,335	13,321	18,229
Sierra Leone	369	241	196	634	364	299
Singapore	137,382	133,684	195,297	186,963	208,472	397,065
Slovakia	14,080	15,485	22,304	20,975	27,248	41,966
Slovenia	22,078	23,587	28,639	34,616	43,131	52,212
South Africa	4,538	3,526	2,960	6,553	5,247	4,674
South Sudan	263	215	166	601	335	246
Spain	35,539	37,818	51,290	53,662	72,111	98,417

Country	Debt per capita (US$)–on total population			Debt per capita (US$)–on working-age population		
	2023	2050	2100	2023	2050	2100
Sudan	1,699	955	595	2,897	1,514	937
Suriname	5,405	4,691	4,856	8,240	7,202	8,379
Sweden	20,161	18,811	18,716	32,408	31,400	34,148
Switzerland	38,474	36,302	37,163	58,481	64,056	68,118
Tajikistan	366	235	182	590	364	291
Thailand	4,581	4,844	7,058	6,389	8,221	13,284
Timor-Leste	203	145	139	329	208	227
Togo	671	390	231	1,148	630	355
Tonga	2,247	2,136	1,906	3,719	3,522	3,117
Trinidad and Tobago	10,761	10,924	17,022	14,511	17,456	30,901
Tunisia	3,209	2,987	3,686	4,846	4,762	6,836
Turkey	3,711	3,508	4,900	5,382	5,574	9,565
Turkmenistan	557	376	365	769	568	593
Tuvalu	467	525	419	856	828	651
Uganda	569	303	214	986	468	345
Ukraine	4,423	4,590	9,663	5,796	7,557	19,420
United Arab Emirates	16,017	10,124	5,953	17,836	12,690	8,491
United Kingdom	49,631	44,779	45,501	77,702	74,305	82,256
United Republic of Tanzania	581	284	140	1,019	467	220
Uruguay	13,064	14,319	20,749	20,998	22,783	40,230
US	99,712	87,744	79,323	149,738	143,885	138,692
Uzbekistan	917	633	444	1,460	1,005	713
Venezuela	5,424	4,630	5,090	7,885	7,222	8,853
Vietnam	1,471	1,342	1,609	2,170	2,128	2,906
Yemen	439	211	136	675	330	211
Zambia	1,591	860	508	2,813	1,360	790
Zimbabwe	1,798	1,124	782	3,231	1,789	1,213

Source: Author's calculations, Countryeconomy.com

APPENDIX 6: Population forecast (millions)

Countries	2020	2030	2040
Afghanistan	39.1	50.0	63.3
Albania	2.9	2.7	2.5
Algeria	44.0	50.2	54.9
Angola	33.5	45.2	59.0
Argentina	45.2	46.6	47.8
Armenia	2.9	2.9	2.7
Australia	25.7	28.2	30.4
Austria	8.9	9.1	8.9
Azerbaijan	10.2	10.7	11.1
Bahrain	1.5	1.8	2.0
Bangladesh	166.3	186.1	202.6
Belarus	9.4	8.7	8.1
Belgium	11.5	11.8	11.9
Benin	13.1	16.6	20.4
Bolivia	11.8	13.4	14.9
Bosnia and Herzegovina	3.3	3.0	2.7
Botswana	2.4	2.8	3.1
Brazil	208.7	216.1	219.2
Bulgaria	6.9	6.5	5.9
Burkina Faso	21.5	26.7	32.2
Burundi	12.6	16.2	20.1
Cambodia	16.7	18.8	20.5
Cameroon	26.2	33.8	42.2
Canada	38.2	41.7	44.0
Central African Republic	5.0	6.5	8.5
Chad	17.2	24.2	31.3
Chile	19.4	20.2	20.5
China	1,426.1	1,398.2	1,342.8
China. Hong Kong SAR	7.5	7.3	6.8

2050	2060	2070	2080	2090	2100
76.9	90.4	103.4	114.7	123.3	130.2
2.2	2.0	1.8	1.6	1.4	1.2
59.6	62.6	63.9	64.8	65.1	64.5
74.3	90.6	107.1	123.0	137.6	150.0
48.3	47.6	46.1	44.0	41.3	38.3
2.5	2.3	2.1	2.0	1.8	1.7
32.5	34.6	36.6	38.7	40.9	43.1
8.7	8.4	8.1	7.8	7.6	7.4
11.2	11.1	10.9	10.6	10.3	10.0
2.1	2.3	2.5	2.7	2.9	3.1
214.7	223.1	226.1	224.1	218.0	208.6
7.5	6.8	6.0	5.4	4.9	4.4
11.9	11.7	11.5	11.4	11.2	11.1
24.4	28.3	31.9	35.1	37.7	39.6
16.1	17.0	17.6	17.9	17.9	17.8
2.5	2.2	1.9	1.7	1.5	1.4
3.4	3.7	3.8	3.9	3.9	3.8
217.5	211.0	200.9	188.6	175.8	163.4
5.4	4.9	4.5	4.1	3.8	3.5
37.3	41.7	45.3	47.9	49.3	49.9
24.1	27.7	31.2	34.2	36.4	37.9
21.9	22.9	23.3	23.4	23.2	22.7
51.1	60.0	68.5	76.3	83.2	88.9
45.6	47.1	48.9	50.4	52.0	53.6
10.6	12.8	14.8	16.5	17.8	18.8
38.9	46.6	53.8	60.3	65.7	69.5
20.3	19.5	18.3	16.8	15.1	13.4
1,260.3	1,135.1	998.8	870.3	744.9	633.4
6.1	5.2	4.3	3.4	2.7	2.1

Countries	2020	2030	2040
Colombia	50.6	55.7	58.6
Congo	5.8	7.3	9.1
Costa Rica	5.0	5.3	5.4
Côte d'Ivoire	28.9	36.7	45.7
Croatia	4.0	3.7	3.5
Cuba	11.2	10.7	10.1
Czechia	10.6	10.4	10.1
Democratic Republic of Congo	96.0	131.5	172.6
Denmark	5.8	6.1	6.1
Dominican Republic	11.0	11.9	12.6
Ecuador	17.5	19.1	20.4
Egypt	109.3	127.1	145.2
El Salvador	6.2	6.5	6.6
Eritrea	3.3	4.0	4.9
Ethiopia	118.9	152.9	188.5
Finland	5.5	5.6	5.5
France	65.9	67.1	67.9
Gabon	2.3	2.9	3.5
Gambia	2.5	3.1	3.7
Georgia	3.8	3.8	3.7
Germany	83.6	82.8	80.6
Ghana	31.9	38.2	44.6
Greece	10.7	9.7	9.3
Guatemala	17.4	20.1	22.6
Guinea	13.4	16.8	20.2
Haiti	11.2	12.6	13.7
Honduras	10.1	11.9	13.5
Hungary	9.7	9.4	9.1
India	1,402.6	1,525.1	1,622.6
Indonesia	274.8	295.9	311.8
Iran	87.7	95.5	99.5

2050	2060	2070	2080	2090	2100
59.4	58.8	57.1	54.3	50.7	47.1
11.0	13.0	14.9	16.8	18.5	20.0
5.4	5.2	4.9	4.6	4.2	3.8
55.7	65.9	76.2	86.2	95.6	104.0
3.2	3.0	2.7	2.5	2.3	2.1
9.4	8.5	7.7	6.9	6.2	5.6
9.8	9.5	9.0	8.6	8.4	8.2
218.2	266.7	314.4	358.9	398.5	430.7
6.1	6.1	6.0	6.0	5.9	5.9
13.0	13.2	13.1	12.7	12.3	11.7
21.3	21.7	21.6	21.1	20.2	19.1
161.6	174.8	185.9	194.3	199.5	201.9
6.7	6.6	6.3	6.0	5.5	5.1
5.7	6.5	7.2	7.8	8.2	8.4
225.0	260.7	293.8	323.2	347.7	367.3
5.4	5.2	5.1	4.9	4.8	4.6
68.2	67.9	67.7	68.0	68.4	68.5
4.1	4.7	5.3	5.9	6.4	6.9
4.3	4.8	5.2	5.5	5.6	5.7
3.7	3.6	3.4	3.3	3.1	3.0
78.3	75.6	73.6	72.1	71.2	70.9
50.6	55.8	60.1	63.6	66.1	67.5
8.8	8.2	7.6	7.0	6.7	6.3
24.7	26.2	27.0	27.1	26.7	25.9
23.4	26.3	28.7	30.4	31.5	32.0
14.7	15.4	15.7	15.7	15.5	15.2
14.8	15.9	16.6	17.0	17.1	17.0
8.7	8.4	8.0	7.8	7.6	7.5
1,679.6	1,701.0	1,689.2	1,645.5	1,580.3	1,505.3
320.7	322.5	320.0	314.5	306.1	295.5
101.9	101.0	96.7	90.8	85.2	80.0

Countries	2020	2030	2040
Iraq	42.1	51.9	62.2
Ireland	5.0	5.5	5.8
Israel	8.8	10.2	11.6
Italy	59.9	57.9	55.2
Jamaica	2.8	2.8	2.7
Japan	126.3	119.6	112.2
Jordan	10.9	12.4	14.5
Kazakhstan	19.5	22.0	24.2
Kenya	52.2	63.1	74.1
Kuwait	4.4	5.3	5.8
Kyrgyzstan	6.7	7.8	8.8
Lao PDR	7.3	8.4	9.2
Lebanon	5.7	6.1	6.6
Lesotho	2.2	2.5	2.8
Liberia	5.1	6.4	7.7
Libya	7.0	7.9	8.7
Lithuania	2.8	2.7	2.5
Madagascar	29.0	36.7	44.8
Malawi	19.5	25.2	31.3
Malaysia	33.9	38.0	41.5
Mali	21.7	29.0	37.4
Mauritania	4.6	6.1	7.7
Mexico	126.8	136.9	144.6
Mongolia	3.3	3.7	4.1
Morocco	36.6	40.0	42.2
Mozambique	30.8	40.8	52.1
Myanmar	53.0	56.4	58.2
Namibia	2.7	3.4	4.0
Nepal	29.0	30.5	32.9
Netherlands	17.6	18.8	19.1
New Zealand	5.1	5.4	5.6

2050	2060	2070	2080	2090	2100
71.9	80.5	88.0	93.8	98.0	100.6
6.0	5.9	5.8	5.6	5.5	5.3
13.1	14.6	16.0	17.4	18.7	19.7
51.9	47.6	43.4	40.2	37.7	35.4
2.5	2.2	1.9	1.6	1.3	1.1
105.1	98.1	90.6	84.7	80.6	76.8
16.4	17.8	19.1	20.1	20.9	21.3
26.5	28.5	30.1	31.5	32.8	33.7
83.6	91.6	97.8	101.7	103.8	104.2
6.4	6.9	7.5	8.2	8.9	9.6
9.6	10.3	10.9	11.4	11.6	11.7
9.8	10.1	10.2	10.0	9.7	9.3
7.0	7.2	7.4	7.5	7.4	7.2
3.0	3.2	3.3	3.3	3.3	3.3
8.9	10.0	11.0	11.9	12.4	12.7
9.3	9.6	9.8	9.9	9.9	9.8
2.3	2.0	1.8	1.6	1.4	1.2
53.2	61.4	68.9	75.5	81.0	85.3
37.4	43.2	48.4	52.9	56.5	59.1
44.3	45.9	46.4	46.1	45.2	44.0
46.2	54.8	62.9	70.0	75.5	79.4
9.4	11.2	12.9	14.5	15.9	17.1
148.9	149.9	148.1	143.8	137.6	130.2
4.5	4.8	5.0	5.3	5.4	5.5
43.4	43.7	43.1	41.8	40.0	37.9
63.5	74.6	84.6	93.0	99.7	104.3
58.6	57.9	56.4	54.4	52.1	49.7
4.5	5.0	5.4	5.6	5.8	5.9
34.6	35.6	35.8	35.1	33.6	31.8
19.0	18.7	18.5	18.3	17.9	17.5
5.8	5.8	5.9	5.9	5.8	5.8

Countries	2020	2030	2040
Nicaragua	6.6	7.4	8.2
Niger	23.7	32.5	42.3
Nigeria	214.0	262.4	312.7
North Korea	26.1	26.8	26.5
Norway	5.4	5.7	5.9
Oman	4.5	6.1	6.9
Pakistan	235.0	276.9	324.9
Panama	4.3	4.8	5.3
Papua New Guinea	9.8	11.7	13.4
Paraguay	6.6	7.4	8.1
Peru	32.8	36.2	38.8
Philippines	112.1	121.4	129.5
Poland	38.2	37.2	35.2
Portugal	10.4	10.3	10.1
Puerto Rico	3.3	3.1	2.9
Qatar	2.8	3.3	3.7
Republic of Korea	51.9	51.2	48.9
Republic of Moldova	3.1	2.8	2.6
Romania	19.4	18.4	17.2
Russia	146.4	141.9	138.3
Rwanda	13.1	16.2	19.4
Saudi Arabia	31.0	37.4	42.6
Senegal	16.8	21.2	25.8
Serbia	6.9	6.5	6.0
Sierra Leone	7.9	9.7	11.4
Singapore	5.6	6.0	6.2
Slovakia	5.5	5.4	5.2
Slovenia	2.1	2.1	2.0
Somalia	16.7	22.9	29.9
South Africa	60.6	68.2	74.0
South Sudan	10.7	13.5	16.1

2050	2060	2070	2080	2090	2100
8.8	9.1	9.2	9.2	8.9	8.6
52.5	62.7	72.2	80.2	86.5	90.8
359.2	399.8	433.5	457.9	471.9	476.7
25.8	24.7	23.4	22.1	20.8	19.5
5.9	5.9	5.8	5.7	5.5	5.4
7.8	8.8	9.6	10.4	11.3	12.1
371.9	414.4	451.3	479.7	499.2	511.0
5.6	5.9	6.0	6.0	6.0	5.9
14.9	16.2	17.2	17.9	18.4	18.6
8.6	9.0	9.2	9.3	9.2	9.0
40.6	41.5	41.6	41.0	39.7	38.2
134.4	135.0	133.0	128.6	121.8	114.2
32.8	30.1	27.1	24.0	21.5	19.3
9.8	9.4	9.1	8.9	8.8	8.8
2.5	2.1	1.8	1.5	1.2	1.0
4.2	4.7	5.2	5.9	6.6	7.3
45.1	39.9	34.5	29.7	25.4	21.8
2.4	2.1	1.9	1.8	1.6	1.5
16.0	14.8	13.5	12.5	11.6	10.8
136.1	132.9	129.7	127.8	127.1	126.4
22.7	25.6	28.1	30.1	31.8	32.8
47.7	52.7	57.5	62.0	66.5	71.0
30.4	34.8	38.9	42.3	45.0	47.0
5.5	5.1	4.7	4.3	4.0	3.7
12.9	14.2	15.2	15.8	16.0	15.9
6.1	5.9	5.6	5.2	4.7	4.2
4.9	4.6	4.3	3.9	3.7	3.4
2.0	1.9	1.8	1.7	1.7	1.6
37.2	44.9	52.0	58.4	63.5	67.4
79.2	83.4	86.9	89.7	92.2	94.3
18.3	20.3	22.0	23.2	23.7	23.8

Countries	2020	2030	2040
Spain	47.7	47.6	46.6
Sri Lanka	22.6	23.8	24.5
State of Palestine	5.1	6.1	7.3
Sudan	46.8	58.6	71.7
Sweden	10.4	10.8	11.1
Switzerland	8.6	9.1	9.3
Syria	21.0	29.4	34.5
Taiwan	23.7	22.6	21.3
Tajikistan	9.7	11.7	13.7
Tanzania	61.0	80.9	104.0
Thailand	71.6	71.2	69.5
Togo	8.7	10.8	13.1
Tunisia	12.0	12.6	13.0
Turkey	86.1	89.0	91.0
Turkmenistan	6.9	8.1	8.9
Uganda	44.5	58.3	72.0
Ukraine	44.7	38.4	35.3
United Arab Emirates	9.4	12.2	13.7
United Kingdom	67.4	71.3	73.8
United States of America	339.4	355.6	370.2
Uruguay	3.4	3.4	3.3
Uzbekistan	33.6	40.2	46.0
Venezuela	28.4	29.2	30.5
Viet Nam	98.1	104.3	108.4
Yemen	36.1	47.7	59.2
Zambia	19.1	25.0	31.6
Zimbabwe	15.5	18.6	22.3

2050	2060	2070	2080	2090	2100
44.9	42.2	39.0	36.5	34.8	33.1
24.8	24.7	24.2	23.4	22.4	21.2
8.5	9.4	10.3	10.9	11.3	11.5
85.2	98.6	110.8	121.3	130.2	136.9
11.3	11.4	11.4	11.4	11.4	11.4
9.3	9.3	9.2	9.1	9.1	9.1
37.8	40.8	43.0	43.9	44.1	43.7
19.4	17.3	15.0	13.0	11.3	10.0
15.6	17.1	18.4	19.4	19.9	20.2
129.6	156.9	184.9	212.5	238.8	262.8
66.4	62.0	57.4	53.2	49.2	45.6
15.6	18.0	20.4	22.6	24.6	26.3
13.1	13.0	12.5	12.0	11.4	10.7
91.3	88.9	84.4	78.6	72.0	65.3
9.6	10.0	10.2	10.3	10.2	9.9
85.4	97.5	107.5	114.8	119.3	120.8
32.0	28.3	24.6	21.1	17.9	15.2
15.4	17.2	19.3	21.6	23.9	26.1
75.5	76.0	76.0	76.0	75.4	74.3
380.8	388.9	398.2	407.1	414.5	421.3
3.3	3.1	2.9	2.7	2.5	2.2
52.2	57.9	62.8	67.3	71.3	74.4
31.1	31.2	31.0	30.5	29.6	28.3
110.0	108.4	105.3	101.0	96.4	91.7
71.0	82.2	91.8	99.8	106.0	110.0
38.1	44.5	50.5	56.0	60.7	64.5
25.9	29.1	32.0	34.4	36.2	37.2

LIST OF TABLES AND FIGURES

TABLES

FIGURES

REFERENCES

1 P.R. Ehrlich & A.H. Ehrlich, *The Population Bomb*, Buccaneer Books, 1968.
2 Meadows, Donella H; Meadows, Dennis L; Randers, Jørgen; Behrens III, William W; *The Limits to Growth; A Report for the Club of Rome's Project on the Predicament of Mankind* (Universe Books, 1972).
3 Mike Eckel, "Uzbekistan Praised For Curtailing Forced Labor In Cotton Harvest", RadioFreeEurope, 4 April 2019.
4 Stephen J. Shaw, "Birthgap—Childless World", 2021.
5 John A. Ross, "Contraceptive Use, Access to Methods, and Program Efforts in Urban Areas", *Frontiers in Global Women's Health*, 23 September 2021.
6 World Bank, "Fertility Rate", accessed 10 September 2022, https://data.worldbank.org/indicator/SP.DYN.TFRT.IN?locations=CN
7 Richard Fry, "The Number of People in the Average U.S. Household is Going up for the First Time in Over 160 Years", Pew Research Center, 1 October 2019.
8 Gretchen Livingston, "Family Size Among Mothers", Pew Research Center, 7 May 2015.
9 Amanda Ruggeri, "The Rise of One-and-Done Parenting", BBC, 10 January 2023.
10 OECD, "Childlessness", OECD Social Policy Division, 21 December 2018.
11 Liao Shumin, "One in 10 Chinese Women Are Childless", *Yicai*, 14 February 2023.
12 John West, "China's Urbanization", Asian Century Institute, 22 March 2014.
13 World Bank, "School Enrolment, Female", accessed 21 September 2022, https://data.worldbank.org/indicator/SE.SEC.ENRR.FE?locations=CN
14 UNESCO Institute for Statistics, "China—Ratio of Female to Male Tertiary Enrollment", Indexmundi.com, accessed 25 September 2022.
15 Ronald F. Inglehart, "Giving Up on God—The Global Decline of Religion", *Foreign Affairs*, September/October 2020.

16 Edan Prabhu, "How Will We Cope When There are Too Few Young People in the World?", Brookings, 10 October 2017. Wittgenstein Centre Human Capital Data Explorer, accessed 3 November 2022.

17 Based on the 5-year average to 2019, to avoid annual distortions.

18 World Bank, "Age Dependency Ratio (% of Working-Age Population)", accessed 7 November 2022, https://data.worldbank.org/indicator/SP.POP.DPND

19 Julius Ballanco, "The Plumbing Census", pmmag.com, 1 June 2010.

20 Nippon.com, "Record 2 Million Foreign Workers in Japan as of 2023", Nippon.com, 1 March 2024

21 Denise Couture, "Facing Critical Labor Shortage, Japan Opens Door Wider To Foreign Workers", NPR, 7 December 2018.
    Adam Taylor, "Japan, Long Closed to Most Immigration, Looks to Open up Amid Labor Shortage", *Washington Post*, 18 November 2021.

22 Nikkei, "Japan's Shrinking Labor Pool Sharpens Quest for Productivity", 1 December 2021.

23 Alessandra Migliacci, Giovanni Salzano, "Italy Is Held Back by 2.6 Million People Who've Given Up on Work", Bloomberg, 3 June 2022.

24 Francesco Pastore, "Youth Unemployment in Italy at the Time of the New Great Depression", Friedrich-Ebert-Stiftung, November 2012.

25 Patrizia Caiffa, "Italians in the World, Emigration Continues Despite the Pandemic", Agensir.eu, 9 November 2021.

26 InfoMigrants, "Italy: Farmers in Puglia Warn of Labor Shortage", InfoMigrants, 16 May 2022.

27 Sergio Goncalves, "Portugal Eases Visa Rules to Tackle Labour Shortage", Reuters, 1 September 2022.

28 LUSA, "Portugal: Wages Increasing in Tourism Sector Facing Labour Shortage", Macaubusiness.com, 27 September 2022.

29 The Local, "Germany Struggles With Growing Worker Shortage", Thelocal.de, 2 June 2022.

30 Sabine Kinkartz, "Germany on the Hunt for Labor", dw.com, 26 July 2022.

31 Thomas Escritt, "Facing Labour Shortages, Germany Sweetens Immigration Offer", Reuters, 6 July 2022.

32 Prof Stein Emil Vollset, Emily Goren, Chun-Wei Yuan, Jackie Cao, Amanda E Smith, Thomas Hsiao, et al., "Fertility, mortality, migration, and population scenarios for 195 countries and territories from 2017 to 2100", *The Lancet*, 14 July 2020.

33 Radiant.com, "The State of Self-Service Checkouts", Radiant.com, 19 February 2021.

34 Nathaniel Meyersohn, "Nobody likes self-checkout. Here's why it's everywhere", CNN Business, 10 July 2022.

35 Edward Humes, "How Online Shopping Has Turned Traffic Into a
    Nightmare", Time.com, 18 December 2018.
36 Robert H Shmerling, "Why men often die earlier than women", Harvard
    Health Blog, 22 June 2020.
    Hannah Ritchie & Max Roser, "Gender Ratio", Published online at
    OurWorldInData.org. Retrieved from: https://ourworldindata.org/gender-
    ratio
37 National Institute on Aging, "Heart Health and Aging", NIH, 1 June 2018.
38 Dana Broach, David Schroeder, "Review of the Scientific Basis for the
    Mandatory Separation of an Air Traffic Control Specialist at Age 56",
    U.S. Department of Transportation, April 2005.
39 US Bureau of Labor Statistics, "Employee tenure in 2022", US Department of
    Labor, 22 September 2022.
40 Eurostat, "40% of 30–34 year-olds have tertiary education", Eurostat,
    24 January 2019.
41 Colin R. Singer, "Here Are The Top 10 Most In-Demand Jobs In Newfoundland
    And Labrador", Immigration.ca, 15 November 2022.
42 World Population Review, "Immigration by Country 2023", Published online
    at Worldpopulationreview.net, Accessed April 2023.
43 The Observers, "Unbearable hours, threats of being fired: The abuse of
    migrant interns in Japan", France24, 15 April 2022.
44 Adam Taylor, "Long closed to most immigration, Japan looks to open up
    amid labor shortage", *Washington Post*, 18 November 2021.
45 OECD, "Italy: Tourism in the economy", OECDiLibrary, Accessed online in
    November 2022.
46 Bill Saporito, "Why I'm Breaking Up With Hand Sanitizer", *Time*, 12 May 2014.
47 Lata Gangadharan, Xin Meng, et al. "Little Emperors: Behavioral Impacts of
    China's One-Child Policy", *Science*, January 2013.
48 Lata Gangadharan, Xin Meng, et al. "Little Emperors: Behavioral Impacts of
    China's One-Child Policy", *Science*, January 2013.
49 SCMP, "From 'lying flat' to 'letting it rot': Why China's frustrated youth are
    embracing 'bailan' way of life", South China Morning Post, 5 October 2022.
50 Ali Francis, "Gen Z: The workers who want it all", BBC.com, 14 June 2022.
51 Ali Francis, "Gen Z: The workers who want it all", BBC.com, 14 June 2022.
52 Emma Ascott, "81% of Gen Z think sharing their salary will create change",
    Allwork, 4 October 2022.
53 Kieran Smith, "The answer to the UK's HGV driver shortage", Driver Require
    Think Tank, 17 June 2021.
54 Langley Research Centre, "NASA Langley Research Center's Contributions to
    the Apollo Program", Nasa.gov, Accessed November 2022.

55 Careerbuilder, "Millennials or Gen Z: who's doing the most job-hopping", Careerbuilder.com, 5 October 2021.

56 Harvard Business Review, "The Best-Performing CEOs in the World, 2019", November-December 2019, https://hbr.org/2019/11/the-best-performing-ceos-in-the-world-2019

57 John Walton, "Why more air travel chaos is on its way", CNN.com, 30 June 2022.

58 Siddharth Vikram Philip, Christopher Jasper, William Wilkes, "Record Flight Delays, Cancellations Make Europe 2022's Worst Place to Travel", Bloomberg. com, 1 July 2022.

59 NL Times, "Many stores cut hours due to worker shortage", *NL Times*, 14 May 2022.

60 Associated Press, "Restoring power to Hurricane Sandy victims takes days to weeks", Pennlive.com, 16 November 2012.

61 Duncan Agnew, "Plumber shortage and supply chain issues are delaying storm recovery efforts in Texas", *Texas Tribune*, 26 February 2021.

62 Keck School of Medicine, "A Public Health Crisis: Staffing Shortages in Health Care", University of Southern California, 13 March 2023.

63 Eli Rosenberg, "Labor shortages are hampering public transportation systems", *The Washington Post*, 28 December 2021.

64 Ian Krietzberg, Amelia Lucas, "Customer service suffers at short-staffed restaurants as Covid takes toll", CNBC.com, 17 July 2022.

65 Alex Trelinski, "Benidorm bars and restaurants forced to close due to lack of staff on Spain's Costa Blanca", The Olive Press, 11 July 2022.

66 Mirror, "Hotels in Spain face staff crisis as they struggle to fill 200,000 jobs for summer", Mirror.co.uk, 4 July 2022.

67 Jason Armesto, "National lifeguard shortage forces pool closures across US", BBC.com, 9 July 2022.

68 Adam Harvey, "The real cost of Australia's worker shortage", Four Corners, ABC News, Posted on 17 October 2022.

69 Jonathan Glancey, "The death of the US shopping mall", BBC.com, 21 October 2014.

70 Adam Clark Estes, "Amazon Is Building a Colossal Warehouse Where America's Biggest Mall Once Stood", Gizmodo.com, 25 August 2017.

71 James Barron, "Water Mains Are Bursting All Over New York. Can They Be Fixed?", *The New York Times*, 12 February 2020.

72 Arpit Gupta, "New York's Subsurface Spaghetti Problem", *City Journal*, 12 August 2021.

73 James Barron, "Water Mains Are Bursting All Over New York. Can They Be Fixed?", *The New York Times*, 12 February 2020.

74 James Barron, "Water Mains Are Bursting All Over New York. Can They Be Fixed?", *The New York Times*, 12 February 2020.

75 Diana Hummel and Alexandra Lux, "Population decline and infrastructure: The case of the German water supply system", *Vienna Yearbook of Population Research 2007*, pp. 167-191, 2007.

76 Kim Kozlowski, "Detroit's 70-year population decline continues; Duggan says city undercounted", *The Detroit News*, 13 August 2021.

77 Danielle Kurtzleben, "Everything you need to know about the Detroit bankruptcy", Vox.com, 15 December 2014.

78 Christine Ferretti, "Last Detroit house demolished in $265M blight-removal effort", *The Detroit News*, 14 August 2020.

79 Alastair Townsend, "Why Japan is Crazy About Housing", Archdaily.com, 21 November 2013.

80 Landlog, "A mismatch between supply and demand due to a shrinking labor force. The construction industry in Japan is facing a crisis now", Landlog. info, Accessed November 2022.

81 Tim Hornyak, "Japan Has Millions of Empty Houses. Want to Buy One for $25,000?", *The New York Times*, 17 April 2023.

82 Nippon, "New Record Low for Japan's Elementary and Junior High School Students", Nippon.com, 30 August 2019.
    Issei Kato, Eimi Yamamitsu, Tom Bateman, "School closures continue as Japan's population declines", *Japan Times*, 9 April 2023.

83 Ben Lefebvre, "Japan's education ministry is repurposing thousands of school buildings, emptied out by the country's shrinking population", *Quartz*, 28 October 2015.

84 Ben Lefebvre, "Japan's education ministry is repurposing thousands of school buildings, emptied out by the country's shrinking population", *Quartz*, 28 October 2015.
    The Straits Times, "School's out forever in ageing Japan", *The Straits Times*, 14 November 2024.

85 Emma Newbery, "You Could Buy a House for 1 Euro in Italy—With a Catch", Nasdaq.com, 2 October 2022.

86 Silvia Marchetti, "This pretty Italian town is paying people $30,000 to move there", CNN.com, 18 November 2022.

87 Gan Li, "China's Epic Property Boom Doesn't Stop for Covid Pandemic", Texas A&M University, 17 July 2020.

88 Graham Scott, "Why The Chips Are Down: Navigating the Global Chip Shortages and Beyond", Jabil.com, Accessed in November 2022.

89 RHA, "A Report on the Driver Shortage", RHA, July 2021.

90 Kieran Smith, "The Answer to the UK's HGV Driver Shortage", Driver Require Think Tank, 17 June 2021.

91 Jacob Bogage, "In a tight labor market, some states look to another type of worker: Children", *The Washington Post*, 11 February 2023.

92 Unicef, "COVID-19 impact assessment and outlook on personal protective equipment", Unicef, 4 May 2020.

93 Laura Ross, "Inside the iPhone: How Apple Sources From 43 Countries Nearly Seamlessly", Thomasnet.com, 21 July 2020.

94 Cheng Ting-Fang and Lauly Li, "TSMC says U.S. plant construction 'more costly' than expected", *Nikkei Asia*, 8 June 2022.

95 Virginia Harrison and Daniele Palumbo, "China anniversary: How the country became the world's 'economic miracle'", BBC.com, 1 October 2019.

96 Unesco, "Education in Africa", Unesco Institute for Statistics, Accessed in November 2022.

97 Nyasha Chingono, "Over 4,000 Zimbabwean doctors and nurses left the country in 2021", Reuters, 21 November 2022.

98 France 24, "Brain drain: Zimbabwe fears losing teachers to the UK", France 24, 16 December 2022.

99 Matt Farah, "A Quick Overview of Nurses' Salaries in the UK in 2023", Nurses.co.uk, Accessed in January 2023.

100 Kevin Kenny, "The Irish diaspora", Aeon Media, 7 September 2017.

101 Antoin E. Murphy, "The Celtic Tiger—An Analysis of Ireland's Economic Growth Performance", European University Institute, April 2000.

102 Antoin E. Murphy, "The Celtic Tiger—An Analysis of Ireland's Economic Growth Performance", European University Institute, April 2000.

103 Ireland Department of Foreign Affairs, "The Irish Diaspora—Its Importance", Gov.ie, 17 August 2019.

104 Jyotika Teckchandani, "Indian diaspora and economic development of India", Wion, 10 January 2022.

105 Jyotika Teckchandani, "Indian diaspora and economic development of India", Wion, 10 January 2022.

106 World Bank, "Migration and Development Brief 40", World Bank, June 2024.

107 The Lancet, "Global fertility in 204 countries and territories, 1950–2021, with forecasts to 2100", *The Lancet*, 18 May 2024

108 World Bank, "Bilateral Estimates of Migrant Stocks in 2017", World Bank, Accessed in February 2022.

109 Amanda Previdelli, "'We need immigration': Austrian minister insists foreign workers are the only solution", *The Local*, 23 August 2022.

110 "History of Anglo-Saxon England", CS.Mcgill.ca, Accessed in August 2022.

111 Office of the Historian, "Unification of Italian States", US Department of State, Accessed in August 2022.

112 Office of the Historian, "Unification of Italian States", US Department of State, Accessed in August 2022.

113 Parliamentary Education Office, "The Federation of Australia", Australian Parliamentary Education Office, Accessed September 2022.

114 Bureau of Labor Statistics, "Spending patterns by age", 16 August 2000.

115 World Bank, "Migration and Development Brief", World Bank, June 2024.

116 OECD Revenue Statistics 2022, "Revenue Statistics 2022—Japan", OECD, 2022.

117 ST. Louis Fed, "Personal Savings Rate", FRED Economic Data, Accessed in January 2023.

118 Landre Signy, "Africa's consumer market potential", Brookings, December 2018.

119 Pensions at a glance: Public policies across OECD countries, "Comparing Pension Policies of OECD Countries", OECD, 2007.

120 AgeUK.org.uk, "Changes to State Pension Age", Ageuk.org.uk, Accessed in March 2023.

121 Department of Social Services, Australian Government, "Age Pension", Accessed at www.dss.gov.au/seniors/benefits-payments/age-pension in March 2023.

122 Silvia Amaro, "France's government outlines plans to raise retirement age despite years of pushback", CNBC.com, 10 January 2023.

123 Marcos Poplawski-Ribeiro, Hamid Davoodi, Carlos Eduardo Gonçalves, Galen Sher, Gabriel Hegab, and Victoria Haver, "2024 Global Debt Monitor", IMF, December 2024.

124 Aayush Singh, "A Tale of Two Countries: A History of the Greek Debt Crisis", *Berkeley Economic Review*, 10 October 2022.

125 Jim Tankersley, Alan Rappeport, "U.S. on Track to Add $19 Trillion in New Debt Over 10 Years", *The New York Times*, 15 February 2023.

126 Mike Dolan, "Debt mountain meets population cliff", Reuters, 14 August 2020.

127 Mike Dolan, "Debt mountain meets population cliff", Reuters, 14 August 2020.

128 Chantelle Francis, "Huge pay for babysitters amid childcare crisis", News.co.au, 30 May 2022.

129 Pia Orrenius and Chloe Smith, "Without Immigration, U.S. Economy Will Struggle to Grow", Federal Reserve Bank of Dallas, 9 April 2020.

130 Adrian Raftery, "The dip in the US birthrate isn't a crisis, but the fall in immigration may be", The Conversation, 21 June 2021.

131 Stuart Anderson, "Fed Chair Finds Trump-Era Immigration Policies Still Harm Economy", Forbes.com, 5 December 2022.

132 Nicholas Riccardi, "Less immigrant labor in the U.S. contributing to higher prices", *Fortune*, 7 May 2022.

133 Matthew Davidson, "Norway is lovely, so why are people leaving?", Norwegian Institute for Urban and Regional Research, 14 February 2022.

134 Danai Christopoulou, "Why Less People Are Moving to Norway Than Ever", Culture Trip, 5 June 2018.

135 Danai Christopoulou, "Why Less People Are Moving to Norway Than Ever", Culture Trip, 5 June 2018.

136 Akshay Kulkarni, "Canada records its lowest fertility rate for 2nd year: StatsCan", CBC News, 30 September 2024.

137 Shelby Thevenot, "Canada sees record-low fertility rates same year as record-breaking immigration levels", 2 November 2020.
Statistics Canada, "Population growth in Canada continues to slow", 17 December 2024.

138 Statistics Canada, "Immigrants make up the largest share of the population in over 150 years and continue to shape who we are as Canadians", 26 October 2022.

139 Bruce Newbold, "COVID-19 has hardened Canadian views on immigration", The Conversation, 1 October 2020.

140 Government of Canada news release, "Government of Canada reduces immigration", 24 October 2024

141 Julien Bérard-Chagnon, Lorena Canon, "The Canadian diaspora: Estimating the number of Canadian citizens who live abroad", Statistics Canada, 13 April 2022.

142 Polly Nash, "Australian study visas fall by 40% as "disruptive" policy changes take hold", The PIE Network, 21 October 2024.

143 Michael Heath, Adam Majendie, "World's Biggest Immigration System Offers Lessons for a Disrupted World", Bloomberg.com, 28 October 2021.

144 ABC Fact Check, "Is Australia's population growth mostly the result of migration, and is that underpinning the budget?", ABC News, 31 July 2019.

145 SBS News, "From skilled visas to ballots: How Australia's migration changes could unfold in 2025", 1 January 2025.

146 Claire Loughnan, "Australia's Harsh Immigration Policy", The Diplomat, 1 September 2019.
Polly Nash, "Australian study visas fall by 40% as 'disruptive' policy changes take hold", The PIE Network, 21 October 2024).

147 Future, "Carbon footprint and price comparison: Secondhand vs. New Clothing", Future.green/futureblog/, 22 August 2022.

148 Jaehyeok Kim, Hyungwoo Lim, Ha-Hyun Jo, "Do Aging and Low Fertility Reduce Carbon Emissions in Korea? Evidence from IPAT Augmented EKC Analysis", National Library of Medicine, 24 April 2020.

149 World Bank, "CO_2 emissions (metric tons per capita)", World Bank Data, Accessed in March 2023.

150 Ian Thomas, "The U.S. Army is struggling to find the recruits its needs to win the fight over the future", CNBC.com, 26 October 2022.
     Dexter Filkins, "The U.S. Military's recruiting crisis", The New Yorker, 3 February 2025.
151 Lolita C. Bandor, "Army sees safety, not 'wokeness', as top recruiting obstacle", *Daily Herald*, 12 February 2023.
152 Jielin Dong, Wei Li, Yuhua Cao, Jianwen Fang, "How does technology and population progress relate? An empirical study of the last 10,000 years", Technological Forecasting and Social Change, February 2016.
153 Tyler Cowen, "The Great Stagnation: How America Ate All The Low-Hanging Fruit of Modern History, Got Sick, and Will (Eventually) Feel Better", Dutton, 2011.
154 Elizabeth Brainerd, "Can government policies reverse undesirable declines in fertility?", IZA World of Labor, May 2014.
155 Poh Lin Tan, "Reversing Demographic Decline: Singapore's experience in trying to raise its fertility rate offers lessons for other countries", Finance and Development, March 2020.
156 Rene Desiderio, "The Impact of International Migration on Fertility: An Empirical Study", *KNOMAD Paper 36*, January 2020.
157 Amy Mackinnon, "What Actually Happens When a Country Bans Abortion", Foreign Policy, 16 May 2019.
158 Matthias Doepke, "How Rosie the Riveter led to the 1950s' Baby Boom", The London School of Economics and Political Science, 4 November 2015.
159 Douglas Belkin, "A Generation of American Men Give Up on College", *The Wall Street Journal*, 6 September 2021.
160 Poh Lin Tan, "Reversing Demographic Decline: Singapore's experience in trying to raise its fertility rate offers lessons for other countries", Finance and Development, March 2020.
161 Kait Hanson, "What you should know about IVF success rates by age", Today.com, 20 July 2022.
162 Testa, Maria & Skirbekk, Vegard & Lutz, Wolfgang, "The Low Fertility Trap Hypothesis. Forces that May Lead to Further Postponement and Fewer Births in Europe", Vienna Yearbook of Population Research. 4. 167-192, 2006.
163 Kyodo News, "1 in 4 singles in 30s not willing to marry: Japan government survey", *Kyodo News*, 14 June 2022.
164 Family Equality, "Building LGBTQ+ Families: The Price of Parenthood", https://www.familyequality.org/price-of-parenthood, Accessed in March 2023.

INDEX

ABOUT THE AUTHOR

Shamil Ismail is an investment analyst, and qualified as a Chartered Accountant and Chartered Financial Analyst. Over the past thirty years he has been involved in various aspects of consumer markets, first working at retailers and later as an analyst researching the markets. He founded Primaresearch in 2015, a specialist research firm focusing on consumer companies. The global trends in demographics and how this will impact consumer markets are of particular interest to him, culminating in this book.

www.ageofdecay.com